COMEDY WRITING SECRETS

by Melvin Helitzer

WRITER'S DIGEST BOOKS

Cincinnati, Ohio

PERMISSIONS

Excerpt from Art Buchwald's column reprinted with permission of the author, Los Angeles Times Syndicate, 1986.

Library of Congress Cataloging-in-Publication Data

Helitzer, Melvin.
   Comedy writing secrets.

   Bibliography: p.
   Includes index.
   1. Wit and humor—Authorship. I. Title.
PN6149.A88H445 1987   808.7   87-2096
ISBN 0-89879-258-4
Illustrations by Jim Benton.
Design by Christine W. Aulicino.

A MAGNUS HOPUS

Dedication
This, my fourth book, is dedicated
to my wife and children, who
bought the other three.

TABLE OF CONTENTS

PREFACE

The study of comedy is the last frontier of literary communication. Until 1982, humor had never been taught as a credit course in a major American university. Until 1984 there wasn't a single published textbook that detailed the structure of humor writing fundamentals. It seemed humor was a fuse too dangerous to enlight. Facetiousness was equated with frivolity.

Today, teaching humor has become a growth industry. The first humor writing course at the Scripps School of Journalism at Ohio University has become such a smash hit that students register a year in advance to occupy one of the twenty allotted seats. Students include members of the faculty, school administrators, and adults from the community—including doctors, lawyers, homemakers, and even one mortician. (We asked him, when trying out his material, if he killed the audience. He said "No, they're already dead when I get there.")

The final exam was suggested by the students themselves. Since humor can't be tested in a vacuum, a pub on campus is taken over for a night and the rowdy audience helps grade the students with their applause. Modest applause is a C, enthusiastic applause is a B, a standing ovation is an A. If they throw fruit it's an F, unless the fruit is edible, in which case it gets marked up to a D.

Now, other universities are starting humor writing courses. In addition to Ohio University, you may find experimental courses in the curriculum of the University of Illinois, Virginia Tech, SUNY in Oneonta, New York, the University of Southern California, and UC at Berkeley. The university with the most humor courses is the New School for Social Research, an adult community college in New York City. Throughout the year, including summers, the school offers noncredit courses in humor writing, stand-up comedy performing and writing, and a comedy workshop. Instructors, including Charles Linder, Elliot Tiber, Scott Blakeman, and Jack Morton, have a long list of writing and producing credits. Except for Los Angeles, no other city has greater resources available to students than New York.

Other well-known humor courses are offered by Stanley Myron Handleman at UCLA (Los Angeles); Lynne Alpern and Esther Blumenfeld at Emory University (Atlanta); Richard Mintzer at the Discovery Center (New York), and Second City (Chicago), the country's most famous school for improvisational training.

And humor workshops are booming. Seminars have recently been conducted at Arizona State, University of Texas (El Paso), University of Pittsburgh, Ohio State, University of Toledo, and internationally at Tel Aviv University in Israel and Cork University in Ireland, to list just a few.

A number of other professionals, notably Danny Simon, the dean of comedy writers, plus Larry Wilde, author of the country's most popular joke books, Art Gliner, Dr. Virginia O. Tooper, Herb True, and Dr. Joel Goodman are booked regularly for lectures on the benefits of humor in personal as well as professional life.

The Ohio University course is only one example of an educational crusade by such outstanding linguists, psychologists, sociologists, and American humor scholars as Don and Alleen Nilsen of Arizona State, Maharev Apte of Duke, Jesse Bier of Montana, Joseph Boskin of Boston, Tony Chapman of Leeds, England, historians H.J. and Barbara Cummings of Washington, DC, Hugh C. Foot of the British Psychological Society, William F. Fry, Jr. of Stamford, Jeffrey Goldstein of Temple, Hamlin Hill of New Mexico, Gerald Mast of Chicago, Paul McGhee of Texas Tech, Harvey Mindess and Joy Turek of Antioch West, Lawrence Mintz of Maryland, John O. Rosenbaum of Southwest Texas State, Victor Raskin of Purdue, Warren Shibles of Wisconsin, authors Robert Orben, Lawrence Peters, and Susan Kelz Sperling, and many more.

Their pioneering efforts have been inspirational and their encouragement has been personally invaluable. This book proudly acknowledges its debt to all of them.

*As the doctor said after he made the first incision,
"How's that for openers?"*

Introducing
the Three Rs of Humor

YOU ARE ABOUT TO LEARN TO WRITE FUNNY. You can learn this creative art for your own personal enjoyment or for financial gain. In either case, you'll find your humor has tremendous value.

I call it the three Rs of humor. Skillful use of humor can create *respect*, cause your words to be *remembered*, and earn you great *rewards*.

RESPECT

There are three ways you can attract attention:

1. You can legitimately achieve some outstanding accomplishment.
2. You can criticize somebody.
3. You can be unconventional.

Humor offers all three opportunities, because humor isn't exclusively entertainment. We use humor primarily to call attention to ourselves. Notice how you react when you start to tell a joke to a small group of friends and, just as you get to the end, someone shouts out the punch line. Your glare will probably be the physical limit of your anger at first, but the second time it happens, you'll try to kill the jerk, and no jury will convict you.

Humor is a universal speech opener because it immediately gets us respectful attention. It's psychologically impossible to hate someone with whom you've laughed. "When we laugh we temporarily give ourselves over to the person who makes us laugh," says Robert Orben.

Laughter is to the psyche what jogging is to the body. Humor, in live performance, offers more immediate gratification than any other art form. You know your audience is appreciative because you can hear their response, and this jury's decision is impulsive and instantaneous.

REMEMBER

When we're successfully humorous—live or in print—people remember. Our best lines are the ones repeated, and retained. An impressive number of the sayings in *Bartlett's Familiar Quotations* are witticisms.

When learning is fun, everybody benefits. Two studies, one at the University of Arkansas in 1980 and the other a few years later at San Diego State, agreed that students who attended a series of lectures which purposely included witticisms and anecdotes achieved higher test scores than students who attended the same lectures where humor was avoided. "When the mouth is open for laughter," wrote Dr. Virginia Tooper, "you may be able to shove in a little food for thought."

All books of quotations have generous portions devoted to witticisms. Jokes are probably our best opportunity for immortality, although Woody Allen once remarked, "I don't want to gain immortality by my humor. I want to gain immortality by not dying."

REWARD

Humor is important in every facet of entertainment, social life, education, and health. Many political candidates, in fact every president since Franklin Roosevelt, have had in-house humorists on their speech writing teams. Big business executives are increasingly hiring writers able to make them gag on every line (and you can read that line any way you want to).

It's been hard for classical culturists to accept that more money is being earned by the art of comedy than by all other fine arts combined. That's no exaggeration. Take a look at the recent record.

- Three of the top-grossing films were comedies.
- Six of the top-rated TV programs were sitcoms.
- Three of the highest-paid newspaper columnists are humor writers.
- Subject of the largest selling greeting cards is humor.
- Eight of the highest-paid nightclub entertainers are comedians.
- Four best-selling books were joke books and humor biography.

Comedy can also be a springboard to more lucrative acting jobs. Stand-up comedians like Robin Williams, Woody Allen, Steve Martin, Lily Tomlin, Harry Anderson, Howie Mandell, Richard Pryor, Eddie Murphy, Martin Mull, Carol Burnett, Redd Foxx, Bob Newhart, Alan King, and Bill Cosby are just a few comedians who've had major movie roles.

The demand for humor writers far exceeds the supply. One reason is that more people want to tell jokes than write them; another is that television is a joke-eating shark. It chews up more humor material in a month than all other forms use in a year. Johnny Carson once remarked that television is the only medium that eats its young, because young writers are the ones most frequently hired to feed the shark day after day and suffer indigestion night after night. While the financial rewards are eye-opening, young writers are only as good as their last joke, and fatigue causes many of them to burn out after a year. A three-year career on any one project ranks them with the true pros of the art.

MAP FOR SUCCESS

The two qualities shared by all successful humor writers are *consistency* and *targeted material*.

This simply means that (1) the ability to write funny isn't a sometimes thing, and (2) the writer doesn't waste precious time preparing the wrong material for the wrong performer, to be delivered to the wrong audience. This is as true in print and broadcast humor as it is for stand-up.

An acronym sums up this second point rather dramatically. I call it the MAP theory. MAP stands for material, audience, and performer. MAP is a triangular comedic constellation which must always be in phase.

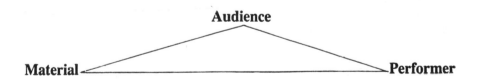

The material must be appropriate to the interests of the audience, and each must also relate to the persona of the performer. Likewise, the audience must complement both the material and the presentation style of the performer. Regardless of where in heaven's name you start, each star in the constellation must relate to both the other stars. The common denominator is *character*. The character of the material must fit the character of the performer and the character of the audience. There are no exceptions in commercial humor.

ATTRIBUTION

One day Milton Berle and Henny Youngman were listening to Joey Bishop tell a particularly funny gag. "Gee, I wish I said that," Berle whispered. "Don't worry, Milton, you will," said Henny.

There are over a thousand examples of humor in this book. I wrote some of it, but most was written by others. In lectures I always credit authors—except for those jokes that consistently get big laughs.

Credit lines for jokes are a researcher's nightmare. There are many standard jokes, but they have thousands of variations. Just who uttered what can rarely be proven.

Tom Burnam, in his book *The Dictionary of Misinformation*, points out that such famous lines as Horace Greeley's "Go west, young man," Marie Antoinette's "Let them eat cake," W.C. Fields's "Any man who hates dogs and babies can't be all bad," and even his tombstone inscription, "I would rather be here than in Philadelphia," Mark Twain's "Everybody talks about the weather but nobody does anything about it," John F. Kennedy's "Ask not what your country can do for you," and Franklin D. Roosevelt's "The only thing we have to fear is fear itself," were all previously written by someone else.

If scholars have this problem with historic lines, then proper credit for jokes, anecdotes, and witticisms can be a never-ending dilemma. If Adam came back to the Garden of Eden, the only thing that would be familiar to him would be the jokes.

The best I can offer for identification is to list the name published in someone else's joke collection, but I wouldn't bet on its accuracy. The library of Shakespeare will always be haunted by the ghost of Marlowe—and that's not an original line either.

PRACTICE, PRACTICE, PRACTICE

Acronyms are my favorite mnemonic device, and in this book acronyms proliferate. The first letter of each word in a group is abbreviated into a more easily remembered word. If you can memorize acronyms like THREES, MAP, POW, and PAP, you'll be able to remember the humor formulas.

While this book is an introduction to humor writing, I don't promise it will instantly transform you into a professional. Learning the fundamentals of humor is easy compared with the dedication required. A woman once rushed up to famous violinist Fritz Kreisler after a concert and cried, "I'd give my life to play as beautifully as you do." Kreisler replied, "Well, I did."

Humor can be taught because it has a structure. It has a memorable list of formulas and a wide variety of techniques. This book promises to teach the mechanics of humor—and that's no grease job!

Part 1

The Basics of Humor Writing

"What if the yogurt spoiled? How would we know?"

CHAPTER 1

Imagination Is Funny: What If. . . . We Take the First Step

THE FIRST STEP IN HUMOR CONCEPTION IS IMAGINATION. It's called "What if?" the two most important words in creativity and the only stimulant a humor writer needs to get started. "Imagination is intelligence having fun," writes George Scialabba.

Look at a clear glass ashtray. What do you see? If you can see beyond its ordinary function, humor writing may be for you. The humorist sees what is logically illogical, perceiving something in a way no one else (at least in the audience) has considered before. To comedy writer Pat McCormick it's not an ashtray at all, but a diaphragm for the Statue of Liberty, a bathtub for Dudley Moore, a contact lens for the Jolly Green Giant, or a yarmulke for a bald rabbi trying to get a suntan.

This realignment of diverse elements into new and unexpected relationships surprises the audience and makes them laugh.

What if mother's milk was ever declared a health hazard, where would they put the warning label?

What if you actually saw McNuggets on a chicken?

What if alphabet soup consistently spelled out obscene words?

9

As a demonstration, let's consider a simple humor exercise. Two Coke bottles are held up—what could they possibly be besides bottles? Scribble down as many exaggerations as possible, without being restrained by practicality. Within five minutes, you should come up with a list like this.

- bowling pins left standing by the first ball
- pins used by a juggler
- a pair of binoculars for a U-boat commander
- portable urinals
- Polish cocktail glasses
- ear plugs for elephants
- Siamese twins formerly joined at the lips
- medical device for reshaping the tongue
- nonworking funnels
- fingernail polish protectors
- golf tees for a very fat man
- spin the bottle for schizophrenics
- corn holders for the Jolly Green Giant
- a newfangled breast implant
- artificial limbs for Iranian soldiers

This humor Rorschach test is more than an exercise. It's the key to comedy's engine, which won't turn over without unbridled imagination. Train your mind to constantly ask "What if?" and brainstorm possibilities. Don't worry if your ideas seem absurd or silly, the idea now is to get your imagination in gear.

Humorists have one cardinal rule: "Don't be inhibited." It's better to take a nihilistic attitude toward *all* subjects than to pussyfoot around "taboos." When writing, write freely. Make uninhibited assumptions. "Put your brains on tilt," says Frank O'Donnell. Write everything down. Editing and self-censorship are the second and third steps. Never the first!

OBSERVATIONAL HUMOR

In observational humor, the humorist focuses a laser beam on a realistic action or logical thought with the sole purpose of trying to destroy it.

> I got an A in philosophy because I proved that my professor
> didn't exist.
> —Judy Tenmuta

Bob Garfield, in *Advertising Age*, described Marty Rackham, a beginning comic, who's constantly writing ideas down and sticking them in his wallet. "The thing is stuffed with miscellaneous business cards, on the back of which he jots random ideas. One says, 'Pulling words from a person who stutters.' Another, 'jumper cables.' Right now he's working on a bit about continental hygiene, 'Did you ever smell a European?' The ideas materialize constantly, in varying degrees of hilarity and sophistication."

Although it sounds impossible, the humorist's mind is a wonderful thing to watch. Sometimes you can even see humorists' lips move as they silently try out the sound of different ideas. Meet them during off-hours at a social gathering; every fact reported, every name mentioned, every prediction made is grist for the humorous association. At the end of a party, if you ask how they enjoyed themselves, they might answer positively only if they'd been successful at collecting new material, which they'll write and rewrite all the way home.

Frequently a cliché is used to set the train of thought in motion—so the humorist can derail it. Notice how Larry Miller does this with "you'll never find anybody like me" in the following example:

I just broke up with someone, and the last thing she said to me was, "You'll never find anybody like me again." And I was thinking: I should hope not. Isn't that why we break up with people? If I don't want you, why would I want somebody just like you? Does anybody end a bad relationship and say, "By the way, do you have a twin?"

JOKE FORMULAS

For years comedy writers have claimed there are only a few basic jokes. What they mean by this is basic construction formulas. But very few agree on just how many formulas there are and how to define them.

I've isolated seven major formulas which can be played like notes of a musical scale—individually or in chords. We'll discuss these formulas later in the book; meanwhile, here they are.

1. *Double entendres*, the plays on words that include cliché reformations and take-offs
2. *Reverses* that trick the audience by a switch in point-of-view
3. *Triples* that build tension and are the framework for an exaggerated finale
4. *Incongruity* that pairs two logical but unconventional ideas

5. *Stupidity* that encourages the audience to feel superior to silly thoughts or actions
6. *Paired phrases* that utilize the rhythms of antonyms, homonyms, and synonyms
7. *Physical abuse (slapstick)* that caters to our delight at someone else's misfortune

But before we get further into the nitty-gritty of funny lines, let's take a more detailed look at the real reasons people laugh. They may surprise you.

"*I don't care what they say. I'm cold.*"

CHAPTER 2

Why We Laugh:
Theories of Comedy

DESPITE THE FACT THAT HUMOR PLAYS AN IMPORTANT PART in our lives, there isn't a lot of literature on the psychology of comedy. Over the centuries, philosophers have devoted only a small portion of their logic to understanding what laughter means, why we tell jokes, and why we do or don't appreciate other people's humor.

Circa 500 B.C., Aristotle studied it and Socrates debated it. In the 1800s Darwin, Hobbs, and Bergson wrote papers on their humor theories. In the twentieth century, Freud, Eastman, Koestler, and even Woody Allen have tried to formulate clear explanations of the purpose of humor. There's been more research on humor in the last twenty-five years than in all previous centuries combined.

Yet, considering the time span and the prowess of the minds that have considered the subject, answers are far from definitive. Like the eternal debate of rabbis over the meaning of the Talmud, every scholar of comedy interprets its subjective phenomenon in terms of his own discipline. Today, there is more diversity of opinion than ever.

So much remains to be done that the student of humor has a real opportunity to make a significant contribution to the field.   —Jeffrey Goldstein and Paul McGhee

The only common denominator is that humor seems to be so subjective that no one theory can possibly fit all influences.

For those interested in creating humor this is good news and bad news. The good news is that if humor has so many tangents, it may have an unlimited variety of benefits. Most of them have yet to be discovered. The bad news is that those who create comedy are not sure they know exactly what they're doing. "I work strictly on instinct," Woody Allen admits.

There are few artists more insecure than humorists. They are traditionally suspicious of any attempt to analyze their creative techniques. In truth, that's because they develop their formulas through trial and error. They discover comedy batting averages; some techniques work more often than others.

> After being an established writer for fifteen years, I remember staring at the typewriter every morning with a desperate, random groping for something funny, that familiar fear that I couldn't do it, that I had been getting away with it all this time and I would at last be found out. [It was] a painful blundering most of us went through.   —Sol Saks

If It Gets a Laugh, Leave It In

But few contemporary humor craftsmen agree on any device, except that "if it gets a laugh, it's funny, so leave it in." Many respected professionals believe the art of comedy writing can never be effectively structured or taught. It's their serious opinion that the skills, let alone the *sense*, of humor are mystically inherited or molded by such factors as ethnic characteristics, early childhood maternal influence, and insecurity.

> Humor is one of the things in life which defies analysis—either you have it or you don't, either you enjoy it or you don't.
>   —Ross MacKenzie

> Nobody can teach you humor writing. The secret is passed on from one generation to another and I will not tell mine, except to my son.   —Art Buchwald

This negativeness, which may be tongue-in-cheek on Buchwald's part, is self-indulgent and more likely self-protective. The current economic growth of comedy is such a major trend that its methodology cannot be left to chance or voodooism. Humor may be a mystery, but it's possible to demystify it.

WHAT'S SO FUNNY?

Humor is an emotional response, extremely subjective, to the vicissitudes of life. Psychologist Patricia Keith-Spiegel has identified the following eight major theories on "Why we laugh."

1. Surprise
2. Superiority
3. Biological
4. Incongruity
5. Ambivalence
6. Release
7. Configurational
8. Psychoanalytical

I maintain that the first two, superiority and surprise, are paramount considerations when your specific purpose is to write commercially acceptable humor.

Surprise

We laugh most often to cover our feelings of embarrassment. We really do! This can be a result of either (1) having unintentionally done or said something foolish, or (2) having been tricked. Surprise is one of the most universally accepted formulas for humor technique. A joke is a story, and a surprise ending is almost always its finale. You'll notice that appreciation of any piece of humor decreases rapidly through repeated exposure, or when the ending is predictable.

Clever word play engenders grudging appreciation from your peers, but surprise word play gives birth to laughter. We smile at wit. We laugh at jokes. The techniques that most often trigger surprise are misdirection, when you trap the audience, and incongruity, which is most effective when the audience is fully aware of all the facts.

Superiority

There appears to be a strong and constant need for us to feel superior. "We're number one!" and its accompanying rebel yell vocalizes that dubious achievement.

"Humor is a reaction to tragedy. The joke is at someone else's expense," wrote Alan Dundes. We even laugh when the baby falls down and goes boom. We defend this sadistic release by saying, "It's cute." It's not cute, especially for the baby. What we're often doing with humor is comparing ourselves with others we consider inferior by ridiculing their intelligence, their social standing, and their physical infirmities.

To those we consider superior, because they are in positions of authority or are more famous, richer, more intelligent, physically stronger, or socially admired, we delight in publicizing their every shortcoming, perceived or real. The greater the prestige of the victim, the greater our desire to equalize. The largest category of contemporary humor and witticisms is insult humor.

> *Congressman to friend:* "The Iran-Contra fiasco is costing the President a lot of sleepless afternoons."

> "Oh, Shirley, what a beautiful coat."
> "Yes, Bernie gave it to me for my thirty-ninth birthday."
> "Really. Well, it certainly doesn't show it."

Humor is social criticism. The object is to deflate. American humor has been an emotional catharsis for every ethnic minority: Irish, German, Polish, Catholic, Jew, blacks, and more recently Hispanics. There are few joke books on Midwestern WASPs.

Humor reassures the insecure. Even if we believe ourselves to be the "haves" (power, money, knowledge, prestige) there is tremendous insecurity about how we got it and how long we're going to keep it. Americans have a tremendous sense of inferiority.

There are two ways to feel superior. The first is to accomplish exemplary work that achieves public acclaim. The second is to publicly criticize the accomplishments of others. This deflates their prestige and focuses attention on ourselves. Regardless of how much the second method might be deplored on ethical grounds, the amount of time and effort exerted to belittle the work of competitors is usually far greater than the amount of time and energy expended to improve our own abilities.

"Humor is the weapon of the underdog," wrote Harvey Mindess. "We must look for avenues through which we can disgorge our feelings of inferiority by discovering the blemishes of our superiors." Our spark of laughter is always ignited by the misfortunes of those we fear. We feel superior because their image has been tarnished and because we aren't in the same predicament.

As individuals (regardless of our status), our humor is generally directed *upward* against more authoritative figures. In a group setting, our humor is directed *downward* toward groups that don't conform to our social, religious, national, or sexual mores.

Freud's explanation is that "A good bit of humor is oriented to maintaining the status quo by ridiculing deviant social behavior and reassuring the majority that their way of life is proper. . . . It is used as a weapon of the 'ins' against the 'outs.' ''

The comic is no El Cid on horseback. If anything, comics are guerrilla fighters—hitting and running, bobbing and weaving, frightened that, with this kind of an act, they've got to keep moving.

The professional humorist, therefore, must always be aware that the audience is happiest when subject matter, technique, and result encourage its members to feel superior. The target of a roast smiles only because he knows everyone is watching for his approval. Otherwise, despite being the "guest of honor," he would rather have stayed home with his wife—where he'd also be insulted, but could have saved a clean, white shirt.

For the record, let's look at all of the other theories one by one. There are important and frequent overlaps, but we'll be looking at how they support the superiority theory.

Biological

This theory emphasizes that laughter is a born and bred instinct. It appears to be a function of the nervous system to stimulate, relax and restore a feeling of well-being.

Primates, with little verbal communicative ability, show friendship with a closemouthed smile. They show anger and hostility with an open mouth, exposing all their teeth, despite the fact they could all use orthodontia.

Laughter is a substitute for assault. If our biological instincts are compulsive, we laugh and joke when we need to "reach out and crush someone." It's an attempt to vent our hostility when physical aggression is not practical—*and that's superiority*.

For example, triumph is often coupled with an openmouthed smile, followed immediately by a roar of laughter and a foot-pounding tribal dance. Watch a pro football player after he scores a touchdown.

Therefore, if laughter is really biologically instinctive, the old adage of never trusting someone who laughs too loudly should be amended to include those who laugh with their mouths open. They may be more influenced by your humor than you'd like.

Incongruity

Why should we put ourselves out for posterity? After all, what has posterity done for us?   —Sir Boyle Roche

There seems to be more than a semantic root shared by the words *ridiculous* and *ridicule*. According to Henri Bergson, a person laughs at incongruity when there is an unconventional pairing of actions or thoughts.

> Conrad Hilton, the hotel magnate, was asked to broadcast his New Year's wish. "I wish everyone would make a New Year's resolution to please put the shower curtain inside the tub."

Whenever someone behaves in a rigid manner which is suddenly ill-suited to the logic of the occasion, these incongruous antics result in a ridiculous scenario.

The comic effect arises from incongruity of speech, action or character revelation.

Some of the best illustrations are the actions of innocent victims to incongruous situations on *Candid Camera*. This program, by design, encourages us to laugh at people trying to maintain dignity in bizarre circumstances. The audience laughs hardest when it knows all the conflicting facts, thereby feeling superior to the perplexed victim.

Allen Funt claims that the "talking mailbox" was the show's top laugh-getter. A man is mailing a letter when suddenly the mailbox starts to talk to him. That part's a practical joke. The apex of laughter comes when the man calls over his friend and asks him to listen to the amazing conversation. He starts talking to the mailbox. At this point, the mailbox doesn't say a word. As the victim gets more and more exasperated and starts shouting at the mailbox, the camera cuts to close-ups of the friend's face, as he is plainly questioning his buddy's sanity.

Incongruity may be a comic plot rather than a basic humor concept. The most frequent plot in TV sitcoms is when one character in the story hides in the closet moments before someone in authority (husband, boss, policeman) unexpectedly enters the room. It's popular because audiences know all the facts, *and that's superiority*.

Ambivalence

> Whatever happened to the good ol' days, when children worked in factories?
>   —Emo Philips

This theory is similar to incongruity in its dependence on incompatible experiences. Nervous laughter covers our recognition of rigid conventions that make us appear foolish when held up to a humorist's strobe light. In a dishonest world, even honesty is amusing.

Greeting card copy: A year ago I bought you a birthday card. Now, here it is a year later . . . and you're getting too damn expensive.

Whereas incongruity tends to stress clashing ideas or perceptions, ambivalence stresses conflicting emotions, such as the love/hate relationships in families. Holding our ambivalent feelings up for comedic inspection is the powerful shtick of humorists like Bill Cosby. A typically funny situation of his is providing an antagonistic response which parents often feel.

Bill Cosby to troublesome son: "Listen to what I'm telling you, damn it, 'cause I brought you into this world, and I can take you out of it."

Ambivalence is one of the most common themes for Jewish humor, such as the son/mother relationship (which makes analysts wealthy).

Mother to bratty son: "I look forward to the day I'll see your picture on a milk carton."

Ambivalent humor covers up our guilt feelings or our foolish errors; it's an attempt to maintain dignity. Self-deprecating humor is just a device to set the audience at ease, so you can be in control—*and that's superiority.*

Release
We laugh in embarrassment when we drop a glass in public or an innocent error of ours has been discovered. The release theory emphasizes that laughter is a planned event, a voluntary reduction of stress triggered by a conscious effort to unlock life's tensions and inhibitions. We attend a Neil Simon play or a Bill Cosby concert because we want humor to help us laugh away our anxieties.

Instead of working for the survival of the fittest, we should be working for the survival of the wittiest, then we can all die laughing.　　　　　　　　　　　　　　　—Lily Tomlin

This release is fortified by group approval. Comedy works best when an audience is not only prepared to laugh but anxious to participate in a shared social experience. So the audience must be encouraged. They must be clued to every plot from the beginning. If the audience and the actor don't know what's behind the door, that's mystery. If the audience knows, but one of the actors doesn't, that's comedy.

When the musical *A Funny Thing Happened On the Way to the Forum* was in out-of-town tryouts, all the audience knew in advance was that the show was a take-off of Shakespeare's *Two Gentlemen of Verona*. Each evening, it got off to a slow start and ended with poor reviews. Then the writers added an opening number, "Comedy Tonight." The audience got the burlesque message immediately and the show became a big hit.

Sigmund Freud wrote, "The most favorable condition for comic pleasure is a generally happy disposition in which one is in the mood for laughter. In happy toxic states almost everything seems comic. We laugh at the expectation of laughing, at the appearance of one who is presenting the comic material (sometimes even before he attempts to make us laugh), and finally, we laugh at the recollection of having laughed."

If we feel the need to laugh, as release theorists claim, it's because we've been whipped by the day's battles and we'd like to see a few others get smacked around. Misery loves company only if it can laugh at them. We'll even laugh wildly watching a catcher chase a foul ball and wipe out seven guys in wheel chairs. That's sadism—*and that's also superiority.*

Configuration

The configurational theorists claim that one factor which makes us laugh occurs when disjointedness falls into place: "Oh, so that's the way it works."

I learned about sex the hard way—from books!   —Emo Philips

We smile, frequently even laugh aloud, when we experience that sudden insight of having solved a mystery or finally conquered a difficult assignment. For example, in humor, we laugh when the material encourages us to instantaneously complete some missing information. If we're successful, and generally the material is so carefully laid out that we can hardly fail, we congratulate ourselves by laughing out loud. We want the world to know we're very smart—*and that's superiority.*

Psychoanalytical

Freud's theory of humor contended that the ludicrous always represents a "saving in the expenditure of psychic energy." Like sleep, it is therapeutic. But even more important, he argued, wit can express inhibited tendencies like the desire to act out regressive infantile sexual or aggressive behavior. A lack of humor can be a sign of mental illness.

"We laugh in order to socially accomplish childish regression without feeling foolish," wrote Flugel. "We adopt a playful mood, excusable as relaxation." This may account for the popularity of comic strips among adult groups. Regardless of one's nationality and culture, they are the most universally accepted format for humor. Therefore, it can be argued, people who write or perform humor are people who, in some way, have never enjoyed growing up.

> We're young only once, but with humor, we can be immature
> forever.   —Art Gliner

Analysts learn a great deal about patients by listening to their humor. And you can learn a great deal about your own psychological makeup by constantly asking yourself, and answering truthfully, "Why did I laugh at *this* joke and not at *others?*"

Our regression into an infantile state of mind through humor, as suggested by the psychoanalysts, is most often practiced in group settings. For group approval, we subjugate our humor appreciation. If the group leaders approve of the humor, we laugh. If the group leaders disapprove, we groan. We rarely enjoy humor if we feel we're laughing counter to the crowd. If we are the first to laugh, we will stifle a hearty ha-ha in mid-ha if no one joins us. Even when acting childish, our desire is to maintain social approval.

In Russia, Yakov Smirnoff reports, a comedian tells a joke and people look around to see who's watching them before they laugh. "It throws the timing way off," he says.

Let's not camouflage our true intentions. We don't use humor just to entertain the world. The value of humor in attack is incomparable, because humor is a socially acceptable form of criticism, a catharsis that combines memorability with respectability.

But the only way you'll survive as a humorist/critic is if your target is equally disfavored by the audience. Understanding what motivates audience appreciation is one of the secrets of writing humor.

"I think you misunderstood when I said every joke must have a target."

CHAPTER 3

The Anatomy of Humor: The THREES Formula

THREE'S NOT JUST A CROWD, IT'S A HUMOR FORMULA

SIX CRITERIA, LIKE INGREDIENTS IN A CAKE RECIPE, make up the essentials of humor. And with few exceptions, the absence of any one ingredient so disturbs the formula that the humor is not only less funny, but in danger of complete failure. Whether the humor is a one-liner, a lengthy anecdote, or a three-act theatrical piece, these same six elements consistently appear.

Target
Hostility
Realism
Exaggeration
Emotion
Surprise

Although there's no absolute prescribed order, in this arrangement, the first letter of each element forms a memorable acronym: THREES.

TARGET

Our instinctive perception is that humor is fun. It isn't! Humor is criticism, cloaked as entertainment, directed at a specific target. Cartoonist Bill Mauldin once wrote, "Humor is really laughing off a hurt, grinning at misery."

Humor does more than grin at misery. It cuts into the target with a knife so razor sharp that no one sees the incision—just the blood. A string of one-liners is less like a necklace of pearls than a crown of thorns designed to scratch our fears. But humor can be group therapy for performer, writer, and audience. It reduces our anxiety and aggression because we're bonding with others in laughter, and we're thereby reassured that the hostility we feel toward the target is acceptable. This frees us from individual guilt; it also indulges our need to feel superior.

Language was invented because we need to communicate. Humor was invented because we need to complain. We use it when we need to focus on the right target. The target can be almost anything—a person, a place, a thing, or an idea.

People as Targets

You can't target an entire audience any more than you can shame the whole world. Humor is an attempt to maintain the status quo, so targeting reaffirms one group's ideas, mannerisms, and prejudices. Thus humor is always unfair. Like editorial cartoons, jokes take a biased point of view. There's no room in one joke for a balanced argument or explanation. As H.L. Mencken put it, "My business is diagnosis, not therapeutics."

Richard Pryor's audiences are easily defined: mostly young, black militants, with a fair percentage of young liberal whites. Thanks to their social lifestyle and political activities, they hold white authority as a common enemy. Pryor uses this bond by targeting police in his humor.

Pick on Somebody Your Own Size

By far the least offensive target is yourself. This is called self-deprecating humor. It's used by those most confident, particularly as a warm-up.

How many people heard my first album? (Crowd screams.)
Well, there goes that material.

They ridicule their own obvious shortcomings first: physical characteristics, finances, intelligence, even their success. For instance, when Bob Hope was being honored for twenty-five years with NBC, he commented: "It's been great. In all those years I've been rewarded with money, adulation, respect and encouragement. And to think I owe it all to the morning that I saw Bobby Sarnoff coming out of the Dixie Motel."

Unquestionably Ronald Reagan is expert at this. He almost always begins each speech, particularly less formal ones, with self-deprecating humor. For example, hundreds of school principals and teachers gathered on the South Lawn of the White House to be honored for their part in the Secondary School Recognition Program. The president's gag writer gave him a typical Reagan charmer:

> "Y'know, I've been out of school for some time now, but I still get nervous around so many principals."

Reagan's humor during the second of his debates with Walter Mondale in 1984 completely spiked the Democrats' best personal attack, the age issue, which had inspired quite a few fossil gags.

> At 76, I'm not afraid that Reagan will push the button. I'm afraid he'll keel over and fall on it.   —Aaron Freeman

Reagan knew this concern would come up during the election debates. When it did, his humorous answer—a reverse that will be a textbook classic for generations—completely deflated the press; even Mondale burst out laughing. According to *Newsweek,* he sealed his election with the following remark:

> I will not make age an issue of this campaign. I am not going to exploit, for political purposes, my opponent's youth and inexperience.

Celebrity Names Are Humor Fodder and Mudder

A second popular target is celebrities, national or local. No doubt it's a cheap shot but, human psychology being what it is, our appetite for a dash of vinegary gossip about our heroes, heroines, or villains is insatiable. Because the public, almost indiscriminately, idolizes the famous and the infamous, the American media love to create new celebrities in entertainment, sports, politics, and letters. Then, paradoxically, no sooner have the *idol rich* reached the apex of their media hype, than we begin to humble them with gossip and humorous digs.

Humor writers take advantage of this illogical mania. Former Senator S.I. Hayakawa admitted that comedians' frequent references to the fact that he had fallen asleep several times at public gatherings so ridiculed his dignity that he retired rather than run for reelection.

> Why can't a girl use sex? Look at Senator Hayakawa. He slept his way to the top.   —Maureen Murphy

Places as Targets

Our need for superiority is the spark plug for ridiculing "where *you* live." Examples are obvious: countries (Russia, China), states (West Virginia, New Jersey, California), cities (New York, Washington, Cleveland, Chicago, Burbank), and local spots in the news (a neighborhood, a street, a bar, lover's lane). Every performer has a favorite dumping ground.

So does every farmer. It's a national psychosis for farmers to target those in a neighboring state for artificial breeding. New Yorkers disparage those who live in New Jersey, who, in turn, tell jokes about Pennsylvania Quakers, who laugh at the Amish in Ohio, who pick on the coal miners of West Virginia, who razz the hillbillies of Kentucky, and so forth westward to Montana "where men are men and the sheep are very nervous."

Things as Targets

There's a veritable Sears catalog of objects that are favorite humor targets. It runs from buildings and automobiles to sports equipment, jewelry, and junk food. The basic rule, again, is that your target be a common bridge between performer and audience. It's easier to start backwards. Don't finalize your position until you've decided it's their position as well.

Tom Brokaw, NBC News anchorman, put his foot in his mouth at an awards luncheon in New Orleans during the height of recruiting controversy. He quipped, "I'm honored you invited me to come, especially when for $10,000 and a new convertible you could have had the top running back prospect at SMU." The laughter was mild; Brokaw didn't realize that the Southern Methodist athletic director and a few of his assistants were in the audience.

Ideas as Targets

Like objects, the list of controversial ideas that can be humor targets is lengthy. It varies depending on audience concern; however, it's the most dangerous target because a person's feelings aren't exposed on the outside like clothes. Targeting homosexuality, for example, is more difficult these days than targeting heterosexual material. Therefore it's easier to be for something than bluntly against it.

> Bisexuality immediately doubles your chances for a date on Saturday night.
> —Woody Allen

As a humor writer you must constantly remember to base your material on an important target shared with your intended audience. If the subject is your cat or dog—who cares?—unless your audience is composed of cat and dog lovers. If it's about cats and dogs who crap up the streets, then you can be sure only if most of the audience comes from your neighborhood.

HOSTILITY

Ridicule should be spelled *rid-a-cruel*. Most comedy is cruel. The words cruel and ridicule not only appear frequently but seem to be closely associated.

There's brutal honesty in Richard Pryor's stand-up routines about race, family, sex, and class savagery. Pryor is a good comedian because he knows how to make his punch lines humorous and not confrontational. George Bernard Shaw once wrote, "If you want to tell a person the truth, make him laugh or he'll kill you."

In order to write commercial humor, it's important to accept this concept of the real thrust of humor—to rid-a-cruel, using mental agility to combat that which threatens to defeat us most often. "The human race," said Mark Twain, "has only one effective weapon, and that is laughter."

All of us have hostility toward some person, thing or idea—unless we are St. Francis of Assisi (or, as Robert Benchley once speculated, "Unless I am getting him mixed up with St. Simon Stylites, which might be easy to do because both their first names begin with Saint"). Did you ever hear a joke about two perfect, happy people? But the cartoon of a beer-bellied, blue-collar worker walking in the front door and saying to his battle-ax wife, "Can you spare a few minutes? I need to be taken down a peg"— now, that works as great humor.

Humor is a powerful pesticide intended to help eradicate many of the hostile feelings in our daily life. The most common are (1) sexual frustrations, (2) intrusion of authority into our private lives, (3) financial concerns, (4) family problems, (5) angst and our feelings of powerlessness in the wake of technology, and (6) the largest group of all, our insecurity about our own physical characteristics, which triggers prejudices and taunts against minorities.

Sex

Mark Van Doren wrote, "Humorists are serious. They are the only people who are." Writers choose their humor subjects seriously. That's why sex makes up close to 50 percent of all humor. All of us, male and female, young and old, are more concerned with sexual activity than any other single subject and perhaps all other subjects combined. It isn't that we're fascinated by exaggerated acts of sex as much as we're frustrated by exaggerated reports of adequacy.

According to Alexandra Penney in *How to Make Love to a Man*, men's greatest sexual fears are size, erection, performance, quantity, premature ejaculation, secret homosexuality, and impotency—pronounced in West Virginia as *"im-poat-tant-cy*—because it's real im-potent to me!" But however you pronounce it, it still means always having to say you're sorry.

Shere Hite in *The Hite Report on Male Sexuality* reported that while men treasure sexuality, "they also dislike and feel very put upon by it." Her report suggests that men feel trapped by sexual stereotypes. They find themselves unable to speak openly about their sexual angers, anxieties, and desires. Many complain about the escalating pressures to initiate sex, to achieve and maintain frequent erections, to control the timing of ejaculations, and to understand, let alone satisfy, their partner's orgasmic needs.

> I finally had an orgasm and my doctor told me it was the wrong kind.
> —Woody Allen

Research on sexual humor indicates that beginning joke tellers are more likely to select themes with sexist content discriminating against males regardless of the gender of the performer or the audience; also that their dominant subjects are those which belittle body parts and sexual performance. Since they normally can't speak openly in public about these fears without seeming to denigrate their own potency, they substitute hostile sexual humor against male inadequacy. The laughter and applause they receive reassures them of a shared anxiety.

> My wife said that her wildest sexual fantasy would be if I got my own apartment.
> —Rodney Dangerfield

> I satisfy my wife every night. We get undressed, take a shower and get into bed completely nude. Then I say, "Darling, I'm very tired and I think I'll go to sleep." And she says, "I'm satisfied."
> —Larry Wilde

To cover their own fear of homosexuality, many comics use humor based upon deviance from the sexual norm. It's the second most common target.

Women are also intrigued by ribald humor about sexual activity, because they're as sexually insecure as men about size, performance, and satisfaction.

> During sex, men confuse me. They suddenly start shouting,

"I'm coming. I'm coming." I don't know whether they want me
there as a partner or a witness.   —Emily Levine

Sex is a concern regardless of age.

Three young boys were reading magazines in a dentist's office.
During a break, the dentist said to one, "I see you're reading
Popular Mechanics. I guess you'd like to become an engineer?"
  The boy nodded.
  He turned to the second, "I see you're reading *Country Gen-
tleman.* I assume you'd like to be a farmer?"
  He turned to the third, who was reading *Playboy.* "Well,
well, well," he said, "and what would you like to become?"
  "I don't know for sure," said the boy, "but I can hardly wait
to get started."

Authority

  While hostility against authority is international, it has always been
an American heritage. Since Revolutionary days, we've enjoyed spiking
the bloated arrogance of authority and watching it bleed. Humor is a great
catharsis, it gives the public an opportunity to blow off indignant steam at
major and minor authority figures.
  "Democracy expresses the notion that power resides with the individual," wrote Joseph Boskin. "And the individual with others has the right to
comment and assess issues and render judgments. The result is humor of
incredible latitude. No subject has been outside its purview, and no person
or group has been blessed with total invisibility."

Artificial hearts are nothing new. Politicians have had them for
years.   —Mack McGinnis

One proof of this hostility is the fact that invariably we ridicule upward, at-
tacking those we perceive to have superior authority. Freshmen ridicule
upperclassmen, but have little interest in writing humor about their younger brothers or sisters. Faculty spend very little effort on humor directed at
students, and much more time on material satirizing the administration. In
the military echelons of command, noncoms bitch about junior commis-
sioned officers, who gripe about major support staff, who in turn snicker
about the general's idiosyncrasies, until—so the story goes—General
MacArthur's wife once asked him to convert to a religion in which he no
longer believed he was God.

Matty Simmons, publisher of the *National Lampoon,* credits the anti-establishment climate of Vietnam and Watergate with the birth and success of his magazine. "Nixon and Agnew had as much to do with the *Lampoon*'s success as I did," he said. "We came along when marvelous people for satire were running the country. They were just so unlikeable."

A humorist tells himself every morning, "I hope it's going to be a rough day." When things are going well, it's much harder to make the right jokes.   —Alan Coren

Here's a story that's double-edged. Some people think it's funny, while others find it tasteless and disrespectful. The question here, however, is which groups—feminists, Republicans, youth, the waiters' union—would find it funny and which would find it distasteful?

Supreme Court Justice Sandra O'Connor went with the other justices to a restaurant for lunch. The waiter asked for her order first. "I'll have a steak sandwich and coffee." "What about the vegetables?" asked the waiter. O'Connor said, "Oh, they'll have the same."

The answer may surprise you. The best group would be a meeting of the Bar Association. Logic? Because lawyers have ambivalent feelings toward judges, this is a case of hostility against authority being released through humor.

Next to government, we frequently feel hostility toward successful people. La Rochefoucauld wrote, "It is not enough to have a success, your best friend must fail." This is especially true of comedy writers.

Comedians and comedy writers talk about friendship, but a lot of us would kill each other. There's something bizarre about guys who do comedy . . . they hate to see other comedians get laughs.   —Johnny Carson

Financial Concerns

"I have a serious investment problem. I have no money."

While men admit they think more about sex than any other subject, a recent *Money* magazine survey indicated that women worry more about finances than sex, by a whopping 51 percent to 12 percent margin.

There's little doubt that money is a constant thorn of irritation and hostility. Said Sophie Tucker, "I've been rich and I've been poor. Believe me, rich is better!"

But even if you have an upper-middle-class income, the Helitzer theory of economic tension maintains that financial anxiety compounds in direct proportion to affluence: the more money you have, the more problems. Just buying a new product, for example, multiplies family anxiety four times: (1) debating whether you really need the product; (2) deciding on a brand, which means reading comparison literature, evaluating alternatives, and physically shopping to find it; (3) haggling over price and agonizing over how to finance it; (4) being exasperated by breakdowns and repairs for the life of the product.

The concern about financial matters starts with your first cry to buy nickel candy and continues to your last breath.

> "Being of sound mind," it was written in the will, "I spent every cent myself."

This thesis is so well documented that we might be better off concentrating on the methods humorists use to take advantage of this universal hostility. First, since everyone has personal money problems, the best way to involve the audience is to show that you share their problems.

> I've got all the money I'll ever need—if I die by four o'clock.
> —Henny Youngman

Second, depending on the audience, business practices are a frequent financial target, since they direct hostility against two subjects at the same time—economics and authority. Consider this company bulletin:

> As you all know, our accounting department has a little red box on its wall with a sign saying, "In case of emergency, break glass." Inside are two tickets to Brazil.

The opportunities for financial subjects are countless: wages, taxes, investments, gambling, lottery awards, credit cards, to name just a few.

> My VISA card was stolen two months ago, but I don't want to report it. The guy who took it is using it less than my wife.

Family Affairs

Hostility against family responsibilities, restrictions and competing interests needs little elaboration. In terms of joke quantity, humor on family conflict runs third only to sex and ethnic humor (which we'll get to in just a minute, under physical characteristics).

> I left my wife because she divorced me. I'm not going to live with somebody under those kinds of pressures. But I still love my ex-wife. I called her on the phone today. I said, "Hello, plaintiff . . ."
> —Skip Stevenson

What's more significant, however, is the growing expansion of targets to include all members of the family, instead of just wives and mothers-in-law. Female humorists, including Erma Bombeck and Lily Tomlin, have come out of the broom closet to use a vacuum cleaner on the bloated male ego.

> I wanted to be an actress. I said to my mother I want to cry real tears. I want to show great emotion for someone I don't really care for. She said, "Become a housewife." She always wanted me to be married all in white—and all virginal. But I don't think a woman should be a virgin when she gets married. I think she should have at least one other disappointing experience. One woman friend of mine told me she hated her husband so much that when he died she had him cremated, blended him with marijuana and smoked him. She said, "That's the best he's made me feel in years."
> —Maureen Murphy

Family targets have always included teenagers and pre-teens. Now the hit list includes even toddlers who are no longer cute but exhibit, according to Bill Cosby, signs of brain damage. Parents are unburdening themselves wittily, even if they can't do it financially.

> They once asked my father what he wanted me to do when I grew up, and he said, "Leave home."

And children are reciprocating in this new birth of freedom which means let's give it to our saintly, gray-haired mother and revered father.

> My parents had a meaningful relationship and stayed together for forty years. Out of love? No, out of spite.   —Woody Allen

Angst and Technology

Angst is an intellectual observation that fairy tales aren't true, it will happen to you—there is an end to every happy beginning. Angst has pointed a devil's finger at anxieties so personal that, in the past, we carefully avoided discussing them even in private: fear of death, coping with deformity, deprivations, or neurotic symptoms such as paranoia, insecurity, narcissism, kinky sexual drives, and a long list of others.

Woody Allen has popularized angst. "I merchandise misery," he wrote. "When I named my movie *Love and Death* the commercial possibilities were immediately apparent to me: sight gags and slapstick sequences about despair and emptiness, dialogue jokes about anguish and dread; finally, mortality, human suffering, anxiety. In short, the standard ploys of the funnyman. . . . It's not that I'm afraid of death, I just don't want to be there when it happens."

Angst is also the hallmark of Lily Tomlin, who even plays a character named Agnus Angst, who says:

God has Alzheimer's disease. He's forgotten we exist.

A philosopher once said: "The best thing that could happen to a person is not to have been born at all. But unfortunately, this happens to very few."

High-Tech Anxiety

Technology can be threatening. Charlie Chaplin exploited frustrations and fears about rapidly growing automation to make people laugh. It's ironic that IBM uses his tramp character as an implied advertising testimonial for computers, because Chaplin was ridiculing machines, not promoting them. The audience vicariously enjoyed his hopeless assembly line dilemmas and mixed-up pursuits with autos that ran in reverse.

The sense of hopelessness that comes from our apparent inability to control the environment is now a universal hostility. Industrial chemicals lead to pollution, drugs lead to suicide, the advertising drum beats for nonsensical fads. The biggies—fear of nuclear war, an invasion of spooks from outer space, and chemical mutation of our bodies and minds—suggest that humor is probably the only rational way of coping.

They asked John Glenn what he thought about just before his first capsule was shot into space, and he said: "I looked around me and suddenly realized that everything had been built by the lowest bidder."

Physical Characteristics

What my comedy is all about is envy, greed, malice, lust, nar-
rowness, and stupidity.   —John Cleese

This is one of humor's most controversial subjects because it caters to our
most primitive instincts—prejudice and insecurity. We hope to maintain
some sense of superiority by ridiculing the characteristics of others, which
appear abnormal to our crowd. We're responding to a primitive form of
group therapy.

We fear control and intimidation by people of different colors or reli-
gions and so, by derision, we attempt to stereotype their physical appearances, ethnic mannerisms, colloquial speech—any unique characteristic
we find odd. We feel the same way about people with different social attitudes from us—about drugs, sex, education, professions, even music, literature, and humor. As long as we're in the majority, we don't hesitate to
criticize.

Humor employs these sins without conscience. A conscience won't
prevent sin, it only prevents us from enjoying it. Ethnic humor is the second most popular category of joke books, and derogatory impersonations
are a favorite comedy foil. This is how Cheech and Chong, whose financial
successes outstripped that of every other comedy team in film history,
described their type of humor:

Our jokes may be fifty years old, but our audience, the youth,
ain't seen shit. To them, it's brand new. If you're white you can
be afraid of people of different color, religious fanatics, but if
you're black or brown, you're afraid of other things, like starva-
tion and not having a place to live. By incorporating the basic
humor of drugs and poverty into our appeal, it makes it universal—the underdogs against the world. We know the humor of
the rough and ready . . . we pander to the worst instincts in
people—caricaturing swishy gays, dumb blondes, illiterate Mex-
icans, greedy Jews. We're shameless panderers. We give our
audience hope. Nobody ever put a gun to a guy's head and
said, "You gotta go down and see a Cheech and Chong movie,
or else." Our fans must have dollars and cents: the sense is inferiority and the dollars are five.

It used to be the blue-collar whites who regurgitated the most hostile ethnic
humor. As long as you joked in your own neighborhood, "kick 'em in the

ass" humor was commercially profitable. Today, black comedians, sensing both an increasing freedom for public humor and an increasing audience of blacks and whites who'll pay to hear it, are coming into a heyday.

Redd Foxx brags about his material being "as outrageous as possible. That's the humor I hear in the ghettos. We don't pull punches, and we don't want to hear about Little Blue Boy and Cinderella—and if they don't like my shit, they can fuck off!"

A popular folk tale, which often reappears as a current event, tells about four doctors' wives from a small Midwestern city who decided to brave a weekend shopping trip in Manhattan. Their husbands were apprehensive about city crime. "If someone wants your pocketbook or jewelry, don't put up a fight. Just do what they say. Promise?"

On their very first morning, as the four were descending in the hotel elevator, a well-dressed black man got on leading a large Doberman pinscher. He looked at the women for a moment, and then commanded the dog, "Sit!" Immediately the four women sat on the floor.

Each writer has his own definition of humor. Shakespeare said, "Brevity is the soul of wit." Somerset Maugham wrote, "Impropriety is the soul of wit." I believe it's hostility. When we all think alike there will be a lot less humor.

REALISM AND EXAGGERATION

"Lateral thinking" is used by business gurus to solve problems and come up with new ideas; it's defined as an interruption in the habitual thought process by leaping sideways out of ingrained patterns. Comedy has been doing this for thousands of years.

That's why humor must include both realism and exaggeration. Since it appears that exaggeration is the logical antithesis of realism, it may seem ludicrous to have both within the framework of one piece of humor. But good humor is a paradox—the unexpected juxtaposition of the reasonable next to the unreasonable—and that creates surprise, another essential in the THREES formula.

"Most good jokes state a bitter truth," says Larry Gelbart. Without some fundamental basis of truth, there's little with which the audience can associate. This technique will be discussed at length in Chapter 10.

The basic two-step in humor is (1) to state some commonly acceptable problem, frequently with a cliché, and (2) in the last word or two change the expected ending to a surprise.

> People who lose sleep over the stock market are lucky. I lose money.

Then there's Abe Burrow's famous parody of the first two lines of Irving Berlin's song, "There's No Business Like Show Business."

> Yesterday they told you, you would not go far. Last night you opened and—they were right!

Incongruous humor is based on the premise of two or more realistic but contrasting circumstances united into one thought. Stephen Leacock once wrote, "Humor results from the contrast between a thing as it is and *ought to be,* and a thing smashed out of shape, as it *ought not to be."* Here's an example by Robert Wohl.

> If you think the world is normal, then how come hot dogs come in packages of ten and hot dog buns come in packages of eight?

Dorothy Parker once wrote, "The difference between wit and wisecracking is that wit has truth to it, while wisecracking is simply calisthenics with words." So realism fathers truisms, those witty bits of philosophy based upon self-evident and generally accepted facts of life.

> What can you expect from a day that begins with getting up in the morning?

> To entertain some people, all you have to do is listen. But there is nothing quite so annoying as having someone go on talking when you're interrupting.

> We shouldn't criticize potholes. They're among the few things left on the road that are still being made in the USA.
> —Robert Orben

Realism becomes even more evident when you consider the humor of children. Their combination of truth and simplistic naiveté delights grown-ups because it gives us a feeling of benevolent superiority—if, like benevolent dictatorship, there is such a thing.

A five-year-old was fascinated by his grandfather's false teeth. He watched as gramps removed his dentures, washed them and replaced them. He asked to see it done over and over. "Okay," said the grandfather finally, "Anything else?" "Yeah," said the kid. "Now take off your nose."

A mother and her teenage daughter were watching an old Clark Gable-Claudette Colbert movie on TV, which ended with the usual clinch and fade-out. "Gee, mom," said the daughter, "your movies end where ours just begin."

To be most effective, the "facts" of humor should be logical—the relationship between people clear and predictable, the time and the locale of the story familiar, the hostility common to the audience and commensurate to the irritation. Major deviations from reality don't prevent humor, but they may reduce the payoff of uninhibited laughter. In essence, then, it should be as realistic as possible.

When Stalin was head of the Russian government he asked a soldier in Siberia, "How's everything?" The soldier said, "I can't complain." And Stalin answered, "You bet your life you can't."

Exaggerated Expectations

How does realism relate to exaggeration? As we accept poetic license, let's accept a humor license that grants permission to expand on themes with soaring imagination and unabashed metaphors. The public is willing to suspend disbelief and skepticism. They permit humorists to utilize hyperbole, blatant distortion, and overstated figures that signal, since the absurd subject matter can't possibly be true, "Hey, it's only a joke." Therefore, the audience laughs at exaggerated banana peel acrobatics because the clown will certainly get up. That's comedy! If he doesn't get up, that's tragedy!

The only way I'll ever be as trim as Robert Redford is if he swallows a steel-belted radial tire.

Another example of the *likely* next to the *unlikely* is the classic photojournalism story about the newspaper that ran two photos: one of a gray-haired matron who'd just been elected president of the local Women's Republican Club and the other of a gorilla who was a new addition to the local zoo—but the captions got switched. That's *likely.* The second stage of the

humor comes from the *unlikely:* the newspaper got sued for defamation—
by the gorilla!

EMOTION AND SURPRISE

Hostility, over- or understated, is not enough. There must be a buildup of
anticipation in the audience. This is really nothing more than the writer's
skill in using emotion to produce tension and anxiety. It's a trick.

Think of hostility—the subject—as a balloon. Tension is the emotional inflation of more and more air, building anxiety as to just how and
when the balloon will burst. The writer's problem is to see that it bursts
with laughter, not hot air!

Each performer has a stage personality, called a persona or shtick.
While others can steal material, they can't steal the nuances that make one
individual funny and another unable to tell a joke or write one. Larry Wilde
believes "there is a melody and cadence to all comedy that is as stringent
and disciplined as music."

A great comedic performer must be an actor with boundless energy.
Many comedians have become good actors in films and sitcoms, but you
rarely hear of a good actor becoming a great comedian. (In the movie *The
Entertainer,* Sir Laurence Olivier played the part of a small-time comic. It
was a brilliant, award-winning performance, and when Olivier was asked
how he had managed to make the comic look so inept, he replied, "I didn't
try to do him badly. I played the role as well as I could.")

Emotion is the ability of the speaker to translate the writer's material
into entertainment through voice, enthusiasm, and action. Emotion is also
experience: knowing when to pause and for how long, the rhythm of inflection, and sometimes nothing more grandiose than a gesture—called a
take, because it *takes* the right gesture.

Tommy Smothers commented in an interview, "One of the hardest
things for a comedy writer is to write in the vague—the spaces, the timing,
the attitude. Woody Allen discovered that stand-up is a funny man doing
material, not a man doing funny material. The personality, the character,
not the joke, is primary."

Emotion is the area most often referred to when critics talk about natural talent—the inexplicable factor that produces stars and champions. It
can't be taught, only encouraged. Performers learn from each other by
scrutinizing timing, characterization, and structure. What can be taught,
however, are five techniques for maximizing emotion. Each is designed to
increase audience tension.

Building Emotion

The first and the most common technique is also the simplest—a pause just before the payoff word. It's called a pregnant pause because it promises to deliver. Even in Henny Youngman's classic, "Take my wife—please!" the slight pause, indicated by the dash, is essential to the reading of that line. (Try to read it any other way!) The pregnant pause creates tension, which is relieved by the surprise ending.

> I know you want to hear the latest dope from Washington.
> Well—here I am.   —Senator Alan Simpson

> Would you be so kind to help a poor, unfortunate fellow out of work, hungry, in fact someone who has nothing in this world—except this gun!

The second technique is asking the audience a question, thereby encouraging them to become involved. This is one of Johnny Carson's favorite devices.

> Anybody see this commercial on TV last night? It claims you can send a letter from anywhere in the country to New York for seven dollars and fifty cents and it promises next day delivery. The Post Office calls it Express Mail. I remember when it used to be called the US Mail.

> Remember how hot it was yesterday? Well a dog was chasing a cat, and they were both walking.

A common technique used by novice stand-up comics to infuse tension is to ask the audience "How many here have ever. . . .?" It's become its own cliché, and the take-offs are even more fun.

> How many here went to grade school?

> How many here paid to get in?

> How many here know what sex is?

The third and fourth techniques are both builds: *triples* and *a joke on the way to a joke,* two or three firecrackers that prepare the audience for one big blast. These will be discussed in more detail in Chapter 7.

The fifth way to build emotional tension is by working the audience, a favorite device of Steve Allen, Howie Mandell, Don Rickles, and his protégé, Pudgy. Each walks out into the audience and throws questions at what appear to be randomly selected members. The audience's tension comes not from their amazement that the comic is able to come up with toppers to every answer, but from the fear that they may be the next victim ridiculed. (Working the audience will be explained in Chapter 19.)

Every playwright builds emotion into a scene. A humor writer does the same thing, but because a joke is the smallest unit of comedy writing, you must be able to infuse tension into a few words. Good humor writers are like professional card cheats. They know how to palm the joker and insert it only when it's needed. When their act is too evident to the audience, they get killed—just like in real life.

Surprise Me

If laughter is the electricity that makes a comedy writer's blood start pumping, then surprise is the power generator. The need for surprise is the one cardinal rule in comedy. It is an absolute must. Without it, clever, pithy remarks may be nothing more than audacious commentary.

"We only laugh because we are surprised," wrote Garson Kanin. Agnes Repplier agrees: "The essence of humor is that it should be unexpected, that is, should embody an element of surprise that should startle us out of that reasonable gravity which, after all, must be our habitual frame of mind."

According to Abe Burrows, the best way to define the construction of surprise is to use baseball terms: a joke is a curve—a fastball that bends at the last instant and fools the batter. "You throw a perfectly straight line at the audience and then, right at the end, you curve it. Good jokes do that." To achieve the unexpected twist of humor language, it's sometimes necessary to sacrifice grammar and even logic for surprise:

He may not be able to sing, but he sure can't dance.

A key word sets up the surprise. It gets the audience to assume they know the ending. Notice how the word *half* works in these examples:

Mother to young son: "Johnny, were you nice to your sister while I was out?" "Yeah, I gave her half my peanuts. I gave her the shells."

My wife and I have many arguments, but she only wins half of them. My mother-in-law wins the other half.   —Terryl Bechtol

Charlie Chaplin defined surprise in terms of a film scene where the villain is chasing the heroine down the street. On the sidewalk is a banana peel. The camera cuts swiftly back and forth from the banana peel to the approaching fall guy. At the last second, the heavy sees the banana peel and jumps over it—then falls into an open manhole.

It's easy to tell if your surprise works, because a live audience's instant laughter is the most honest of emotions. You can give a bad speech, a poor theatrical or musical performance and the audience will still politely applaud. If you perform bad humor, the jury's icy silence may be just a preliminary to their unsolicited advice.

No matter how well written, some jokes don't come off in performance because the comedian gets too anxious and telegraphs the surprise. Many performers tip-off the funny line with a lick of their lips or a gleam in their eyes. They hold up their hand and stop the audience from laughing all out ("Hey, you ain't heard nothing yet"), so the audience is primed for a big topper. But then there's no surprise, and no laughter. This can have a domino effect because the performer loses confidence in the material, then starts to press and loses other laughs, because the audience has a sixth sense about "flop sweat"—when a performer is anxious and trying too hard.

"Comedy is mentally pulling the rug out from under each person in your audience," wrote Gene Perret. "But first, you have to get them to stand on it. You have to fool them, because if they see you preparing to tug on the rug, they'll move."

Coming up with a surprise ending takes a good deal of thought, testing and rewriting. Let's try an example of a surprise ending for different audiences. Which ending would you select?

1. He was complimented when the editor called his work sophomoric because he had flunked out of college in his freshman year.

2. He had flunked out of college in his freshman year, so he was complimented whenever anybody called his work sophomoric.

It's obvious that the second version works better, because the surprise word (*sophomoric*) is held to the last instant. The next time you hear a joke you instinctively laughed at, take a moment to analyze it. Where did the surprise come? Now take one of your favorite funny stories. Can it be rewritten to be even *more* effective?

A POP QUIZ

Let's see how the entire THREES formula works on a contemporary story. Does it have a target, hostility, realism, exaggeration, emotion, and a surprise ending?

> An elderly truck driver was eating lunch at a roadside diner when three shaggy young hoodlums, sporting black leather jackets garishly decorated with swastikas, skulls, and crossbones, parked their motorcycles and came inside. They spotted the truck driver and proceeded to taunt him, taking his food away, pushing him off the seat, and insulting his old age. He said nothing but finally got up from the floor, paid his bill and walked out. One of the bikers, unhappy that they hadn't provoked a fight, said to the waitress, "Boy, he sure wasn't much of a man, was he?" "No," said the waitress, looking out the window, "and he's not much of a truck driver either. He just backed his truck over three motorcycles!"

Did the formula of THREES work? Was there:

T = Target: Yes, the young American hoodlums.
H = Hostility: The story exploits public frustration at the escalating growth of juvenile crime.
R = Realism: There's little doubt that the aggressive actions of the bikers could happen.
E = Exaggeration: Plenty! The motorcyclists, three against one (note the number three again), their crude behavior exemplified not just once but with three incidents of hostile action, and, of course, the truck driver's final action—not a simple thing to do quickly.
E = Emotion: Obviously carefully written to squeeze out every drop of audience hostility in the opening: the stereotypical fascist appearance of the bikers, their childish aggression meant just to provoke a fight with an outnumbered, aged opponent, even our disappointment when the truck driver appears—for a moment—to be a coward.
S = Surprise: The climax of the story is withheld until the last two words.

The THREES formula will maximize an audience's humor interest. It's the battle plan. Now, let's look at some of the ammunition.

"It's hot, Moses. Very hot. Just change 'adultery'
to 'playing around' and the double entendre possibilities are limitless."

CHAPTER 4

POW Is a Play on Words

WHERE DO JOKES COME FROM? Well, funny things do happen to us every once in a while. If we're extroverts, we dramatically recount the bizarre features with exaggerated overtones. We get laughs. And we think we're pretty funny.

But professional humorists can't wait for absurd things to actually happen. They have to produce every day, so they create what they can't find. They do this in one of two ways—by rephrasing old material, or creating new humor.

There's no such thing as an ad-lib (a term called "sans script" by Antoni Tabak). But Tabak's pun is more clever than accurate, because ad-libs are scripted and then used at the right time by comedians.

Fans savoring the pros' "quick" turn of phrase are really admiring their memory and their ability to instinctively transfuse old material into a new situation. Ninety-nine percent of the time their "on stage" performances are rewritten, rehearsed, and retaped. And while ad-lib opportunities do come along, professionals are actually just pushing keys in their memory banks at such speed the audience believes they're originating humor on the spot. They're not originating, they're adapting—whether the material is "their own" or not.

The top professionals like Bob Hope, Johnny Carson, Milton Berle, George Burns, and Red Skelton have been in comedy for over *fifty* years.

And that's seven days a week, because the comedic mind doesn't stop even when the body is resting. They have delivered thousands of jokes, one-liners, anecdotes, and skit vignettes—and heard hundreds of thousands.

While fifty years of experience is great to have, as a beginner you can't depend on joke files even if you've read every joke book written, and about twenty-five new ones come out every year. You have to learn the second method: how to create from scratch.

You start by *watching* the antics of people in public, on TV, in films, and you read about them in news stories. You fantasize "what if" situations, and you play with words.

TO MAKE 'EM LAUGH—POW!

More than 50 percent of all humor is based on a *play-on-words*, which provides the obvious acronym of POW. Reminiscent of a sound effect in superhero comics, POW does pack a punch—and a punch line. POW is a twist on familiar clichés, bromides, metaphors, aphorisms, book, movie, and song titles, famous quotes, national ad slogans—in fact any expressions widely known by the public.

I prefer to lump these play-on-words groups together under the title clichés, for all famous expressions ("Where's the beef?" or "Go ahead, make my day," etc.) soon become trite through overuse. Like salt indiscriminately tossed on food, clichés are sprinkled liberally into every conversation, every letter, every political speech and, unfortunately, in too many major literary efforts. In fact, they're a dime a dozen. A cliché is an expression that has lost its original impact. It's a stereotype shortcut to comprehension when we are creatively lazy or mentally bankrupt. But the humor writer uses audacious and surprising interpretations of clichés to shock an audience into laughter.

> As the farmer said to his disappointed cow, "I'm sorry I gave
> you a bum steer."
> —John Murtaugh

Clichés are the basis of practically all puns, limericks, and clever witticisms. They run the gamut from childish idioms to erudite double entendres. Cliché practitioners have included S.J. Perelman ("One of our stagecraft is missing," and "Stringing Up Father"), Tom Stoppard ("I have the courage of my lack of convictions"), and every stand-up comedian.

The First Step for Mankind Is a Little Cliché

Clichés are perfect first-launch vehicles for the neophyte humor writer, because one-liners are the most salable humor form today. I'm not sure just why "shorter is better." Perhaps it's because comics used to say, "Stop me if you've heard this one," and too many people did! In any case, the simplicity of cliché humor can be put to immediate use in a wide variety of formats such as photo and cartoon captions, greeting cards, news and advertising headlines, bumper stickers (a rear view of pop culture), titles of books and articles, and monologues.

Its great value in humor is that the ending of a cliché is predictable, so the audience's thoughts are headed in a predictable direction. The humor writer has a number of formulas for altering a cliché so that its final direction tricks the reader or listener. The result is surprise laughter, the payoff of comedic effort.

The key word is *predictability*. Since surprise is the most important initial stimulant for laughter, the easiest way to achieve surprise is to use a vehicle that takes the audience for a ride in a predictable direction—a direction you will change at the last possible moment. This is done visually on roller coaster rides or in magic; both are a last-second switch of an optical illusion. In humor, it's a last-second switch of a verbal conclusion.

The most obvious example is children's poetry. We expect the lines following "Roses are red, violets are blue" to rhyme. When we're tricked, we are surprised and we laugh, or at least smile, depending on how clever the twist.

Here's an example of a simple poem with a predictable ending. It turns out to be funny—and wise—when our expectation turns out to be erroneous. The following rhyme was written in a school yearbook:

> Think of Sidney,
> Think of Lee.
> If you ever need money,
> Think of Sidney.
> —Red Buttons

Clichés are more common in speech than rhyme, but their ending must be just as predictable. In fact, one definition of a cliché is a phrase so predictable you can finish it after you've heard the first few words.

CLICHÉ MASTER

There are five basic techniques for using clichés. We'll study these point by point in this chapter, but first let's take a look at the list.

1. *A Double Entendre* is an ambiguous word or phrase that allows for a double interpretation of words, images, and associations—the second of which is generally spicy.

2. *The Simple Truth* is the opposite of a double entendre. It takes the explicit meaning of a key word in an idiom and interprets it literally.
3. *Reforming* alters either the word order of the cliché or the spelling of one or two words by adding or deleting letters, in effect substituting a homonym or a word that rhymes.
4. *The Take-Off* first offers the acceptable interpretation of the cliché followed by a realistic but highly exaggerated commentary, frequently a double entendre.
5. *Associations* utilize combinations of clichés or titles by relating different subjects.

1. THE DOUBLE ENTENDRE

Secretary to boss: "I've got good news and bad news. The good news is that your wife is *keeping a cat around the house* so she won't be lonely when you travel. The bad news is that the cat's six-foot-two and plays jazz clarinet."

The reason double meanings are used so often (perhaps as much as 40 percent of all cliché humor), is that they're so easy to do and so much a part of our vocabulary.

Fast food restaurants are not only mushrooming—they're adding the whole salad bar.

More simple examples abound. Consider these names and slogans:

Waukegan, Illinois Radiator Repair: A good place to take a leak.

Art supplies: Honest, I Was Framed. —Collected by Rance Crain

Sign over boss's son-in-law's desk: If you think I'm dead wood, just try to fire me!

Jeans ad: Survival of the fittest.

Business card: Fenton Baked Goods
J.P. Fenton, President
"One Tough Cookie"

Let's take the expression "wire ahead for reservations." We instinctively believe we know what that cliché means, but three of the four words have several double entendre possibilities. That's where the humor writer starts his "What if . . ." mental calisthenics. When he is satisfied, after many rewrites, that he can recast the cliché, he finds the path to his pun easy to construct:

> The Sioux tribe sent one of their brightest braves to engineering school. After graduating, he returned home and was immediately assigned to install electric lights in all the latrines. He became famous for being the first Indian to wire a head for reservations.

The more sophisticated your linguistic ability, the more opportunity for the double entendre. Even Supreme Court decisions have used humor of this type, but it doesn't do them justice.

> Every night I had a strange girl. Same girl—she was just strange.
> —Michael Davis

The logic behind double entendre humor is as basic as its French translation: two meanings. The audience assumes one meaning; the comic is sneaking in another.

> Irving made a lot of money one year in the garment business and decided to buy a racehorse. One day he brought all his friends to the stable as the vet was laboriously working on the horse. "Is my horse sick?" asked Irving. "She's not the picture of health," said the vet, "but we'll pull her through."
> "Will I ever be able to race her?"
> "Chances are you will—and you'll probably beat her, too!"
> —Myron Cohen

As new expressions come into the vernacular, the professional humor writer looks for every opportunity to play around with words—the most socially acceptable form of playing around.

> We call our maid a commercial cleaner, because she cleans only during commercials.

Lately the computer industry has inspired hundreds of double entendre cli-chés, such as "terminal condition," "Take a byte out of this," and "There's nothing new about computers: Eve had her Apple and Adam had his Wang."

Double entendre is the formula in the most memorable comedy sketch of all time: Abbott and Costello's "Who's on First," in which Who, Why, Yesterday, etc. are supposedly the names of players. Where'd that routine come from? I don't know—(all together, now: THIRD BASE!).

Everybody's Doin' It

The most popular double entendre is the word *it*, which can be used to mean a hundred different things, but none more than the synonym for inter-course.

Lawyers do it in their briefs.

Doctors do it with patience.

Publishers do it by the book.

Bankers do it with interest.

Carpet layers do it on their knees.

Elevator operators do it going up and down.

Math teachers do it with unknowns.

MC, after bombing with an anti-feminist joke: "Boy, am I going to get it when I get home. Or maybe, I'm not going to get it when I get home."

The second most common double entendre is the word "in," which also has an obvious sexual connotation.

"Isn't it great to be in June?"
"Yes, but her sister, Barbara, was even better."

Patient on phone: "Is the doctor in yet?"
Nurse: "No, we're just up to foreplay."

Since the second meaning of a double entendre is frequently considered risqué, broadcast censors cross-examine every word in a script. Some sitcom writers will purposely put in expressions like "There's a fruitcake in the parlor," just to watch the censor sweat. (In children's advertising, their paranoia is sometimes more comic than the jokes. I spent six months arguing with a young lady of the National Association of Broadcaster's TV Code Office for permission to use the jingle line "Two in the bathtub is more fun than one," for a washable doll called Rub-a-Dub Dolly. The censor, an attractive twenty-five-year-old, who unfortunately had a five-second broadcast delay built into her mind, once challenged: "Can you prove that two in the bathtub is more fun than one?" I looked at her for a moment and then said, "I'm about to suggest a wonderful idea!")

They're Everywhere

Other fertile sources of double entendres are clichés from one activity that can apply to another.

> The heart patient refused the transplant saying he'd already had
> a change of heart.   —George Carlin

The above double entendre is an example of a first-degree transition. The next higher grade are those clichés which offer opportunities for clever adroitness.

> While driving through the Kansas farmlands, I suddenly had the
> need to urinate. Since no restrooms were immediately availa-
> ble, I pulled my car off the road and went into a wheat field.
> As I was getting back in my car, a state trooper arrested me.
> The charge: "Going against the grain."

> My son and I, attending a wedding, were asked by the usher if
> we were on the groom's side or the bride's side. My son was
> shocked. "Are they taking sides already?"   —Lillian Koslover

A common source of double entendre humor is the misunderstanding most foreigners have with English. It makes Americans feel superior.

> Johnny Yune, a Korean comedian who moved to Los Angeles,
> says he took a date to Bakersfield. On the drive home the date
> suddenly said, "I want you to know I don't go all the way."
> Said Yune, "So, I dropped her off in Encino."

But be warned. Amateurs make the mistake that since double entendres are so plentiful they are easy to harvest. Unless they are properly planted, they'll turn out to be crabgrass.

> He was a millionaire golfer, so he used his chauffeur as his driver.

They are also so often used in humor that even unsophisticated audiences can detect a telegraphed punch line.

> One man walking his dog met a friend on the street who admired his pet.
> "I just bought him for fifteen hundred dollars," said the owner.
> "Isn't that a lot of money for a mutt?" his friend asked.
> "Why, he's not a mutt. He's part Airedale and part bull."
> "Yeah, what part is bull?"
> "The part about the fifteen hundred dollars."

If the double entendre isn't hidden, there's no surprise.

Irony

Double entendres on the highest level tend to be ironic figures of speech—sarcastic statements that generally mean (to insiders) the exact opposite of what's being expressed. Bob Hope would walk into the ward of a military hospital and shout to the wounded GIs: "Please don't get up!" Another example is the suggestion, during a hurricane, that we invite our neighbors (whom we don't like) over for a swim in our pool, "because they're a bunch of drips, anyway!"

> He's such a skilled professor he can tell you everything he knows in one breath.

Irony can be expressed in many ways, but it's often the result of associating an absurd double entendre with a hostile product.

During the Tylenol crisis, humorists had a cabinet of pill-gotten gains with ironic double entendres like these:

> *Doctor to patient:* "Please note that each bottle of Tylenol has two expiration dates—one for the pills and one for you. . . . I recommend you take two every four hours and have your next-of-kin call me in the morning."

The Oral Misunderstanding

Since an audience laughs when they feel superior, the following cliché uses dialogue built on one character's misunderstanding:

When I told my gentile girlfriend I was bringing the bagels for brunch, she set two extra places.　　　　—George Furth

The Usage Blunder

English teachers like to collect and publish student spelling and usage errors; perhaps it's some compensation for the daily pain they must bear without baring. While these examples are, purportedly, a result of ignorance, humor writers are frequently inspired by the double entendres crafted by a fool.

For her birthday, she asked her boyfriend for designer genes.

The girl was affluent in both French and Spanish.
　　　　　　　　　—Collected by Judith Ramos

My marital status is singular.

Three classes of professors compromise the teaching staff, and faculty are chosen as committee chairmen on the basis of senility.　　　　　　　　　—Collected by Grove Day

This is a mid-evil story and Hester was A-moral person.

In my whole college carrier, I enjoyed this coarse. I had you before, if you remember, but never like this.
　　　　　　　　　—Collected by Jesse Bier

Malaprops

Malapropisms are twisted language innocently spoken by a dolt. They were the format of Burns and Allen's act for more than thirty years. Today, entertainment columns are big users of celebrity witticisms, and publicity agents, when they can't find something positive to say about their clients, may credit them with reformed cliché wit that turns into malaprops. In the 1940s, movie mogul Sam Goldwyn was quoted in the entertainment columns so often with examples of mistaken grammar that the classic malaprop was retitled Goldwynism.

A verbal contract isn't worth the paper it's printed on.

Every Tom, Dick and Harry is named William.

For your information, I would like to ask a question.

Now, gentlemen, listen slowly.

In two words: im-possible!

And his most famous: Include me out.

Baseball managers Casey Stengel (in the sixties) and Yogi Berra (in the seventies) used the same device to cement their immortality in reference books.

Stengel

I guess I'll have to start from scraps.

If people don't want to come to the ballpark, nobody can stop them.

What do you want—egg in your beard?

It's *deja vu* all over again.

Berra

That restaurant is so crowded, nobody ever goes there anymore.

I want to win 100 or 105 games this year—whichever comes first.

Asked by Mack McGinnis, editor of *Speaker's and Speechwriter's Guide,* if he was actually responsible for all those quotes, Yogi explained, "I really didn't say everything I said."

Oxymorons
A more recent humor category of incongruous double entendre ex-

pressions goes by the suggestive name *oxymorons*—a contradiction in terms that makes an excellent source of humor material, particularly for greeting cards and T-shirt copy. Consider the following:

Military Intelligence
Friendly Enemy
Sweet Sorrow
Closet Exhibitionist
Friendly Criticism
The Silent Scream
Pretty Ugly
Old News

2. THE SIMPLE TRUTH

The simple truth is just that—simple and true. By taking the literal meaning of a key word, we surprise the audience, who's automatically interpreted the expression with its traditional reference. It makes logic illogical. It's commonly referred to as the "Call me a taxi" or "Call me a doctor" formula. ("Call me a taxi." "Okay, you're a taxi"; or, "Call me a doctor." "Why, are you sick?" "No, I just graduated from med school.")

My wife went *window shopping* yesterday and came home with seven windows. —Rodney Dangerfield

Caveman to child: "When I was your age, my parents used to *rock me to sleep.* The rocks were as big as your head." —Mel Brooks

It appears almost childlike in its comprehension. One of the ways to study it is to think like a child. For example:

Grandma Elden was baby-sitting and every five minutes Adrienne had another request to keep from going to sleep. Exasperated, she said to her four-year-old granddaughter, "Adrienne, if you call Grandma one more time, I'm going to get very angry." Five minutes later she heard Adrienne say quietly, "Mrs. Elden, can I have a glass of water?"

Another way is through a childish riddle, which uses simple truth as its touchstone.

"I bet you I can say the capital of all fifty states in less than a minute."

"Impossible. It's a bet. Ready, set, go!"

"Okay. The capital of all fifty states in less than a minute. I said it. You lose!"

The innocence of children is an example of the simple truth in humor.

Art Linkletter once interviewed a young boy on his "House Party" program.

Linkletter: What did your mother tell you not to say on this program?

Boy: Not to announce that she's pregnant.

Linkletter: Being pregnant is a wonderful thing. Why not announce it?

Boy: Mainly, because she ain't.

A six-year-old asked his mother: "Ma. Tell me the truth. Where did I come from?" The flustered mother thought, "Must I really start explaining the details of sexual reproduction already?" So she asked, "Tell me, Hubert, why do you want to know?" And Hubert said, "Cause the kid next door said he came from Detroit. I wanna know where I come from."

As we mature comedically, the simple truth techniques permit a whole series of formula jokes.

Teacher to student: "When's your birthday?" "October 17th."
"What year?" "Every year!"

Coed to prof: What kind of husband should I get?
Prof: Get a single man and leave the husbands alone.

I spilled spot remover on my dog—and now he's gone.
—Steven Wright

Thanks for sending me a copy of your book. I shall waste no time reading it.   —Benjamin Disraeli

A bum said to me, "I haven't eaten in three days." I said, "Force yourself."   —Henny Youngman

How the Simple Truth Works
On the surface, the mechanics of the simple truth seem easy to understand and structure, and therein lies the danger. Despite the word "simple," we must train ourselves to re-examine every major word in the cliché, reject its most common connotation and go back to basic English. This is not a simple task.

> President Reagan has taken the position that nothing is too good for our elder Americans, and that's exactly what they're going to get—nothing.

In addition, because the simple truth is so juvenile it's frequently denigrated as a "smart-ass" remark (which used to be called "smart-alec" until they discovered Alec had nothing to do with it).

> "What would you say to a martini?" "Depends on what the martini said to me first!"

Let's take a peek under the comedy tent to see how the simple truth works. We're looking for the surprise opportunity in the following cliché: "I like a girl with a head on her shoulders."

Although you know what we're looking for, even now your natural inclination may be to say, "What's funny about that idea?" But we aren't concerned with the logic of *ideas*; we aren't philosophers. We are linguistic specialists concerned with the logic of *words*. So we must first visualize a girl with a round head *on* her shoulders. What's missing is her neck.

That's 20 percent of the humor equation. The other 80 percent is finding a second line that holds the surprise until the last word, so the audience can feel superior. Different lines work with different audiences. Steve Martin's punch line ". . . because I hate necks," would be acceptable to just about everybody, whereas "because . . . when I was eighteen I gave up necks and went for the whole thing," might offend those with delicate sensibilities.

Let's join in with another example. And that's the word: *join*. It's not only a double entendre, it has three definitions: (1) to unite, to bring together, to touch; (2) to cooperate, to become a member, to enlist; and (3) to argue, to quarrel, to engage in battle. In humor writing the choice is up to us.

When a friend asks you, "Will you join me?" the obvious understanding is that he's using the second definition, "to get together"— whether it's to sit down at his table or go with him to an event. But if your answer is based on the first definition, uniting, touching, or bringing two distinct parts together, your reply catches your friend by surprise: "Why, are you coming apart?"

If, on the other hand, he asks you to "Please join me in a cup of coffee," the incongruity of the second definition allows you to respond: "Of course, if you think there's enough room."

Such elementary humor will get you a physical reaction: a laugh or, more likely, a kick in the pants. In any case, remember that one of the rewards of humor is attention, and people will admire your courage.

In pictorials, a literal interpretation of a word or phrase often results in humorous physical action. In several Mel Brooks movies the hero and his cohorts ask the heroine, "How do we get there?" And the woman says, "Walk this way." Then she proceeds to swish and sway away from camera and the men imitate her feminine walk.

The Basic Rules

There are thousands of phrases that lend themselves to this simple truth construction. The basic rule is that the first part or first sentence is a cliché. The second part (the punch line) is an unexpected interpretation that's realistically literal.

> *Doctor:* I don't like the looks of your husband.
> *Wife:* Neither do I, doctor, but he's good to the children.
> —Larry Wilde

> *Boss to employee:* I'd thank you, Harrison, but, as you know,
>   yours is a thankless job.   —Frank Modell

As your mind gets more practice, your ear will amplify countless opportunities to make humor using the simple truth technique.

> *Wife:* You never look out for me!
> *Husband:* Of course, I do. And when I see you coming, I run
>   like hell.

> The president of the synagogue addressed the congregation:
> "Lefkowitz just lost his wallet with six hundred dollars in it. If
> anyone finds it, Lefkowitz said he'd give a reward of fifty dol-
> lars." A voice in the rear: "I'll give seventy-five!"

> *Clerk to judge:* The bar association wondered if you'd like to

contribute ten dollars to a lawyer's funeral?
Judge: Here's a hundred. Bury ten of them.

Quality humor doesn't just deliver one gag and then tax the audience's patience developing a new setup. Once you've got the audience laughing or on a roll, it's better to stay with toppers—a series of punch lines, each related to the previous one. Here are two examples, the first uses one simple truth pay off and the second tops the same story with a second *simple truth* punch line. The length of the pause between the two punch lines is a matter of judgment which separates the amateur from the pro.

The forest ranger approached an Indian riding his horse up the steep canyon trail, his aged squaw trudging slowly along behind him. "Chief, I've been noticing for months now that you always ride up the trail and your wife always walks. How come?"
"Because," said the Indian solemnly, "she no gottum horse."

Here's the topper version of the same story. Note how the change in locale keeps the simple truth relationship realistic:

During World War II in North Africa, a GI approached an Arab who was riding his donkey along the military highway. His aged wife trudged along ahead of him. "Hey, Abdul," said the GI, "I've been noticing for months that you always ride and your wife always walks. How come?" "Because," said the Arab, "she no got donkey." "But why does she always walk ahead of you? Arab politeness?" "No! Land mines."

Research reports and statistics are excellent sources for simple truth humor material.

If a single dolphin has as many as two thousand babies, can you imagine how many she'd have if she were married?

Married daughter to mother on phone: "Ma, I gave birth to triplets. Isn't that exciting? You know triplets are conceived only once in every three million times!"
"My heavens, Deborah, when did you have time to do housework?"

Prof: Every fifteen minutes in the U.S. some student is contract-
ing VD.
Coed: I think I know him.

Simple Truth Exercises

Having read the above jokes, now you should be able to finish some
on your own. Read the first part of each of the following clichés, and see if
you can come up with a simple truth tag. To help you get started, the key
word with the best possibility for a double entendre is in italics. Check your
pay-off line with the ones suggested on page 64.

1. Every twelve and a half seconds, *some woman* in the US is giving birth.
2. Boy: Are you *free* tonight?
3. My girlfriend was faithful to the *end*.
4. We never *serve* women at the bar.
5. Why was George Washington *buried* at Mount Vernon?
6. Cleanliness is *next* to godliness.
7. Judge: The *court* awards your wife $200 a week for support.

The Non Sequitur

Another category of humor that's similar in many ways (although not
technically a cliché) is the non sequitur, an illogical statement which is humorous because of the juxtaposition of two elements. "One must have
some grasp of logic even to recognize a non sequitur," wrote Allen Paulos.

I shot an elephant in my pajamas. How he got in my pajamas,
I'll never know.   —Groucho Marx

A hundred years from now the works of the old masters will be
a thing of the past.   —Grove Day

Roadhouse sign: Clean and decent dancing every night but
Sunday.

Store sign: Big Sale—Last Week!

A Few for the Road

A famous actor, Edmund Kean, on his deathbed, was reported to
have said, "Dying is easy. Comedy is hard." In the same vein, reading
about cliché construction is easy. Creating original humor material using
these techniques is hard, because it's just not funny while you're examin-

ing it. E.B. White once wrote, "Dissecting humor is like dissecting a frog. They both die in the process." You'll understand this better in a minute.

What's the best way to structure literal truth humor? Take the line: "Can you tell me how long to milk a cow?"

This is a straight question, but a questionable straight line. The joke isn't apparent because the language of humor isn't applied. But "How long should a cow be milked?" is a question that permits a *take-off* rebuttal (we'll come to that technique shortly), but there's no literal truth possibility. However, if we transpose a few words and the question is restated "Can you tell me how *long cows* should be milked?" it's obvious we now have a long cow. An answer could be: "The same way as short cows."

Try a few yourself. Complete the last lines of these two setups:

I've been on the road for three weeks . . .

I have to get on a plane . . .

They're starting to get easy now, aren't they?

The Simple Truth on Stage

Many professional comedians use the simple truth technique from time to time in their monologues. Several use this technique most of the time. One of its most famous practitioners is George Carlin, whose shtick is examining words closely for incongruous variations. He is truly the first serious linguist of comedy.

Steven Wright is another of the young stand-up comedians who uses the simple truth as basic material. In his first HBO special, nearly 40 percent of his material was non sequiturs. Here's a sample; by now, you should be able to quickly anticipate most of the humorous conclusions.

I bought some batteries, but they weren't included. So I had to buy them again.

Why is it a penny for your thoughts, but you have to put your two cents in? Somebody's makin' a penny.

I parked my car in a tow-away zone. When I came back, the entire zone was gone.

I took my dog for a walk around my building—on the ledge. A lot of people are afraid of heights. Not me, I'm afraid of widths.

I woke up one morning and my girlfriend asked me if I slept good? I said, "No, I made a few mistakes."

One time the police stopped me for speeding. They said, "Don't you know the speed limit is fifty-five miles per hour?" I said, "Yeah, I know, but I wasn't going to be out that long."

And I hate it when my foot falls asleep during the day because that means it's going to be up all night.

Simple Truth Punch Lines
Here are just some payoff line possibilities to the Simple Truth exercises on page 62. How do yours compare?

1. Every twelve and a half seconds, *some woman* in the U.S. is giving birth.
   We've got to find that woman and stop her.
2. Boy: Are you *free* tonight?
   Girl: Of course. Did I ever charge you?
3. My girlfriend was faithful to the *end.*
   Unfortunately, I was the quarterback.
4. We never *serve* women at the bar.
   You'll have to bring your own.
5. Why was George Washington *buried* at Mount Vernon?
   Because he was dead!
6. Cleanliness is *next* to godliness.
   No, in the dictionary go-getter is next to godliness.
7. Judge: The *court* awards your wife $200 a week for support.
   Defendant: Gee, that's very nice of you, judge. I think I'll throw in a few
   bucks myself.   —Henny Youngman

3. REFORMING

This is the most common cliché category that coins new double entendres. The results are often puns such as this tire ad: "We skid you not," or fast food restaurant-names like: Mustard's Last Stand, Blazing Salads, and Aesop's Tables.

That restaurant inspired the TV show: "That's Inedible!"

The humor here comes from altering one or two letters in a word of the cliché and arriving at a twist which cleverly changes the point of view. The reformulated word will most likely be a homonym or a rhyming variation.

There are three ways to reform clichés. The first is to alter or transpose the words and create a new related thought. After considering clichés appropriate to the theme of your subject, you try to reform one of them by juggling the words or by reversing the order and placing the last word first. Drama critic Walter Winchell did this in a review of a season opener: "Who am I to stone the first cast?" Then there's the classic drug joke: "I'm not as think as you stoned I am."

The second, and most frequent, use of reforming is replacing one or two letters in a key word of the cliché in order to achieve a surprise turn of phrase.

I will not cut off my nose to spite my race.　　—Golda Meir

The third way to reform a cliché is with a homonym, a similar sounding word with a double entendre interpretation.

The things my wife buys at antique auctions are keeping me
Baroque.　　　　　　　　　　　　　　　—Peter De Vries

Different types of reformed clichés work best in different mediums: homonyms usually come off better orally, whereas typos are more effective in print. We'll discuss each in turn.

The Oral Cliché

Here the ear transmits to the mind the most familiar interpretation of each word. Actually, *here* is one of the most popular words to use because it sounds like *hear, hair,* and *hare.* Just by mixing them up, you can concoct simple combinations like: "An adolescent rabbit is a pubic hare," and "Hair yesterday, gone today."

Shrimply Awful

Try reforming words using homonyms from one subject group (like fish names), just for the pun of it.

Did you hear about the Norwegian who brought his harpoon to Israel because he knew he'd be visiting the Wailing Wall?

You can make up scores of gags using this list compiled by Rosemary Williamson:

O sole mio
Oh, my cod!
A lofty perch
Future shark
My brother's kipper
What the hake

Or string the words in one sentence: "I got a haddock herring that tuna blow 'salmon chanted eel-ing' and, upon my sole, he did it on porpoise."

Here's how the homonym technique would sound as a dialogue conversation between two phantoms:

"Witch way, ghost thou?"
"My house."
"Haunted?"
"Of corpse."
"Howl you go?"
"Broom."
"May I ghoul along?"
"Sure. Always broom for one more."
"What'll I wear?"
"Shroud."
"Why?"
"Because behind every shroud is a shiver lining."
"Sounds frightfully expensive."
"Ya' gotta take scare of yourself, Halloween."

A Barrel of Pun

These examples seem pretty obvious after you've seen them. They're a bit harder when you have to create them from scratch, so a lot of second raters "know a good joke when they steal one." It becomes instinctive to look for words that convey double entendre sounds. These can be in the form of riddles:

What does a grape say when you step on it?
Nothing, it just gives a little whine.

Or they can be simple quips.

"Asphalt" is another way of describing rectal problems.

With friends like you, who needs enemas?

She was chaste, very chaste. Of course, sometimes they caught her, too. —Norm Crosby

Probably the very first spicy jokes we learned as children were homonyms that worked orally, like "spreading roomers" and "smelling moth balls."

Many of the AIDS jokes are created using this technique. The four letters form a convenient and common suffix for nouns and brand names: maids, Gatorade, Band-Aid, Rolaid, etc. So the humor, as in the following examples, becomes pretty obvious:

What's an incurable disease for a JAP (Jewish-American princess)?
Maids. She dies if she doesn't have one.

What do you call a queer in a wheelchair?
A Rolaid.

Daffy definitions also use this same homonym method. It can work either way; some humor works best when the homonym is listed in the question, other times it works best when the homonym is a key phrase of the daffy definition.

Homonym in Question and Definition

What's a fahrenheit? A moderately tall person.
An ICBM? Eskimo doo-doo.
Infantry? A very young sapling.
Fanfare? A hot dog and beer.
Fireproof? A tenured professor.
Gigolo? A fee male.
Food poisoning? The rite of imminent ptomaine.
Horse food? Oat cuisine.
Hope chest? The breast is yet to come.
Metallurgist? An expert who can look at a platinum blonde and tell whether she is a virgin or a common ore.

Lettuce Get Started
Now it's your turn to do it—no, not *that* "it"! Take a word that seems

appropriate to the occasion and put down as many sound-alikes as come to mind. Then, write the joke.

For example, hormone sounds like: whore moan, her moan, harmony, etc. Now it's not difficult to write such bits as Tom Padovano's "Hormone could be heard clear across campus," or that old classic "How do you make a hormone?" *"Don't pay her."*

Okay, so far so good. But how many double entendre homonyms can you make from these words?

Two is fair, four is good, five or more is excellent; if you can't come up with any, take up accounting.

Caesar	Dewey
Tudor	read
fowl	liquor
atoll	Czech
bore	bigamy
maker	hoarse
wurst	bare
Hebrew	

Fractured Clichés

Another homonym device is split-reforming, which separates one word into two to get a surprise double meaning.

The 86-year-old lady was being interviewed by the quizmaster on TV. "You look wonderful," he said. "Yes," said the old lady, "I've never had a sick day in my life." The MC was astonished. "You've never been bedridden even once?" he asked. The old lady said, "Oh, many times, and three times in the haystack."

The most common category of splits are words that begin with the letter "a" (such as *alone, around, abreast, abroad, apparent, apiece,* and *ahead*).

Two partners on a sinking boat are thrown into the sea. "Can you float alone?" one asks the other. "I'm drowning," says the other partner, "and he's talking business."   —Larry Wilde

"Would you like to play around?" the young man asked his girlfriend. "Are you asking that as a lover or as a golfer?" she replied.

One actor to another: "I was abroad myself for two years, but fortunately a psychiatrist fixed me up."

Similar to the "a" words are those that change their meaning when the prefix can be separated by a space or a word can be divided into two:

An elderly man and woman meet for the first time at a Miami Beach social: "And how's by you the sex?" asks the woman. "Infrequently," replies the old man. "Tell me," demands the woman, "is that one word or two?" —Myron Cohen

Juggler to audience: "Don't worry. I've got a backup system. So everybody, back up!"

Another category of split-reform words invite *her* in. They end in "er" (such as *catcher, licker, freezer,* and *player*), or start with the sound of "her" (such as *harass*). Words that invite *him* in work, too (such as vitamin, Himalayan, hemisphere).

One frosh to another: "I can hardly wait to read the book the English prof assigned us: J.D. Salinger's *Catch Her in the Rye.*"

"I was a diesel fitter in a shoe store."
"They don't have diesels in shoe stores!"
"Sure they do. I stood around and said, 'Dese'll fit 'er.' "

Other words can be reformed by adding, deleting, or separating prefixes (such as *a, an, I, pre, un* or *in*).

An atheist is someone who has no invisible means of support.

At Ohio University students owe so much money they changed the initials of the college from OU to IOU.

Plagiarism: the unoriginal sin. —Roy Peter Clark

Words can also be reformed by using suffixes as homonyms (such as *-ize*).

"Do you want this pasteurized?"
"No! Just up to my mouth'd be fine!"

Another way of simulating homonyms is by combining broken English with Yiddish, Italian, Spanish or any other familiar foreign words or names. For example, youngsters who emulate the style of a famous Swedish tennis champion are known as "Bjorn-Again Borgs." And an Italian prostitute was known as Mille Grazie.

Print Clichés
Because the sound difference in reformed homonyms is so subtle it's necessary to see many alterations in print. That's why they're so popular on signs and graffiti. But spoken aloud, these homonym clichés will only earn you groans for an outrageous pun.

> I know a transsexual who only wants to eat, drink and be
> Mary.   —George Carlin

Here are a few examples of the thousands of reformed homonym combinations that work best in print.

A zebra is twenty-five sizes bigger than an A bra.

Humor writers prefer gag lunches.

Celebrity in snowstorm talking to reporter: "If I had a good
   quote, I'd be wearing it!"

The boy had a lot to be spankful for.

Familiarity breeds attempt.

Note from meter maid to ticketed car owner: "Parking is such
sweet sorrow."

*Young boy to star baseball player walking out of DA's office
during drug investigation:* "Say it ain't snow, Joe!"

Homonyms are particularly popular in print advertising headlines, and one of the most common reformed words is *sight* to *site*: shot on site, what a site, out of site.

Other examples of homonyms appear often in advertisements, T-shirts, signs, and store names. The bumper sticker "I owe. I owe. It's off to work I go!" uses a homonym effectively, as do the following store names:

Mattress shop: Desperately Seeking Snoozing
Dry Cleaner: F. Spotts Fitzgerald
Dog Emporium: Groomingdale's   —Rance Crain

Signs

Bird food—cheep
For sail—boats
Lenten special—filets of soul
Your money tearfully refunded

In skits and humorous short stories authors will frequently reconstruct cliché homonyms into character names.

Fashion designer: Natalie Attired
Roof designer: Eaves St. Laurent
Religious fanatic: Delores Mae Shepherd
Military lawyer: Marcia Law
Material girl: Phyllis Teen
UN translator: Polly Glott
Bone specialist: Arthur Itis
Wine expert: Sherry D. Cantor
WAC drill sergeant: Bella Kose
Mortician: Maude Lynn
President of Hispanic Workers Union: Manuel Labor

There's no limit to the number of reformed clichés you can have in one sentence. With paired words, two *homonyms* are required in one joke.

In matters of humor, what is appealing to one person may be appalling to another.

Then there's the overweight jogger who ignored advice and panted himself into a coroner.   —Bert Murray

Definition of a stockyard: flesh in the pen.   —Robert Fitch

Do under others as you would have them do under you.

No nukes is good nukes.

Writing a Reformed Cliché for Print

Our paper carried the notice last week that Mr. Herman Jones
is a defective in the police force. This was a typographical error. Mr. Jones, of course, is a detective on the police farce.
                              —The *Ootlewah Times* (Tennessee)

Most newspaper bloopers, known as typos, fall in this category, but you
can also write a reformed cliché for print.

In the summer of 1985, two Czechoslovakian tennis stars, Ivan Lendl
and Hana Mandlikova, respectively won the US Open men's and women's
tennis championships. The fact that they were both Czech gave writers of
photo captions, cartoons, headlines, and newscasts a field day in homonym witticisms.

Imagine you are a newspaper or newsmagazine editor. You've got a
photo of the two winners, each holding a US Open trophy and a check for
$170,000. Your assignment is to come up with a photo caption or headline.
You choose to do a reformed homonym. It's an obvious choice.

Step One
First write down all the homonyms associated with the sound of
Czech. A sample list would include all those connected with bank checks:

bounced check	bad check
good check	rubber check
cashed check	deposited check
big check	paid check
returned check	endorsed check
cancelled check	the check is in the mail

But the word *check* has many other meanings. It's used in chess to check
and checkmate an opponent. There's the game of checkers and the cliché
"check and double check." In ice hockey one player body checks an opponent. In a roll call, one checks off names with a check mark. You can ask
for separate checks in a restaurant. And when you've completed this list,
be sure to check it out completely!

Step Two
Now substitute the word *Czech* in all the above expressions and determine if the caption or headline syncs with the specific picture described
above. How many different ones can you come up with? This assignment

is for *quantity*. There should be five to ten possibilities from the above list, for instance, "Czech-mated" or "cashed Czechs." Only after you've examined many possibilities should you select the best one.

The Computer Mind

It seems like a lot of work for one photo caption. It *is*. But before long, your mental computer will have a file of all the different possibilities that you can call up at a moment's notice.

Do all those steps really become automatic? Think of it like the moves Jimmy Connors has to make setting up for a tennis shot. As the ball approaches, Connors decides to move diagonally forward or backward, left or right. At the same time, he is getting his racket back, planting his feet properly while keeping both eyes on the ball to judge its speed and spin. He now makes decisions on his shot, the velocity of his swing in order to block, punch or slam the ball. With his peripheral vision he determines where his opponent is and guesses where he'll go. It is not necessary to drag this analogy out. Connors does all this and more in less than a second while the ball is traveling nearly a hundred miles per hour—and that's for every shot.

Unlike a champion tennis player, as a writer you have a lot more time to run through your gamut of double entendre clichés. The second time is not only better than the first, it's a lot easier, too. The five thousandth time will be easier still.

Writing a Reformed Cliché as a Pun

In this assignment you'll be a copywriter writing an advertisement to encourage the public to use your bank for personal loans. Again, we'll go through similar steps.

Step One

Locate the important word or phrase you would like to remodel. In this case, concentrate on the word *loan*. Then write as many words as you can think of that rhyme with *loan*. Go for quantity.

Step Two

Select the words from your list that seem to have double entendre possibilities: groan, lone, moan, phone, postpone, own.

Step Three

Now, start eliminating. *Groan* and *moan* have negative associations. *Postpone* is the opposite of what you wish to recommend. But we still have *lone*, *own*, and *phone*. That's not bad!

Step Four

Write as many clichés (according to our umbrella definition of clichés) with the word *loan* or *lone* in it, and try some spelling reforming. Humor permits us to take some liberties with the language, so our list (longer than this) includes:

Can you float a loan
You'll never be a loan
The loan ranger *(Hey! That could work.)*

Step Five

With a little reforming the Lone Ranger can become the *loan arranger* supported by (who else?) his loyal sidekick, Tonto, who now becomes *pronto*. Now, with the loan arranger, phone, and pronto you have an ad headline that suggests action:

Santa Monica Bank
Phone the loan arranger—and pronto!

Variations on a Theme by Stravinsky

To appreciate the innumerable variations this technique provides, let's take the title of Stravinsky's famous ballet *The Rite of Spring*. Okay, the sound *rite* can be spelled in the following ways: rite, write, right, and wright. Each spelling, singular or plural, contributes to a variety of humor possibilities, such as these examples of newspaper photo headlines.

Over a photo of a high school commencement: The rite of spring.
Over a photo of a book on spring gardening: The writes of spring.
Over a photo of the Wrights' annual garden party: The Wrights of spring.

In addition, the word *spring* can now be replaced with one of the following nineteen words which rhyme:

bing	bring
ding	cling
fling	king
ling	Ming
ping	ring
sing	sling
sting	string
swing	thing

wing   wring
ying

Thus, a picture of Ted Williams instructing hitters at training camp could carry the headline: "The rites of swing."

By multiplying those nineteen words by the four variations on *rite*, we now have a total of seventy-six possible variations on *one cliché*. And we're not finished! Just as we did with *spring,* let's take the word *rite* and replace it with one of the twenty-seven words that are close in sound. Here your *Webster's Rhyming Dictionary* (Castle Books) will be of help.

bright	brite
cite	dike
dyke	fight
flight	height
hike	kike
knight	like
mike	might
pike	plight
sight	site
spike	strike
tight	trike
tyke	vike
white	yike

This changes the first *rite* combination from four to thirty-one, and with the nineteen *spring* variations, we now have (31 x 19) the possibility of 589 variations—from just one cliché! Of course, only a handful of these combinations could probably ever be used, but you never know when odd opportunities will turn up: a college president named Ping shows up at his children's birthday party, so now you can have a news photo caption that reads: "The Tykes of Ping."

Three Prerequisites
There are three strict prerequisites for a reformed cliché to be funny.

1. The take-off cannot be obvious—it must be a surprise.
2. It must be, at least, mildly outrageous (it's all in good pun).
3. The original cliché or title must be immediately familiar to the audience. The *Rite of Spring* exercise, for example, would earn few laughs from the

non-musical or even those who know Stravinsky's ballet as *Le Sacre du Printemps*.

A time-honored rule in comedy is to never do more than three jokes on one topic, and some comedy writers will argue that two is plenty. Yet here's an example of a radio commercial for City National Bank of Los Angeles which uses the malaprop technique seven times and holds the audience for a cute twist at the end.

(phone rings)
Daughter: Smith residence.
Father: Hi ya, sport. Let me talk to Mom.
Daughter: Hey Mom. It's Dad.
Mother: Ask him what he wants, hon. I've got my hands in dishwater.
Daughter: What do you want, Dad? Mom's got her hands in fish water.
Father: Just tell her I've been to City National.
Daughter: He's been pretty bashful, Mom.
Mother: What about?
Daughter: What about?
Father: About the trust.
Daughter: About the truss.
Mother: Truss? What truss?
Daughter: Which one?
Father: The life-insurance trust, kiddo. The one from City National.
Daughter: The lighting shirt's truss, Mom.
Mother: The lighting shirt's truss?
Father: The one that keeps the tax man from being one of my beneficiaries.
Daughter: The one that keeps the Pac-Man from eating bony fishes.
Mother: Ask him what in the world he's talking about, honey.
Daughter: What in the world are you talking about, Dad?
Announcer: Come in and talk to a City National trust officer. We'll show you how a truss can protect your lighting shirts.
Daughter: That's "life insurance."

Again, by ridiculing the speaker's confusion with English, we feel superior, so we laugh.

4. THE TAKE OFF

I said to my wife "All things considered *I'd like to die in bed,"*
and she said, "What, again?"　　　　—Rodney Dangerfield

The take-off is the most traditional of all humor techniques. It not only features the double entendre, it compounds the element of "audacious realism" by completing the cliché with a bizarre reference.

　　The idea behind the take-off is that the cliché is *implicit*—it implies something more than what's explicitly stated. It's the opposite, therefore, of the simple truth, which accepts the literal meaning of a key word in the cliché. With the take-off, the cliché can either start the joke or be the punch line. The most common choice is as an introduction; then a surprise take-off is the big payoff.

My father never liked me. *For Christmas he gave me a bat.* The first time I tried to play ball with it, it flew away.
　　　　　　　　　　　　　　　　—Rodney Dangerfield

When the Cliché Comes First
Here are a few examples with the cliché first, then the take-off.

Let a smile be your umbrella—and your hair will be a big mess.

If an infinite number of monkeys sat typing at an infinite number of typewriters—the smell would be unbearable.

Clichés are often the formula for humorous aphorisms, like the Peter Principles of Laurence J. Peter.

If you can fool all the people some of the time—that's enough!

To examine this technique more closely, let's start with the aphorism that has more variations than any other in comedic literature: *If at first you don't succeed, try, try again.*

Don't think of it as a failure. Think of it as time-release success.　　　　　　　　　　　　　　　　—Robert Orben

The full line sparks a take-off in either direction.

If at first you don't succeed, try, try again—she expects you
to.   —Guido Stempel

If at first you don't succeed, then quit. There's no sense being
a fool about it.   —W.C. Fields

The shortened version is the most popular springboard for a take-off. The
procedure for writing a take-off is to add a clever and surprising ending to
the cliché opening. As in these examples, it isn't necessary to use the full
cliché. Frequently, just the introduction or suggestion of the appropriate
cliché is enough.

> *If at first you don't succeed*
> —you're fired!
> —you're not related.
> —get out of bed and go home.
> —you'll get plenty of advice.

And an opera singer would be given this advice:

If at Faust, you don't succeed. . . .

Here's an example of another abbreviated cliché:

A fool and his money were lucky to get together in the first
place.   —Harry Anderson

The best way to learn is to practice. Write a better ending for each of
the following examples:

Every once in a while they send an innocent man to Congress.

He was *a self-made man* who owed his lack of success to nobody.   —Joseph Heller

Comedy is in my blood. Frankly, I wish it were in my act!
                                                —Rodney Dangerfield

I wouldn't hurt a fly, unless it was open.   —Mae West

Sign on hot chestnut stand: *I don't want to set the world on
fire,* I just want to keep my nuts warm.

Sign at 19th Hole: *If you drink, don't drive.* Don't even putt!

Whatever goes up must come down, but don't expect it to
come down where you can find it. —Lily Tomlin

The race isn't always to the swift, nor the battle to the strong,
but that's the way to bet! —Damon Runyon

Blessed are the young, for they shall inherit the national
debt. —Herbert Hoover

Nobody knows the trouble I've seen, but I keep trying to tell
them. —Mignon McLaughlin

When the Cliché Comes Second

It's a more difficult construction when the cliché is in the second
clause or sentence. As with puns, a groan is the most frequent reaction.

The dog's breath smelled terrible, so *his bark was worse than
his bite.*

Wife to friend: "I'm in trouble. I broke my husband's favorite
golf club." "What did he say?" "He said, *'What hit me?'* "

Sign in Berkeley, California: Hubert Allen—Accountant
Many Happy Returns

Guest of honor at roast: "I'm standing so you'll know *I don't
take insults lying down.*"

If you don't want the dentist to hurt you, *keep your mouth
shut.*

What do you say to a three-hundred pound baked potato?
Anything, but be sure *to butter him up.*

You can combine cliché formats. Here's one, inspired by S.J. Perelman,
which combines reforming with a take-off (and the cliché comes second).

The hooker was chasing the comedian down the street—a
unique case of the tail dogging the wag.

The Big Pay-Off

Whether you put the cliché first or second depends on which ending evokes the biggest surprise. The importance of holding the surprise phrasing to the last possible moment cannot be overemphasized.

On the West Coast they say that not waiting until the last word to divulge the surprise is going past the "post office window." On the East Coast, more racetrack oriented, they call it going past the "pay-off window."

Again, remember that humor is written backwards. That means you first find the cliché you want to work on, then build a story around it. The trick is *not* to telegraph it. Here's one that was so obviously stretched, it looks more like taffy than good humor:

> A construction worker discovered his wife in the back seat of a Thunderbird making love to another guy. He got into his cement truck, drove up to the car and dumped an entire load of concrete all over it. Then, he drove away thinking, *"The longer they go, the harder it gets."*

While this is an example of a labored anecdote "just to make a joke," it does follow one other essential rule: make sure the joke is the last possible thought, and don't add other words to the sentence after the joke. If you do, the audience will think that your take-off was only a setup for a bigger laugh coming up.

Double Your Pleasure

You can put more than one cliché in one sentence. It doubles the work, but it also doubles the fun.

> *Give a man enough rope* and he'll get *tied up in the office.*

> Some girls *fight against being kissed.* Others *take it lying down.*

Why do people groan rather than laugh at outrageous puns? I'll tell you the truth. I have no idea, and neither does anyone else.

5. ASSOCIATIONS

Creativity is putting together two activities that haven't been previously associated into a plausible but audacious scenario. Association is a more formal word for teaming. This is humor's variation of a metaphor. We combine two simple elements that are logical but impossible. While that sounds strange, the humor comes from the unexpected, off-beat relationship. Our laughter covers our surprise, and our appreciation is enhanced by tinges of envy. ("Why didn't I think of that?")

Associations have many possible formats. Some of the most popular are listed here.

1. *Association of a cliché with a celebrity name* whose fame is a result of a physical or mental reputation.

My opponent has done the work of two men: Laurel and
Hardy.   —Governor James A. Rhodes

It's been so hot, Mickey Rooney has been using Dolly Parton
for shade.   —Bob Hope

The last time I told that joke, Yul Brynner had hair. Come to
think of it, so did I.   —Robert Orben

2. *Association is the teaming of two clichés.* This technique frequently produces incongruous humor, and is the backbone of improvisation.

Wife to friend: "I call Herb's salary a phallic symbol because it only rises once a year."

3. *Association is the teaming of verbs or adverbs with nouns.* The results of this technique are often referred to as "Tom Swifties."

Verbs

"So you think you're a big wheel," he spoke.
"Make a canoe of that tree," he barked.
"This spotlight is really helpful," she beamed.
"It's a dog's life," he muttered.
"The faucet's broken," she gushed.
"I wish I were back in the forest," she pined.

Adverbs

"The smog is really bad today," he cried breathlessly.
"What kind of cheese is this?" he asked sharply.

"They have a funny name for streets in France," he said ruefully.
"I've finally won the Academy Award," said Henry fondly.

—Gene Perret

"My feet hurt," Tom said flatly.
"They do?" she asked archly.
"Yes," said Tom soulfully.
"Tough," she answered callously.

—Neal Robison

Did you hear about the two worms in the cemetery who made love in Ernest?

Associations as Warm-ups

A humorist's funnybone is like an athlete's muscles or a singer's vocal cords. They work best when they're warmed up first. (The same can be true of lovers, but that's another book.) Writing teachers insist that students do fifteen to thirty minutes of brain-stretching exercises each morning to clear away the fog.

Robert Orben warms up writing twenty-five one-liners inspired by the morning paper. Then, he gets to work. Others like to imagine funny captions to news photos. Art Gliner, famous Washington, DC disc jockey and humor lecturer, gets his seminars warmed up using an association exercise. He has them write down words that might describe how tired firefighters, police, dog catchers, plumbers, etc. feel when they come home at night. For example:

FIREFIGHTER	POLICE OFFICER	DOG CATCHER	GARDENER
burned up	beat	muzzled	hosed
alarming	flat-footed	bone-tired	potted
torched	half-cocked	bitchy	plowed under
fired up	run-down	run-down	bogged down
plug nickle	blue	pooped	bushed
steaming	shot	hounded	raked over
ladder day saint	charged	licked	mulched
not too hot	holed up	dog-tired	dug up
made ash of myself	badgered	collared	seedy
	it was a riot	the paws that	all wet
	that's the ticket	refreshes	rocky

Gene Perret, humorist and publisher of *The Comedy Roundtable* newsletter, likes to associate puns on famous names. (For the address of this newsletter, see Appendix B.) First, you find a name with homonym possibilities. Then, write an anecdote to fit.

The Italian-American farmer who erected a tombstone for his beloved wife, Nellie, that read: "Here Liza Minelli."

Before she became Madonna, she was a pre-Madonna.

—K.C. Conan

Take pity. I'm Jung and Freud-ened.

"I just can't Handel the Messiah."
"Then you'd better go into Haydn."
"Oh, get off my Bach, or I'll give you a karate Chopin the neck."

A microcomputer that draws geometric patterns on the screen is called a "Micro-Angle-O."

Slogans for famous artists.
  Seurat: Que Seurat, Seurat.
  Monet: A lasting impression.
  Van Gogh: Lend me your ear.
  Henry Moore: Moore for your money.
  Warhol: The new Warhol—uncanny.
  Gauguin: Here we Gauguin.
  Goya: You can be Jewish and still love a Goya.

—*Advertising Age*

Humorists take themselves seriously, but no one else. The more you can combine realism and exaggeration, the more humorous it will be. That's why disrespectful association of the rich and famous with book or movie titles is a frequent warm-up for professionals:

Elizabeth Taylor in *Once is Not Enough*.
Ted Turner in *Raging Bull*.
Ronald Reagan in *Heaven Can Wait*.
James Watt in *To Kill a Mockingbird*.
Claus von Bulow in *The Big Sleep*.   —Maureen Murphy

Associating the last names of two different celebrities is another humor writing exercise in association teaming.

If Isadora Duncan had married Robert Donat, would their child be a Dunkin' Donut?

If Betty White had married Soupy Sales, would they have called her Betty White Sales?

Ohioan Mike Harden writes for the *Columbus Dispatch,* and in one of my favorite Harden columns he recommends new state mottos.

Arizona: Bring us your sinuses.
Colorado: Don't eat yellow snow.
Florida: Ponce DeLeon, the first man to come here without his wife.
Idaho: Baked, mashed, or fried?
Indiana: No one stops here on purpose.
Kentucky: Buy it here. Drink it somewhere else.
Maryland: Birthplace of the Indianapolis Colts.
Mississippi: Wake us if you need anything.
Nevada: Three to one says you can't.
New Hampshire: Don't take us for granite.
New Jersey: This looks like a good place to dump it.
New York: Watch your wallet *or* Tipping is a *must.*
North Carolina: Don't believe everything the Surgeon General tells you.
North Dakota: General Custer, the first man to wear an Arrow shirt, was healthy when he left here.
Oregon: Visit here. Live somewhere else.
Rhode Island: Just don't blink.
Texas: Big deal!
West Virginia: Our children live in Ohio.
Wisconsin: Eat cheese or die.

If all this is just the first step in humor writing, you're probably reminded of the ancient warning: Watch out for that first step, it's a doozy! But with patience and practice, you'll soon be sliding down the bannisters.

CHAPTER 5

Brainstorming POW
Associations

BRAINSTORMING IS THE TEDIOUS, TIME-CONSUMING PROCESS which
eventually uncovers a new *play-on-words* (POW). Humor writers spend
more energy in word play than they do in foreplay.

The procedure seems simple enough. You take the main subject and
break it down into groups of associated activities, then rearrange these
groups into smaller and smaller subsections.

Regardless of your humor assignment, the technique is the same.

To show you how this works, let's imagine you need to write material
on golf, a favorite topic for humorists because so many VIPs play golf.

The first rule is to chart the subject. On a piece of paper (or in the case
of golf, four or five pieces of paper), divide the subject into different head-
ings. For example:

1. Golf equipment
2. Golf course
3. Golf play
4. Golf players

Now chart each heading with as many subheads as you can think of, and
keep adding to the list every time you have another brainstorm. Don't censor yourself. The quantity of ideas is important here; quality comes later.

Therefore, under *golf equipment* we might list:

flag	cart
tees	caddy
headcovers	lucky ball
clubs	balls
bag	shoes
scorecard	optic yellow
clothes	hats
socks	gloves
glasses	Argyle socks
spikes	pencil
cap	rake
towels	ball washer

That's not good enough. We can break down the clubs into another major subdivision:

driver	woods
irons	wedge
putter	

And, of course, even the woods and the irons can be listed by numeric designation: two wood, nine iron, etc. That's only category one (golf equipment). Now do the same with category two, *golf course*.

country club	18-hole course
9-hole course	dogleg
men's tee	women's tee
pro tee	trees
fairway	green
clubhouse	rough
woods	lake
apron	sand trap
divots	practice green
bunker	driving range
19th hole	groundskeeper
locker room	shower
out-of-bounds	ball wash
water hazard	

And now with category three, *golf play:*

score	par
birdie	stroke
eagle	bogie
hole-in-one	Mulligan
handicap	"fore"
lost balls	drop ball
foursome	play-through
tournaments	double bogie
Pro-Am	championship
trophy	skyball
hook	slice
shank	chip

Finally, with category four, *golf players:*

betting	double-up
Nassau	duffer
hobby	fanatics
exercise	pair
curses	bragging
cheating	hustler
pros	amateurs
hackers	sandbagger
lessons	expense
disgust	slicer
foursome	partners
opponents	hooker

The next part of the chart is a list of as many cliché expressions as possible associated with each entry. For example, in category one (equipment) we could list:

Clubs

Got a new set of clubs
He hit a 300 yarder
Make a six-footer
Practice swing
She knows how to putt

Balls

They've gotcha by the balls
Kiss his balls for good luck
She addressed the ball
He lost his balls
Keep your eye on the ball
Don't stand too close to the ball
Hit a pair of beautiful balls

Bag

That's not his bag
She's a bag lady
In the bag

And in category two, *golf course,* a suggested list of cliché expressions might include:

Name of the game
How many strokes per round
Let's play a round
Great way to meet people
She gave the caddy a tip
A rich man's sport

In categories three, *play,* and four, *players,* you might include:

He knows the score
It was a playable lie
It's a gimme
She got out of the trap
I lie three
He's a poor sport
She moved heaven and earth
What's par for the hole?
That shot was a prayer
She shoots in the low 70s
He's a scratch player
He's a hooker
She's a slicer

She's a weekend hacker
The woods are full of them
He got out of a hole
He got distance off the tee
How do you like the greens?

As you read over the list you can already see a number of humor possibilities, particularly with double entendres. Now is the time to list double entendres, synonyms, antonyms, and homonyms that have a connection with golf. Here's a sample list.

Double Entendres
Golf words or expressions that have two or more meanings:

hole	sport
hooker	trap
ball	nine holes
lie	socks
lost ball	hole in one
out-of-bounds	tip
play	play through
lucky ball	bag
birdie	putt
slicer	stroke
swing	scratch
rough	handicap
game	make
a six-footer	score
long ball hitter	ball wash

Synonyms
Two or more words that have approximately the same meaning. Some golf synonyms:

club = sticks	green = carpet
oath = curse	hat = cap
good shot = beauty	drive = tee-off
putt = tap	bar = 19th hole
lake = drink	gimme = concede
locker room = showers	tip = gift
par = scratch	away = longest distance

Antonyms
Words that have comparatively opposite meanings in golf:

birdie = bogie   opponent = partner
play = practice   match play = lowest score
lost ball = found ball   hold head down = hold head up
flubbed = on the nose   wager = friendly game
tip = advice   country club = public links
stand close = stand away   men's tee = women's tee
eagle = double bogie

Homonyms
Words used in golf that sound similar to other words:

fore = four, for, foreplay, foursome
course = enter course (sign), intercourse, curse
play a round = play around
caddy = Caddy (Cadillac)
70s = 70s (Fahrenheit temperature)
putts = putz (Yiddish for penis)

Now the Hard Part

Using all this research, the assignment is to come up with humorous material for your monologue (or sketch) on golf. Remember that to be funny, the final line of the scenario must end in a surprise. Depending on the speed of the performer, four jokes a minute is maximum or two jokes plus one anecdote is average. So if the assignment is for five minutes of material, at the maximum you need only twenty one-liners, or seven anecdotes, or an assortment.

The beginner writes just twenty pieces. The professional writes three times what's needed, as many as sixty different bits, keeps trying them out on small groups (but never your own family), rewrites, discards, rewrites some more, then finally settles on the twenty which work best for that specific audience. It's hard to get students to believe that all this labor and editing is necessary.

Let us take the exact material listed above and try a few jokes. For this exercise we have deliberately stayed with one scenario, the standard hacker/caddy dialogue, so that we can concentrate on humor technique. These stories would all benefit from personalizing—substituting a VIP's name for either member of the cast. Many of them would work whether the hacker is male or female.

Category One (Golf Equipment)

Caddy to hacker: "No matter how you slice it, sir, it's still a golf ball."

Hacker: I got some new clubs for my wife.
Caddy: I know your wife, sir, and you know, that wasn't a bad trade.

Caddy: I don't get it, sir. First you slice your ball into the woods. Then you hook it onto the highway. Now you top the same ball into the water. And you still insist on my finding it?
Hacker: Of course. It's my lucky ball.

Hacker: I hit two beautiful balls today.
Caddy: The only way you could do that, sir, would be to step on a rake.

Caddy: Here's a lost ball I found on the golf course.
Hacker: Gee, thanks. But how did you know it was a lost ball?
Caddy: Because they were still looking for it when I left.

Hacker: This is my first time playing golf. When do I use my putter?
Caddy: Sometime before dark, I hope.

Category Two (Golf Club)

Did you hear about the rich Texan who bought his son a set of fourteen golf clubs? All but one had a swimming pool.

Hacker: I'm moving heaven and earth to do better.
Caddy: Try moving heaven. You've already moved plenty of earth.

Caddy: The traps on this course are certainly annoying, aren't they, sir?
Hacker: Yes, and would you please shut yours.

Hacker: How does one meet new people at this country club?
Caddy: Easy. Try picking up the wrong ball.

Sign in the locker room: Please do not wash your balls with
   towels. Use a wire brush.

The hacker was playing in his first big tournament and asked
his new girlfriend to kiss his balls for luck. She looked at him
for a second and then said, "Your golf balls?"

Category Three (Golf Play)

Hacker: I play golf in the 70s. When it gets hotter, I quit.

The hacker was sentenced to be hanged. As he climbed the
scaffold he said, "Do you mind if I take a few practice swings?"

Hacker: Golf is sure a funny game.
Caddy: It wasn't meant to be, sir.

Hacker to caddy: "This hole should be good for a long drive
   and a putt."
After he flubbed his first shot the caddy said, "Now for a
   helluva putt."

Hacker: Any ideas on how I can cut about ten strokes off my
   score?
Caddy: Yes, quit on 17!

Sammy Davis Jr. to caddy: "I'm black, I'm Jewish, and I've only
   got one eye, and you ask me 'What's my handicap?' "

Caddy: How come you're not playing with Mr. Anderson today,
   sir?"
Hacker: Would you play with a man who lies, cheats and moves
   his ball? Well, neither will Mr. Anderson.

The expressions *head up* and *head down* can be played either way:

Hacker: With my score today I'll never be able to hold my head up.
Caddy: Why not? You've been doing it all afternoon.

Priest: I wonder if it would help if I prayed before I teed off.
Caddy: Only if you pray with your head down.

Caddy: Father, is it a sin to play golf on Sunday?
Priest: The way I play, it's a sin to play any day.

Hacker: Ever seen such a long ball hitter as me?
Caddy: Sure, the woods are full of them.

Category Four (Golf Players)

Give me my golf clubs, the fresh air, and a beautiful blonde partner—and you can keep the clubs and the fresh air.
—Joe E. Lewis

Hacker: "My wife says if I don't give up golf, she'll leave me. And you know, I'm going to miss her."

Did you hear about the golf pro who made a six-footer on the practice green and his wife sued for divorce?

Hacker: What do you think I should do about my game?
Caddy: Well, sir, first I'd relax, then stop playing for six months, then give it up entirely.

Tourist booklet: In North Carolina there are more golf curses per mile than anywhere in the United States.

Why Work So Hard?

This seems like an unusual amount of labor just to create a few one-liners. Well, it is and no humor writer will deny that the work is laborious, tedious, time-consuming, and frustrating when it doesn't come out right. Like most creative people, humor writers spend a lot of time gazing blankly out the window looking for the right figure of speech. And just as you're about to find it, your spouse will come up and say, "As long as you're not doing anything, take out the garbage."

Now let's put a few of these double entendre ideas, combine them with some comedic rhetoric and put them together in one anecdote.

A young man in his twenties went to Las Vegas, met a girl, had a fabulous night, got drunk, got married and woke up the next morning. He said to her, "Look I've got a surprise for you. Last night when I said I don't have a handicap, I meant I am a no scratch golfer. I spend all my time out on the golf course, and you're the first girl I ever went out with." The girl said, "Well, I have a handicap too. I'm a hooker, and I can't stop." So the kid took out his club and said, "Look, I can help. Next time, before you swing, just put your right hand high on the shaft. You'll do fine."
           —Bob Hope

"I think of my boss as a father figure—which makes her very angry."

CHAPTER 6

The Next Giant Step: Reverses

THE TERM *REVERSE* HAS MANY DEFINITIONS in humor writing. Some define it as the device of adding a contradictory tag line to the opening line of a cliché.

> I couldn't wait for success, so I went ahead without it.
> —Jonathan Winters

Some writers define it as a situation in which the "outs" take over from the "ins."

> I have a job at the local radio station. I get in my car at rush hour and report on helicopter traffic.   —Joe Bolster

Other writers combine it with the old switcheroo, a concept which takes a standard humor bit and switches the characters and the setting to fit the existing situation.

> *T-shirt slogan:* I survived the coldest day in New York history—27 below. I got this shirt from an aunt—who didn't.

Finally, others believe a reverse is changing the point of view of a cliché 180 degrees.

Sign in Bureau of Printing and Engraving: "The buck starts here!"
—Ronn Brachin

By far, the most common definition of a reverse is an unexpected switch in the audience's point of view. The object is to catch the audience off guard because we cover our embarrassment with laughter. Surprise comes from a basic change in direction—a reversal of habitual thinking or activity. A good example is this reverse:

A man and woman are making passionate love in the bedroom. Suddenly the apartment door opens and a man comes in: "Darling! I'm home, my love." He walks into the bedroom, looks at the naked couple and says, "What is she doing here?"

The writer must drop at least one clue to push the audience in a false direction (man shouting, "Darling!"). Then the standard reverse is a simple statement whose original point of view is effectively cancelled out by the last few words:

I sold my house this week. I thought I got a good price for it— but it made my landlord mad as hell.   —Gary Shandling

"I have a brother in Harvard Med School."
"What's he studying?"
"Nothing, they're studying him."

The reverse is a standard ploy for MCs' openings:

Is everybody having a good time? Well, we'll put an end to that right now!

We usually go for the best in live entertainment. But tonight we have to settle for. . . .

Now, here's a little song I wrote after catching my girlfriend in bed with my wife.

Retaliatory Humor
The reverse is also a favorite device for delivering an insult or a surprise compliment.

Goldie Hawn is funny, sexy, beautiful, talented, intelligent, warm, and consistently sunny. Other than that, she doesn't impress me at all.
—Neil Simon

Howard Cosell is America's greatest sportscaster. And that's not only my opinion, it's his, too!

Casper Weinberger is one of the most maligned, ridiculed and insulted administrators in government today—and rightly so!

When I wrote my first humor book, *Comedy Techniques for Writers and Performers*, I asked Steve Allen for a testimonial for the jacket. I could have predicted his reply, since he frequently uses reverses:

As an author, myself, of humor techniques, I'm delighted to add Mel Helitzer's book to my library—and someday I may even read it.
—Steve Allen

CHANGING THE POINT OF VIEW

Why are we so often surprised by humor reverses? After all, the ending is logical (realistic) and, unlike a magician's sleight of hand which has us looking in the wrong direction, the comic can only hope that the audience goes off on the wrong train of thought.

Since surprise is one of the basic elements of the THREES Formula (as discussed in Chapter 3) a reverse becomes a basic tool. The technique is to offer a solution which is both logical and diametrically opposite of what is expected.

When I was young, I thought that money was the most important thing in life. Now that I'm old—I know it is. —Oscar Wilde

The language of effective humor is carefully scripted. Very little is left to hope. Each phrase, each idea, each fact is carefully designed to sidetrack our train. That creates surprise.

Take this story by Emo Philips, whose male persona dresses as an emaciated Alice in Weirdoland. We know that doors open in two directions, but throughout the anecdote Philips plants clues to let us assume we are following the *ins* not the *outs* of the story. We are wrong!

One day I was playing—I was about seven years old—and I saw
the cellar door open just a crack. Now my folks had always
warned me, Emo, whatever you do, don't go near the cellar
door. But I had to see what was on the other side if it killed
me, so I went to the cellar door, pushed it and walked through,
and I saw strange, wonderful things—things I had never seen
before—like . . . trees, grass, flowers, the sun—that was nice!

Note how the following material helps build up to the surprise reverse:

"I was about seven. . . ." It's important for realism that the age be logical, that a child could be confined up to that age. If it weren't for that simple insert, the fallacy of the story—even though we know it's mythical—
would suffocate our laugh mechanism.

"I saw the cellar door open just a crack." This sets up the first of the
two reverse possibilities by introducing tension.

*"My folks had always warned me . . . whatever you do, don't go near
the cellar door."* This is the impetus for assuming the thrust is going from
outside to the inside since we're now sure the comic is talking about enter-
ing some mysterious, horror-filled dungeon. Why do we automatically
dismiss the reverse possibility? Because we're not professional humor
writers, that's why!

"I had to see what was on the other side if it killed me." The mystery is
being cleverly exaggerated by the "kill" reference.

"I saw strange, wonderful things—things I had never seen before."
Now we are sure that the cellar is filled with relics from King Tut's tomb.

"Like . . ." This is a long pause, which completes the tension cycle.
Philips is ready to spring the surprise reverse, and the laugh response is as-
sured.

To test this analysis, just read Philip's anecdote and leave out any one
of the above statements. The joke will fail.

D. L. Stewart, humor columnist for the *Dayton Daily News*, is a master of the reverse technique. In his book *Fathers Are People, Too!*, Stewart
tells a story about how he helped chaperone his son's high school choir on a
trip to New York:

That evening we drive to the place where the buses are to pick
up the choir. The buses arrive, the suitcases are loaded into the
luggage compartments and the choir scrambles aboard. Not
surprisingly there are a few cases of last-minute changes of
heart as a vague future adventure becomes a frightening reality.
Some are openly sobbing as they plead with their families to let

them stay home. But eventually, the choir director convinces all chaperones to get on the bus.

How are we going to herd fifty kids around Manhattan on that crowded, dirty subway system? And what's going to happen when fifty apple-cheeked young boys from middle America come into contact with the lowlife of New York? The muggers. The junkies. The prostitutes. But it's too late to worry about that now. We're here. The muggers, the junkies, and the prostitutes are going to have to protect themselves as best they can.

There is an unwritten law in humor that only one reverse is permissible in any one story or script. Two is pushing and three or more so conditions the reader to anticipate the reverse that the surprise is telegraphed.

A man finds a chimp in the middle of the street. A police car drives by and he asks, "Hey, what do you think I should do with him?"

"Take him to the zoo," yells one policeman.

The next day the police notice the same man with the same chimp.

"I thought I told you to take it to the zoo," said one officer.

"I did," said the man, "and we had so much fun, today I'm taking him to Disneyland."

In each of the following examples, the writer wants you to be thinking in terms of the first mentioned point of view. Despite the careful step-by-step analysis above, you may be so accustomed to the logical thought process that many of these reverses will still catch you by surprise.

Boy: Can I take your picture in the nude?
Coed: Absolutely not! You'll have to wear your socks and a tie.

An executive walks into his boss's office. "I'm afraid I'll have to leave early today. I've got a terribly sore neck."

The boss says, "Whenever I get one like that, I go home and my wife makes love to me. She knows how to massage every muscle in my body and when she's finished all the tension is gone. You ought to try that."

The next day the boss walks over to the executive: "Did you try what I told you?"

"Yes, I did," says the executive, "and it worked just fine. By the way, you have a beautiful house, too!"

Now You Do It

The standard reverse should now be easy to spot. After you've seen three or four, you should be able to finish the last line of the following reverses. Compare your best effort with a pro's version on page 110.

1. A woman walking down the street with her dog passes a bum sitting on the sidewalk. The man looks up and says, "You've got the ugliest pig I've ever seen."
   "Why you drunken bum," says the woman. "It's not a pig, it's a dog." And the bum says. . . .

2. A bum walks into the doctor's office with a frog on his head. "What seems to be the problem?" the doctor asks. . . .

3. The ugly girl was walking down the street with a pig under her arm. She meets a friend who asks, "Where did you get the pig?" (The last line, please?)

4. They just took away the license of one of our doctors for having sex with his patients. And that's too bad, because. . . .

5. A friend of mine took up weightlifting—got broad shoulders, huge arms, muscular legs, rippling chest. . . .

IF YOU'VE GOT A MESSAGE, DON'T TELEGRAPH IT

Here are a few more reverses, but the jokes are *telegraphed*, which professionals work hard to eliminate. You don't want the audience to anticipate the ending. The following are examples of jokes that are too easy because they're too obviously laid out.

I know an actor with a figure like Sophia Loren, sings like Dolly Parton, can be as dramatic as Jane Fonda, but can't land a job. The reason is he's a man!

"Sorry to hear your wife ran away with your gardener."
   "Oh, that's all right. I was going to fire him anyway!"

After two drinks, my wife turns into a screaming witch. After five drinks, I pass out completely.

I saw a picture of that new tank that can go forty-five miles an hour, has a six inch armor plate, a 105 mm cannon and, thanks to our defense budget, the army will have 100,000 of them by 1989. Not the tank, the picture.

The trick, on a reverse, is to lay out the plot line of a story so realistically that the joke isn't telegraphed and the audience is carefully set up for the surprise ending.

A man was driving on a narrow, winding mountain road when he almost collided with a car wildly careening around a blind curve.

"You stupid fool," he shouted at the other driver. The other car came to a dead stop. A woman rolled down the window, looked at the man and yelled, "Pig!" and then quickly drove off. Furious at the insult, the man slammed his car into gear, roared around the mountain curve and slammed head on into a giant hog standing in the road.

Walking down the street, I saw a blind man being led by a seeing-eye dog. Suddenly, the dog pissed on the blind man's leg. His owner took a biscuit out of his pocket, bent down and gave it to the dog. I walked over and said to the man, "Sir, I couldn't help noticing what you did. It's one of the greatest acts of kindness I've ever seen." The blind man said, "Kindness, hell, I just want to find where his head is so I can kick him in the ass."

An anecdote is a tall tale told as a small story with a sudden climax. With the setup, we mean to confuse the audience. So we include just enough information in the body of the story to encourage them to proceed automatically in the direction we'll reverse at the end.

"Let me tell you about my big spending husband," one woman said to another. "It was our anniversary, so he took me to the most famous restaurant in town and told me to order the most expensive dish on the menu. I did . . . a Big Mac."

Two old men were watching a Great Dane lick his balls. One turned to the other and said, "All my life, I wished that I could do that!" The second one said, "Better pet him first, he looks mean as hell."   —Billy Crystal

Taking a Brake
Films and plays lay groundwork for plot solutions with seemingly insignificant dialogue or clues sprinkled throughout the scenario. But jokes can't take an hour and a half (although some storytellers seem to take that long), so one-word clues are shuffled into anecdotes which, when combined with a reverse, prove to be the surprise detonator cap.

A worker on a construction site would wait until the end of the day and then walk out past the guards with a wheelbarrow filled with dirt. Management was positive he was stealing supplies, but every check of the wheelbarrow accounted for nothing but plain sand. After the job was completed, the foreman walked up to the construction worker, who had his last paycheck, and said, "Mike, I know you were stealing something. Tell me the truth, what were you takin'?"

Mike said, "Wheelbarrows!"

Two Jews met on a Brooklyn street corner. "How are things?"

"I'm doing fine," said the second. "I now own that office building on the corner. Say, do ya wanna buy it?"

"How much?" asked the first.

"Seeing you're an old friend, ninety million dollars."

"It's a deal. Lend me your pen. Here's your check. Good-bye."

A third man, overhearing the exchange, asked the buyer: "What was all that nonsense about? You know he doesn't own his own apartment let alone an office building. And he knows that you don't have millions of dollars. What do you get out of this?"

"Well, I'll tell you," said the buyer. "I got his pen."
                                                —*Jerusalem Post*

Jack Hanna, director of the Columbus, Ohio zoo, was displaying a toucan to David Letterman on his NBC TV show. Letterman was tossing grapes to the bird, "One, two, three," *throw*.

The bird caught each one to the roaring approval of the audience. Suddenly, Letterman said to Hanna, "Jack, why don't you try one?"

"Fine," said Hanna.

"Here we go," yelled Letterman, and he began tossing grapes into the air for Hanna to catch in his mouth.

OTHER BENEFITS

One delight of the reverse is that it can be used in innumerable ways to make a point, not just tell a joke. It's an excellent technique for speeches and essays.

> Two competitor manufacturers were attending an industry association outing at a mountain resort. They were roommates in the same small cabin when they heard scratching outside the door. One went to look, came back and started to put on his running shoes. "What's the trouble?" asked his roommate. "There's a giant bear outside," the other man said, "who's so hungry he's gonna smash his way right into this room." "Well," said the other, "why put on sneakers? You can't outrun a bear." "I know," said the other, "but all I need to do is outrun you."

To be told most effectively, the reverse must *not* be *telegraphed* by an introduction like "Talking about survival, let's make sure we keep our eye on our competitors. . . ."

Reverses are also very practical for deflecting insults. If the critic isn't carefully specific, the target has the thrill—and it is a thrill when that opportunity comes—to reverse the point of view and change the javelin into a boomerang.

> *Redneck:* What did the doctor say about your big, fat ass?
> *Wife:* I don't know. Your name never came up.

> My brother once had a job dressed as a polar bear in order to promote soft drinks at shopping malls. One day a man strolled up to him and asked, "Don't you feel stupid dressed up in that thing?"
> My brother said, "I feel stupid? You're the one talking to a bear."　　　　　　　　　—Martha Miller

At the height of an argument, I once said to my wife, "You're

not only incredibly beautiful, you're incredibly stupid!" Then,
realizing I had gone too far, I started to apologize. "That's all
right," said my wife. "It's God's fault."
  "What do you mean by that?"
  "Well, God made me beautiful so you would be attracted to
me. And he made me stupid, so I'd be attracted to you."
—Gene Perret

Again and again, faulty construction not only decreases the delight (because the surprise is anticipated), it also reduces the effectiveness of humor communication.

A Texan, visiting Vermont, asked a farmer how much acreage
he had. "Oh, I got a big farm," said the farmer. "Over 150
acres." The Texas swelled up and said, "You know, mister, I get
into my car in the morning, drive all day and still can't get to
the end of my property." The farmer said, "I know what you
mean. I've got a car just like that."

It is apparent, by now, how a reverse works in a long anecdote, but it can actually be done in only two sentences, as long as the first one carefully sets the false direction.

My boyfriend and I broke up, even though we're still deeply in
love. He wanted to get married and I didn't want him to.
—Rita Rudner

I divorced my first wife because she was so immature. I'd be in
the tub taking a bath and she would walk in whenever she felt
and sink my boats.   —Woody Allen

LET'S WRITE A REVERSE

When school is out, there's always the tearing up of homework, screeching and giggling. You would think professors
would act more dignified!   —Paul Sweeney

The basic reverse of students and teachers is a favorite humor subject, since it's familiar to all of us. So let's practice writing a reverse using that very subject. We'll use the beginning of the school term, when summer is over and mothers are obviously ecstatic about getting the house back. But because parents have guilt feelings, they need to be reassured that this progeny rejection is shared by other parents. To a humorist, guilt feelings are fertile ground for comedy. Guilt permits you to publicly ridicule a shared hostility.

But just saying, "We all feel relieved when our kids go back to school and the house is quieter and neater" is not wit. Your first efforts using clichés may look something like this:

When my kids go back to school, I go back to sanity. (*Where's the cliché?*)

When school starts again, my kids think they're going back to hell, and I think I'm going back to heaven.

The meaning of life, liberty and the pursuit of happiness gets a lot clearer the first day my kids go back to school.

For parents, Thanksgiving takes place in September—on the day school starts.

These first tries aren't totally satisfactory; they're too obvious. By talking about the benefits to mother all along, the punch line is telegraphed.

Now, let's try it as a reverse. We know we must set up the audience to think in a false direction. The simplest reverse, therefore, would be if we can get the audience to believe we're talking about the children while our real point of view is the mothers. So we try this:

The setup: September is the month when millions of beautiful faces radiating happiness turn toward school . . .
The reverse: they all belong to mothers.

Voilà! A great speech opening for a PTA-type group—guaranteed to get an appreciative laugh because of two humor ingredients: shared ambivalent hostility and surprise.

Internal Revenue Agent to taxpayer: "The first thing you've got to do is stop thinking of it as *your* money." *—Wall Street Journal*

Here are just some punch lines for the reverses on page 104. Yours can be even funnier.

1. A woman walking down the street with her dog passes a bum sitting on the sidewalk. The man looks up and says, "You've got the ugliest pig I've ever seen."

"Why you drunken bum," says the woman. "It's not a pig, it's a dog."

And the bum says, "I was talking to the dog."

2. A bum walks into the doctor's office with a frog on his head.

"What seems to be the problem?" the doctor asks.

And the frog said, "Well, it's about this wart on my ass."

3. The ugly girl was walking down the street with a pig under her arm. She meets a friend who asks, "Where did you get the pig?" And the pig says, "I won her in a raffle!"

4. They just took away the license of one of our doctors for having sex with his patients. And that's too bad, because he's the best veterinarian in town.

5. A friend of mine took up weightlifting—got broad shoulders, huge arms, muscular legs, rippling chest—she looks awful!

"I had everything: money, a beautiful apartment and a sexy, wealthy woman. Then bang, one night my wife walked in."

CHAPTER 7

Bewitched, Bothered, and Bewildered: Triples

If peanut oil comes from peanuts
and olive oil comes from olives,
where does baby oil come from?

—Lily Tomlin

EACH JOKE STRUCTURE HAS ITS DEVOTEES: the one-liner (Bob Hope), the epigram (Carl Reiner and Mel Brooks), the anecdote (Buddy Hackett and Bill Cosby), free association commentary (Richard Pryor and Robin Williams), word association (George Carlin), the insult (Don Rickles), working the audience (Steve Allen), and dozens of combinations of the above. But the triple is one format that all humorists use and have used. A triad grouping of examples or a sequence of three actions, comments, or categories, the triple increases tension with its longer buildup. That's why triples are one of the most common humor formulas—the payoff laugh is usually bigger than that you'd get with just the final point.

Prof: Mary Wilson, what part of man's anatomy enlarges to ten times its normal size during periods of great emotion?
Coed: I'm too embarrassed to answer that in public.
Prof: The correct answer, Mary, is the pupil of the eye—which leads me to three conclusions. One, you didn't read your textbook. Two, you have a dirty mind, and three, when you get married, you're in for a major disappointment.

THE HOLY TRILOGY

The triple, sometimes called "the holy trilogy," was the format of innumerable minister, priest, and the rabbi anecdotes fifty years ago. In those stories the order of appearance was dependent upon the religious interest of the audience, because the last mentioned was always the comic hero who outsmarted his colleagues. No one seems to know why or how these stories got started. But since they provide many opportunities for personalizing ethnic superiority, they'll probably remain popular as long as we have religious differences.

A minister comes home to his apartment early and finds his wife nude in bed and the room filled with cigar smoke. He looks down from his tenth-story window and sees a man smoking a big cigar just leaving the building. Enraged, he picks up his refrigerator and throws it out the window, killing the man instantly.

"Why did you do that?" someone yelled from the street. "You killed my priest."

The minister was so distraught that he threw himself out of the window.

A few moments later, three men—a priest, a minister, and a rabbi—approach heaven's gate and an angel asks each how he died. "I don't know," says the priest, "except suddenly a refrigerator smashed me into the ground." The minister says, "I threw it. But I was so filled with remorse, I jumped out of the window and killed myself."

"What about you, rabbi?" asks the angel.

"You got me. All I know was I was minding my own business, sitting in a refrigerator. . . ."

The Power of Three

The mystical power of the unit three has been known for centuries. The Bible is filled with triple designations: the three wise men, the Trinity, the Hebrew forefathers Abraham, Isaac, and Jacob, etc. And it may be an odd number in math, but its even *da-da-Ta-da-da-Ta-da-da-Ta* cadence makes it the most important number in comedy. And that's (1) the truth, (2) the whole truth and (3) nothing but the truth.

It is a dramatic speech heightener for orators, and the most famous speech triple in American history is Lincoln's "of the people, by the people, for the people. . . ." The Declaration of Independence's "life, liberty, and the pursuit of happiness" takes in a lot of ground, but (really now!)

couldn't Jefferson have thought of more benefits if he also wasn't enamored with the rhythm of speechmaking's "holy trinity"?

Children learn about Goldilocks and the three bears and the three little pigs. Aesop's fables made frequent use of triples. People in the theater are superstitious about numbers: actors will knock on stage doors three times and only three times.

> There are three ways to be ruined in this world. First is by sex, the second is by gambling, and the third is by telling jokes. Sex is the most fun, gambling is the most exciting, and being a comedian is the surest.
> —Paul Roth

Humor's PAP Test
According to a comedy theory developed by William Lang, a triple is one of the most perfect formats for a joke, because there are only three parts to most comedic bits. I call these three elements humor's PAP test.

P = Preparation (the situation setup)
A = Anticipation (triple)
P = Punch line (story payoff)

Here are a few examples of how the PAP test works.

> *Preparation:* The reason my wife and I have been happily married for forty years is because we go out to dinner once a week . . .
> *Anticipation (The Triple):* some candlelight, a little wine, soft music.
> *Punch line:* I go out on Friday night, she goes out on Saturday.
> —Henny Youngman

In each of the following examples note how anticipation is set up by the triple:

> P = My wife and I don't get along.
> A = I take my meals separately, I take a separate vacation, and I sleep in a separate bedroom.
> P = I'm doing everything I can to keep this marriage together.
> —Brickman, *Washington Star*

> P = Jews, Protestants, and Catholics:

A = let's all get together, give up our prejudices, and love each other
P = so we can give it to the damned Iranians.

It's possible, of course, to abbreviate the PAP rule by combining two of the elements in one sentence. In these examples, the third part of the triple also includes the punch line:

My wife is an angel. She's constantly up in the air, she's continually harping on something, and she has nothing to wear.

Hollywood star in TV commercial: "Now all of you know I can buy any product. So you think I'm endorsing Royal gelatin because of the flavor. No, you're wrong. Or you think I'm pleased that it tastes delicious and has so few calories. No, you're wrong again. It's because they're paying me a helluva lot of money."

If you want to be seen—stand up!
If you want to be heard—speak up!
If you want to be appreciated—shut up!

To see how the triple sequence sets up the value of the last line, reread the last joke and leave off the first or second line. Then the triple reads this way:

If you want to be heard—speak up.
If you want to be appreciated—shut up!

The humor is still there but the punch is softer because without the buildup of the triple there's less tension. Now try adding a few more examples in each piece and you'll find that by unnecessarily stretching out the sequence you'll be impatient to get to the punch line.

If you want to be involved—show up!
If you want to be seen—stand up!
If you want to be heard—speak up!
If you want to be appreciated—shut up!

There's no reason to give four examples when three will accomplish all the preparation you need to pay off the last hostile line.

You can take the same idea and add a reverse to make it sound very fresh for an after-dinner speaker.

> I was told to be accurate, be brief, and then be seated. . . . So
> I promise I shall be brief as possible—no matter how long it
> takes me. —Willard Pearson

PUTTING THE TRIPLE ON HOLD

A common formula is to set up a joke with a triple. Then a question refers to some outside physical occurrence and the payoff line, again, goes back to the triple. Once you learn this formula the variations multiply.

> *Waitress, in hoarse voice:* "For dessert, we got ice cream—
> vanilla, chocolate, and strawberry."
> *Customer:* "You got laryngitis?"
> *Waitress:* "No, just vanilla, chocolate, and strawberry."
>
> *(Same joke, different disease)*
> *Waitress, scratching her behind:* "Our specials today are steak,
> chicken, and pot roast."
> *Customer:* "You got hemorrhoids?"
> *Waitress:* "No. Just what's on the menu."

Do's and Don'ts for Triples
There are a number of rules specifically geared to the number three. Tension is important in humor structure and a triple helps build tension, but be wary of too much of a good thing.

1. Never tell more than *three* jokes about one subject at any one time.
2. Don't spend more than *three* minutes on any one theme.
3. *Three* themes of about *three* minutes each are optimum for a ten minute stand-up monologue.
4. *Three* minutes is the best length for a skit.
5. Don't use more than *three* voices in a radio skit or commercial.

The following story is also an example of how the triple can be personalized by the substitution of a local name for the third designation:

> I had a terrible dream last night. Three of our leaders suddenly
> passed away. St. Peter took each to his new chambers, an ugly,

foul-smelling cell. The first one was for President Reagan, and
as he entered he noticed a huge gorilla, and then a deep voice
intoned, "Ronald Reagan, because of all your sins, you will
spend the rest of your life making love to this female gorilla."
St. Peter then showed Senator Kennedy his cell, which also had
a gorilla tied up, and as he entered the same deep voice intoned, "Senator Kennedy, because of all your sins, you will
spend the rest of your life making love to this female gorilla."
Then [add local name] was shown to his cell, and inside was
Dolly Parton tied up. I was aghast, until I heard the deep voice
say, "Dolly Parton, because of all your sins. . . ."

Word Economy

Humor writing is a lesson in word economy. An anecdote is not a
short story. It's a small story told in the fewest possible words. That's why,
even in a long triple, you need to give just enough information to set up the
payoff line. Humor takes even more literary effort than the average editorial story because the climax must cause an immediate physical reaction in
the audience.

Three sons, with their wives, were celebrating their parent's fiftieth anniversary. At the dinner, the first son stood up and said,
"Dad. Mom. I'd have brought you a present, but Suzy and I
spent the summer in Europe, so we're kinda broke, but we do
wish you the very best." The second son said, "My dear parents. I, too, would have brought a present, but I just bought
Nancy a diamond necklace, and we're short right now." And
the third said, "Folks, we purchased a powerboat which left us
strapped, but we wish you good health and love for years to
come." "That's okay, sons," said the father. "I know how it
feels to be broke. I never told you this but when your mother
and I decided to get married fifty years ago, we didn't even
have the money for a license, so we never had a ceremony."
One of the sons burst out, "My god, Dad. You know what that
makes us?" "Yes, I do," said dad, "and cheap ones, too!"

We can tell the story without a triple in half the words:

A son attends a fiftieth anniversary dinner for his parents. He
apologizes that because of personal luxury expenses he
couldn't afford a present. The father sympathizes, "We know

how it is. When mother and I were courting we were so poor we couldn't afford a license, so we never got married." "My god," says the son, "do you know what that makes me?" "Yes," says dad, "and a cheap one, too!"

We cut the words and even eliminated two sons (so much for family planning), but the elimination of the triple decreased the suspense and minimized the buildup of hostility against three selfish sons. It isn't that *one* example isn't funny; it's just that ridiculing *three* is more pleasurable.

By listing a series of three conditions the triple is just one structure of a joke. Then, as in the pay-off technique with clichés, it must be concluded with an audacious and surprising climax.

THE TRIPLE TAKEOFF

Bride to marriage broker: "Your prospect is old, his eyes squint, and he has no teeth."
Broker: "No need to whisper, he can't hear either!"

With triples, you have established a formula that can easily work by just substituting different occupational features. Note these sound-alike twins—one for a professor and the other for a humorist.

The thing about being a professor is that if you can make just one student successful, if you can make just one student see the light, if you can make just one ready for the outside world, then you're still stuck with nineteen failures.

The thing about being a humorist is that if you only get one laugh, if you only get one smile, if you can make only one person happy, then you know your act stinks!   —Gene Perret

The Triple Reverse
A very popular combination of techniques is to start off with a triple, then switch to a reverse.

I'd like to introduce a man with a lot of charm, talent, and wit. Unfortunately, he couldn't be here tonight, so instead. . . .

Any of you see *Hollywood Wives* on TV last night? Talk about plot, drama, great acting—it had none of those things.

My wife's family consisted of three brothers and a dog: Tom,
Dick, Harry, and Rover. Harry was the dog.

A Joke on the Way to a Joke

Triples can also be used to enhance a mild piece of humor. Topping
the first bit of humor with two additional comments should encourage the
audience to build a laugh track and not judge the first part as "If that all
there was to it?"

Bob Nelson does a visual triple during his monologue about college
football players being interviewed on camera. He places two balloons under an oversized sweater to indicate shoulder pads. But as he is putting
them under the sweater he starts off with a visual triple. He first pushes the
two balloons underneath from the bottom and leaves them momentarily
side by side. "Wanna see my grandmother?" he asks. Then he moves the
balloons midway up the sweater and says, "This is my idea of what my
dream girl looks like." Then he moves the two balloons, one to each side
of the sweater, and says, "My dream girl lying down." Finally, at this
point, he puts them in the shoulder pad position for his football segment.

This is called *a joke on the way to a joke*. It's an effective device when
changing props takes more than an instant. Except for pregnant pauses,
silence is a comic's deadly enemy.

Here are a few more examples of triples written as toppers. The idea
is that each one of the three is a small laugh. After a short pause, when the
audience laughter comes halfway down (never wait until it stops completely because it's so hard to restart), the second (or third) line is added. This
build, when it works, is one of the techniques which contributes to a burst
of jokes called a roll, equal in comedy to a home run with the bases loaded.
That also means "For God's sake, don't stop me now."

A gossip is one who talks to you about other people.
A bore is one who talks to you about himself.
A brilliant conversationalist is one who talks to you about
yourself.   —Dr. William King

How Many Does it Take to Change a Lightbulb?

The lightbulb jokes often consist of triples. The first and second lines
are setups for the third. Here, as an example, is a group based upon
needling a neighboring state, a common inspiration for hostile humor.

How many Louisianians does it take to change a light bulb?
Three: one to hold the ladder, one to screw in the bulb, and
one to bribe officials for the permit.

How many Virginians? Three: one to hold the ladder, one to screw in the bulb, and one highly refined lady to remark how much lovelier the old bulb was.

How many Oregonians? Forty-two: one to hold the ladder, one to screw in the bulb, and forty to draft the environmental impact statement.

How many New Yorkers? A hundred and two: one to hold the ladder, one to screw in the bulb, and one hundred cops to make sure the first two aren't mugged.   —*Wall Street Journal*

"When I went to college a girl got pinned. Today,
she gets nailed."

CHAPTER 8

The Harmony of Paired
Elements:
Synonyms, Homonyms, and
Antonyms

HUMOR IS A FEAT OF VERBAL GYMNASTICS, and paired elements are examples of clever speechwriting commonly used in political addresses,
philosophical sermons, academic oratory, and toasts.

Solely as humor, this device appears in formats as varied as Shavian
wit, ad slogans, and bumper stickers. We find paired elements regularly as
"a thought for today" in calendar memo pads. They are a bit classier than
words of advice like "pay the butcher today" or "clean out the garage."

There are four variations of paired elements:

1. Paired phrases
2. Paired sentences
3. Paired words
4. Paired statistics

PAIRED PHRASES

To be most effective, paired phrases must be parallel—equal in grammatical structure and rhythm. Some need an introductory setup line: most do
not. But they all have a simple declarative statement that's craftily repeated
by reversing the order of the last few words. The result is an aphorism, almost lyrical in its repetition and valuable because it's easy to remember.

Two of our greatest gifts are imagination and humor.
Imagination compensates us for what we are not,
Humor compensates us for what we are.

Ask not what your country can do for you. Ask what you can
do for your country.   —John F. Kennedy

If guns are outlawed, only outlaws will have guns.
                                   —National Rifle Association

When the going gets tough, the tough get going.

Figures don't lie but all liars can figure.

Better a witty fool than a foolish wit.   —William Shakespeare

As a humor technique, paired phrases are facile but not necessarily simple. The basic rule, common in most humor, is that the last line is written first, because that's the point you want remembered. Then you try to reinforce the theme by reversing the words so that the first line incorporates the same rhythm.

Nobody cares how much you know until they know how much
you care.

Pilot over intercom to impatient passengers: "We're having a
short delay for engine repairs. Aren't you glad you're down
here wishing you were up there, rather than up there wishing
you were down here?"   —Joan White Book

I've got what it takes to take what you've got.   —Jim Boren

Paired phrases are so popular as clichés that they afford many opportunities for take-off humor.

Boss to his new employee: "Relax, Bitler. You have nothing to
fear except fear itself. And me, of course!"   —Robert Mankoff

They are frequent applause-getters, and writers know that the audience is more stimulated by the turn of phrase than by its logic. Homonyms get laughs even when they don't make much sense.

It is better to have loved a small man than never to have loved
a tall.   —Mary Jo Crowley

Sing Along with the Bouncing Ball

As a general rule, audience participation is an excellent technique for increasing appreciation. It's like singing along with the bouncing ball. The audience laughs and applauds its own perspicacity. Therefore, it isn't necessary to write both parts of the paired phrase if the second part is obvious. You can flatter the audience by letting them complete it themselves.

The difference between herpes and mono is that you can get
mono from snatching kisses.

PAIRED SENTENCES

This technique consists of two paired phrases, but used in separate sentences, generally by two different people. Instead of a take-off on a cliché ("The world may be your oyster, but you have to crack the shell to get it"), the responder's wit comes from the ability to reverse the order of the words and toss them back in the originator's face.

Telegram from play producer to George Bernard Shaw: "Send
manuscript. If good will send check." Shaw replied: "Send
check. If good will send manuscript."

A creditor sent a dunning letter to a customer, enclosed a picture of his fourteen-year-old daughter with a note: "This is the reason I must have the money." Customer replied with a picture of a voluptuous blonde in a bikini and a note: "This is the reason I don't have the money."

PAIRED WORDS

Pairing is an English professor's ballpark, because the majority of paired elements falls into the four classifications known as *synonyms, homonyms, antonyms,* and *groupings.* No professional humor writer is without a good resource book, such as *Webster's Dictionary of Synonyms, Homonyms and Antonyms,* on the desk.

Synonyms

Synonyms are different words that have a similar meaning ("Women sweat but ladies perspire"). Humor usage stretches the definition a bit but a close relationship must exist.

Definition of the upper crust: A bunch of crumbs held together by dough.

Once you learn the formula, a whole series of jokes falls into place:

It's difficult to act youthful without acting childish.

Synonyms are popular word pairings. There are so many words in the language which have a similar meaning that there are countless double entendre opportunities. It's popular because it's easy.

I call my girl friend candy because she makes my peanut
brittle.   —Rudy Lerch

The simplest technique is a cliché that focuses on a key word, which is repeated by a synonym.

She was an earthy woman, so I treated her like dirt.
                                                —George Carlin

Shoe salesman: Don't worry about the shoes. They'll stretch.
Woman: Then don't worry about the check. It'll bounce.
                                                —Rita Rudner

In this second group of examples, the key words have similar meanings, but at least one must be highly exaggerated.

She wasn't just throwing herself at him. It was more like taking careful aim.

He only acts mean. But down deep in his heart, he's thoroughly rotten.

The paired take-off, like any cliché take-off, uses the synonym as the first statement and a surprise or unexpected insight for the punch line.

Man does not live by bread alone, but by additives and preservatives, as well.   —Lou Stoddard

A lot of motorists could afford to be a bit more superstitious—
like believing in signs!

Redneck arguing against women's lib: "I told her to stick to her
washing, ironing, sewing, cooking and cleaning. No wife of
mine is going to go to work."   —J. N. Boblitt

Homonyms
Homonyms are words that have the same sound but are spelled differently.

She was a girl who preferred men to liquor.

The boy in the tragic explosion had blue eyes. One blew right
and the other blew left.

Ad for Honeywell Communications System: From high tech to
hi, mom.

Antonyms
Paired antonyms generate a lot of humor material because opposite
words are the simplest form of reverse. The first key word starts you in one
direction; the antonym flips you in the opposite.

The more double entendre antonyms you can put into one-liners, the
more likely you are to reach a wider audience, since each person gives the
words his own interpretation. For instance, trade terms are only funny to
those on the inside. But here's one that has two interpretations and the
choice is yours:

A Chinese casting director once said, "Girls who put up good
front most likely to be called back."

When *Saturday Night Live* was having a bad season, critics were quick to
dub it "Saturday Night Dead."

Antonyms as paired words can be used in three structures: as opposite
words, as a prefix that reverses the first word, and as a rhyme with homonym characteristics.

Opposite Words

A pessimist is someone who once put money behind an optimist.

In this structure, the first line includes a simple declarative statement and frequently employs a cliché.

The trouble with telling some guys a good joke . . .

Now the antonym pairing is added, but stated in a hostile manner.

. . . is that it always reminds them of a bad one.

This pairing takes place in the same phrase:

The only thing more disturbing than a neighbor with a noisy, old car is a neighbor with a quiet, new car. —*Los Angeles Times*

There are good and bad politicians in the government: some are trying to clean it up; some are trying to clean it out.
—Robert Orben

When we talk to God we're said to be praying, but when God talks to us we're said to be schizophrenic.   —Lily Tomlin

Boy to friend: "If I'm too noisy they give me a spanking. If I'm too quiet, they take my temperature."

The three most frequently used groups of antonym pairings are (1) *good and bad*, (2) *right and wrong*, and (3) *good and lousy*. All have a variety of double entendre possibilities.

Father to pre-teen daughter: "There are two words I want you to stop using. One is *swell* and the other is *lousy*. Promise?"
"Sure Dad, now what are the two words?"

Today, most humor has the life of a daylily, but here's one written two hundred years ago that's still funny.

Your manuscript is both good and original, but the part that is good is not original and the part that is original is not good.
—Samuel Johnson

Since the humor comes as much from the appreciation of clever word play even antonym non sequiturs can get laughs.

Let's get out of these wet clothes and into a dry martini.
—Robert Benchley

It's no wonder foreigners are confused by our language. Here a slim chance and a fat chance mean the same thing.
—Joyce Mattingly

The Prefix

There are hundreds of words that become antonyms of the subject just by adding a prefix—*uninteresting* is the antonym of *interesting, impatience* is the opposite of *patience*, and *dehumidifier* works opposite to the way a *humidifier* operates.

I left journalism because I met too many interesting people at an uninteresting salary.

The reasonable man adapts himself to the world. The unreasonable man persists in trying to adapt the world to himself. Therefore, all progress depends on the unreasonable man.
—George Bernard Shaw

I bought a humidifier and a dehumidifier. I put them in the same room and let 'em fight it out.   —Steven Wright

As a Rhyme Which Has Homonym Characteristics

The prerequisites for being in the diplomatic corps are the ability to handle protocol, alcohol, and Geritol.   —Wallace Rowling

Brainstorming Antonyms

But now another hard part. The first step of humor writing (and it *is* a pain until you get instinctive about it) is *listing*. You must dredge up every related idea and expression, every possible association. When we hear the expression "right and left" the normal train of thought is a pairing of directional tracks. But not for humorists. Their train dispatchers check to see just how many different tracks can be run on. They quickly see that "right" is also part of the antonyms "right and wrong." So, the most sophisticated (and appreciated) humor uses one meaning from one antonym pair and one meaning from another pair.

Most running experts and bankers recommend that you wait

until you've completely paid for the right running shoe before
you plunge in and buy the left.   —Dave Barry

Antonyms in comedy need not fit Webster's definition perfectly. As long
as the suggestion of an opposite is inferred, the humor can work.

The older an athlete gets, the faster he ran as a child.
                                                  —Red Smith

Have you ever wondered where the flies go in winter? Well, I
wish to hell they'd go there in summer, too.

A beautiful girl walked into my hotel room. She said, "Oh, I'm
sorry. I must be in the wrong room." I said, "No, you're in the
right room. You're just forty years too late."   —George Burns

It is important, however, not to mix up proper antonym combinations. The
antonym of "born" is "died" and the opposite of "started" is "finished."
So we can use the following line either way:

In this nightclub a number of famous comics were *born*—and
tonight, a number just died.

A number of famous comics *started* here—and tonight, a number just *finished* here.

It would be wrong to interchange them. The audience rarely pardons the
amateur who says, "A number of famous comics *started* here—and tonight, a number just *died* here."
    Here's how an important joke, using a paired antonym, was actually
written. When he was running for president in 1956 against President
Dwight D. Eisenhower, the Democratic candidate, Adlai Stevenson, was
being viciously attacked by the Republicans as having homosexual affilia-
tions. The stories circulated about Stevenson were malicious and untrue.
Governor Stevenson had few choices. To defend the charges in public
would only give them wider currency. To sue would take too long. The
Democrats decided to use humor to get the voters on Stevenson's side and
began working on a joke he could use in an upcoming speech. The bottom
line was to get Eisenhower, or his associates, to stop telling lies, so the first
time the joke was drafted it went like this:

Eisenhower must be worried. Just as soon as I started telling stories about him, he started telling lies about me.

That was the thrust, but the way this sequence is written the last line is *not* what Stevenson wanted the people to remember. So they tried a number of other variations until they found a paired antonym that worked. This is still heralded as one of Stevenson's great lines.

President Eisenhower and I have a pact. He'll stop telling lies about me, and I'll stop telling the truth about him.
—Adlai Stevenson

Antonym Doubles
Humor, like music, is more interesting when used in harmony like chords. Here's how to write two antonyms in the same bit:

A beauty salon is where a woman gets a faceful of mud and an earful of dirt.

When we're young we want to change the world. When we're older we want to change the young.

Antonym Triples
And here are antonyms that work as a triple:

There are three books my daughter felt were the most important influences in her life: the Bible, her mother's cookbook,
and her father's checkbook. —Joyce Mattingly

The real meaning of movie ratings are:
G = the hero gets the girl.
R = the heavy gets the girl.
X = everybody gets the girl.

Groupings
The final classification of clever word pairing is a miscellaneous cat-
egory called *groupings*. They aren't quite synonyms or antonyms. Instead, they are a group of two or more words loosely associated with a particular activity or profession. There is a good deal of controversy over this category, but who cares if the purists argue as long as the audience laughs?

A political candidate must learn not only to stand on a platform, but to sit on the fence and lie on the spot. —Frank Tyger

I come from out west, where men are men and women are
women, and you can't ask for a better setup than that.

—Red Skelton

I come from New York, where men are men—and women are
men, too!   —Robin Williams

PAIRED STATISTICS

The mechanics of constructing paired statistics require you to save the surprise number for the very last, just as if it were a word.

Sheriff to outlaw: "I'll give you a fair chance. We'll step off ten
paces and you fire at the count of three." The men pace off,
the sheriff shouts, "One, two," and then he turns and fires.
The dying outlaw says, "I thought you said fire on three." The
sheriff said, "That was your number. Mine was two."

My tennis coach told me I was one year away from being a
good player. And next year, I'll be two years away.

Professional humor writers use numbers if they have sequence possibilities, but the sequence doesn't necessarily have to be exact, as in the one,
two, three examples above. The numbers can go up, they can come down,
or they can even be repeated. The only rule is that the sequence be logical
and rhythmic. Note the numbers on the following examples:

Numbers Up

(#3-4-5)
Did you hear about the Polish race driver at Indianapolis who
had to make sixty-two pit stops? Three for fuel, four to change
tires, and fifty-five to ask directions.   —Larry Wilde

(#6-7-8)
MC at old age home: "We're going to give a prize to the oldest
person here."
First voice: "I'm 63."

Second voice: "I'm 73."
Third Voice: "I'm 83."
Fourth Voice: "I'm dead!"

(#5-10-25)
There are still things you can get for a dollar—like nickels,
dimes, and quarters.   —Charles Lindner

Numbers Down

(#10-9-8-7)
Professor to class: Don't be afraid of rewrites. Just remember
the first draft of Dickens' book was called *A Tale of Ten Cities*.
The second draft was called *A Tale of Nine Cities*, then it was
eight, then it was seven. . . ."   —Kathy Leisering

Number Repeated

(#20/20 and 5/5)
I wanted to be an FBI man, but you have to be 5 feet 7 and
have 20/20 vision. Then I toyed with becoming a master crimi-
nal—but you have to be 5 feet 7 and have 20/20 vision.
                    —Woody Allen

To have twenty lovers in one year is easy. To have one lover for
twenty years is difficult.   —Zsa Zsa Gabor

The kind of humor I like is the thing which makes me laugh for
five seconds and think for five minutes.   —William Davis

LET'S WRITE A PAIRED PHRASE

Following a misfortune, we have certain options. We can turn pessimistic
and curse the frequency of bad luck, or we can be optimistic and consider
that fate has provided a costly learning experience.

This is the base for an aphorism—a concise expression containing
truth or wisdom. The comic writer is trained by necessity to see humor
through woes-colored glasses. In this case we look for wit through paired
elements, since we already have an obvious optimist-pessimist pairing.
Our first effort might read something like this:

A pessimist curses fate; an optimist looks for benefits from
every decision.

There is some wisdom in that line but nothing particularly marketable. So
we try again, using some repetitive adjectives and subjects.

An optimist sees benefit in every disaster; a pessimist sees re-
currence in every disaster.

Still nowhere, but certain possibilities are starting to appear. We not only
have antonym pairings ("optimist/pessimist"), but we also have a double
antonym pairing with the words for *good luck/bad luck* ("benefit/disas-
ter"). However, the word *disaster* seems too exaggerated for our problem.
Perhaps, one peg down, *calamity,* might be more appropriate. We try
again:

An optimist sees a benefit in every calamity; a pessimist sees a
calamity in every benefit.

There's something wrong, now, with the sound and the connotation of *benefit*. We try other words. *Opportunity* could work, but not every decision is
an opportunity. All of them test us, however, so we go on to *test,* and finally, *challenge*. (Ah, that sounds better!) Now we write:

An optimist sees a challenge in every calamity. A pessimist sees
a calamity in every challenge.

The result is a double pairing that, in reality, doubles as an aphorism for humor writers. It's good writing and it's good advice, too!
    Paired elements are another example of how humor is written back-
wards—joke first! And whichever medium is used for humor, writers find
paired elements increase commercial value. In other words:

The work will get funny, and the funny will get work.

CHAPTER 9

Funny Words:
The Spark Plugs of Humor

An egg is funny, an orange is not!

—Fred Allen

IN HIS PLAY *THE SUNSHINE BOYS*, Neil Simon wrote about funny words. One of the main characters, Willy, says to his nephew: "Fifty-seven years in this business, you learn a few things. You know what makes an audience laugh. You know what words are funny and which words are not funny. Alka Seltzer is funny. You say 'Alka Seltzer' you get a laugh. . . . Words with 'K' in them are funny. Casey Stengel, that's a funny name. Robert Taylor is not funny. Cupcake is funny. Tomato is not funny. Cookie is funny. Cucumber is funny. Car keys. Cleveland. . . . Cleveland is funny. Maryland is not funny. Then, there's chicken. Chicken is funny. Pickle is funny."

No pro disagrees. There are phonetic values in certain words that almost guarantee a laugh. Mel Brooks recommends, "Instead of saying salmon, turkey is a funnier sound. It just helps. (The 'k' sound doesn't have to even be the first letter.) Like a line I wrote for Sid Caesar. He was playing the part of Jungle Boy, a man who comes out of the jungle. He's asked by a reporter, 'What's your greatest enemy?' And Jungle Boy says, 'Buick! Only way to kill Buick, punch in grill. Hard! Buick die!' "

Why is the "k" sound funny? Research indicates that, as babies, it's the sound we associated with comfort and joy. Think of all the words we coo to babies, and you'll notice they have a "k" sound, even though most of them begin with the letter "c." Here are just a few:

cutie	cookie
kitten	cuddle
curls	cozy
cat	catch
candy	car
carry	careful
cold	comb
come	count
coo	cootchie-coo
cow	ca-ca
creep	crib
cry (don't)	kiss
kiddie	clean
cupcake	

No other sound has such a universal humor kick. As you say "kiss," for example, your mouth smiles, it doesn't pucker up.

There are literally thousands of funny words that act like spark plugs to kick over the laugh motor. Unlike key (surprise) words which come at the end of a sentence, funny words work best in the middle of a joke and are frequently used in groups, as a list of names, foods, or unusual activities. All writers have their own favorite buzz words, and they're jealous of them, even to the point of uncontrolled anger when someone else uses them. Fortunately, these words are not private property.

To be categorized as funny, a word has to have at least one of the following three characteristics: a funny sound, a double entendre, or an association with a famous person. For examples we'll take the single classification of funny names.

1. *It must have a funny sound.* Jonathan Winters' characters have names like Granny Frickert, Melvin Gohard, Lamargene Gumbody, and Elwood P. Suggins. Other comics have used names like Faith Popcorn, Hortense Powdermarker, and Daphne Kugelmass.

S. J. Perelman, the master of humorous appellations, invented Professor Motley Throng, Ernest Void, Irma Voltaire, the Flagellation Trust Company, and the Cutlass and Blintzes Pub. His version of Sleeping Beauty starts off with "Once upon a time, there was a king and queen named Morton Steinberg and his wife, Fanny. . . . They made up their minds that if they ever had a child they would name it Shirley, even if it was a boy."

Was it only a coincidence that Jack Roy (nee Jacob Cohen) gained fame and respect only after he changed his name to Rodney Dangerfield? Or that the Marx Brothers' act went into high gear when Julius became Groucho and his brothers Leonard and Adolph became Chico and Harpo?

Zero Mostel's real name was Sam. He said he changed it to Zero so he could make something out of nothing.

2. *It must have a double entendre sound.* It's hard to forget a name like John Dough. And it's easy to understand a character's habits when he has a name like Lionel Bedwetter or Sandor Needleman.

As children, our first cloakroom exercises in homonym humor were originating book titles with off-color names of authors:

"The Yellow Stream" by I. P. Standing
"The Open Kimono" by Semour Hare
"The Hawaiian Prostitute" by Wanna Layahora
"My Shotgun Wedding" by Himalaya Last
"The Russian Rabbi" by Ikan Kutchadikoff

3. *It must be a name of a person recently in the news whose activities (sometimes unfairly) encourage our ridicule, hostility, or derision.* As soon as these names hit the headlines, they also hit the top of the humor charts. Old jokes—new names! Colonel Kaddafi, Ayatolla Khomeini, Klaus von Bulow, John DeLorean, Kurt Waldheim, etc.

IT WAS BIGAMY TO GIVE HIM CREDIT

At least one of these same three qualifications must apply to all funny words. Here are just a few hundred examples, listed by the most popular categories.

Names
Every ethnic group has names that encourage a smile.

Jewish

Mendel	Becky
Sidney	Sadie
Bernie	Shirley
Irving	Lena
Mr. Teitelbaum	Mrs. Goldberg

A grasshopper walked into a bar and ordered a drink. "My god," said the bartender, "a talking grasshopper. You know, we

have a drink named after you?" The grasshopper looked at him
in amazement and asked, "Irving?"

English

Percy	Humphrey
Reginald	Victor
Hortense	

Italian

Guido	Tony
Concepcion	Giuseppe

Chicano

Margarita	José
Speedy Gonzales	Pablo
Manuel	

French

Lucky Pierre	Francois
Henri	Pepe
Suzette	

American
Funny American names are short and often have a double entendre.

Pop	Spud
Doc	Fatso
Dick	Champ
Chuck	Ace
Phil	Spike
Bunny	Biffy
Trixy	Penny
Buffy	Babs

Most male comedians purposefully take short names, more often than not a
nickname: Woody, Soupy, Henny, Bobby, Shecky, Mel, Billy, Joey, etc.
Female humorists names are just short: Goldie, Lily, Lucy, Carol, Erma
and Shari.

Cities and Places

There seems to be no limit to the names of cities, small towns, street names, local restaurants, bars, hotels, colleges, and department stores that can be used as humor fuses. The more localized they are, the better.

> Everybody needs someone to ridicule so they'll feel superior, and everybody feels superior to West Virginians.

Years ago, such expressions as "How will it play in Oshkosh?" or "You couldn't even make it in Paducah!" were terms for funny hick towns. Today, because a large portion of comedy is played to New York audiences, no state seems to be a target more often than New Jersey. ("Isn't it a shame that the light at the end of the tunnel is New Jersey?") For the same reason, no borough gets kidded more often than Brooklyn. Although Sheboygan is a funnier word, no city is the butt of more jokes than Cleveland (either because of the "k" sound or because Cleveland is proof that God had a quality control problem!).

Sometimes the sound alone permits humor from mispronunciation.

> You know how Van Nuys got its name? Well, one day my little old Jewish mother was visiting me, and I took her to the top of the Hollywood Hills and had her view the valley below just at sunset. 'Well, mama, what would you call that?' And she said, "Ver nize."
>
>   —Joey Bishop

Foods

Many food names, both generic and brand names, just sound funny. There's probably no more guaranteed laugh in comedy than the word "Twinkie." Use it at the end of a list of foods you ate last night, and an involuntary smile comes to the lips of your audience. Archie Bunker used it ad nauseam, because it sounds a lot funnier than "Hostess Cupcakes."

Generic

pea	jelly bean
peanut	frankfurter
salami	cherry
all-day sucker	tutti-frutti
fruit	lollipop
sarsaparilla	fruitcake
prune	macadamia nuts
hot dog	lemon

pepper	applesauce
noodles	chicken soup
coconut	nectarine
chopped liver	shrimp
fortune cookie	castor oil
kumquats	garlic
meatball	

Household and Brand Names

Jell-O	Tums
Tide	Fig Newton
Whopper	Tootsie Roll
Tidy Bowl	Fab
Scotch Tape	Preparation H
Ex-Lax	Buick
Saran Wrap	Sanka
McDonald's	Dr. Pepper
Serutan	Crazy Glue
Winnebago	Kotex
Tylenol	Moxie
Popsicle	Chock Full o' Nuts
Dairy Queen	Ben Gay
Pinto	Alka Seltzer
Arm & Hammer	

The orchestra conductor asks for musical requests from the au·
dience and someone shouts, "How about the second movement by Ex-Lax?"

I understand the Tidy Bowl man comes from Flushing.

I wouldn't say Nancy Reagan is designer conscious, but when
she was a baby, the first words out of her mouth were "Gucci.
Gucci. Gucci."

The Ten Commandments are just chock full o' nots.

Ethnic Expressions
While ethnic jokes are a major category in contemporary humor the
utilization of ethnic expressions requires precise knowledge of their meaning and cadence.

Yiddish

As more Jewish comedians are assimilated into mainstream American society, the main question is whether Yiddish expressions will retain a major humor value. Probably not, but they still sound funnier than their English counterparts, i.e., *bar mitzvah* sounds funnier than *confirmation*, and *rabbi*, because of unfortunate stereotyping, conjures up more humorous possibilities than the title of *minister*.

schnook	klutz
fagalah	zaftig
nebbish	bubbe
meshuggener	kosher
chutzpah	kvetch
schvartza	seltzer
schlepp	shpritz
gevalt	putz
gefilte fish	matzo balls
schlock	schlemiel
schmuck	goyim
latkes	tzuris
shtick	

George Jessel was famous for his many gold-digger wives and girlfriends. Once, roasting golfer Arnold Palmer, Jessel said, "Arnie has made a fortune with his putts and my putz has practically broken me!"

German

Closely allied in humor with Yiddish expressions are German names and foods, probably because a good deal of Yiddish originated from German.

When the monster makes love to Madeline Kahn in Mel Brooks's *Young Frankenstein* film, he thrills her with his enormous "shvantzenstucker." And Sid Caesar's stupid German professors had names like Kurt von Stuffer, Siegfried von Sedative, and Rudolf von Rudder.

Exclamations

These sound a lot funnier than "Oh, my!"

wow	yuck
wham	ugh
bang bang	zonk

gee whiz   zoowie voom
lalapaluzza

Customer to waiter: What have you got to eat?
Waiter: Klochomoloppi. Also have lich lock, slop lom, stock-
   lock, rishkosh, and flocklish.
Customer: Yuck!
Waiter: We've got yuck, too. Boiled or braised?
                              —Sid Caesar and Carl Reiner

DOUBLE ENTENDRES

We've already discussed this most basic of all humor techniques so let's
concentrate here on some of the tricks of the trade. As usual, most funny
double entendres are made up of words that have a sexual connotation.

Sex Objects
Many products have features that can be associated with the parts of
the human body. For example, an auto has two big, beautiful headlights, a
cute tail, ball bearings, nuts, a gear shift, a dead battery, a filter, a belt, a
stiff rod, fingertip or push-button controls, it backfires, and there's a loose
screw at the wheel. The U.S. Army instructs recruits on rifle assembly by
using double entendres. Even the basic weapon is called a piece.

Sex and Media
Thousands of book, movie, and song titles, such as *Moby Dick, The
Secret Policeman's Other Ball,* and *Once is Not Enough, Play It As It Lays,
Much Ado About Nothing,* and *I Wonder Who's Kissing Her Now?* fill a
small dictionary in this category. The skill is finding not any word, but the
right word. We've already covered the word "it."
   Most comic references are inspired by words in three categories:
hard-core, soft-core, and bedpan.

Soft-core and Hard-core
It's easy to be prudish and say that hard-core expressions aren't funny, they are just intended to shock. But it's much more accurate to say that
the decision of whether to use soft-core (ass) or hard-core (asshole) is determined by the character of the performer and of the audience.
   There are three reasons why professional writers will work very hard
to avoid hard-core words.

1. The soft-core word can be just as funny when it is the definition rather than the shock of the word which sparks the humor.

"Do you handle condoms?" the young man asked the drug store
  clerk.
"Yes, I do."
"Well, wash your hands, I want a ham sandwich."

2. The soft-core word is acceptable to a wider range of audiences. Therefore, it's more commercial—if earning money is an important consideration.

One chorus girl to another: "This guy's idea of oral sex is talking about himself."

3. Soft-core may suggest the act and encourage the audience to fill in the missing word. Then, who can complain about the language?

When we are told by doctors that our teens were our peak sexual period, we feel bad that we let so many good years slip between our fingers.

Sexual Verbs
There are endless possibilities—all too obvious—with such descriptive words as:

blow/suck	coming/going
eat/swallow	bang/screw
finger/feel	

Here, the problem is not to find them but to avoid them. They're just too easy a joke. As humor vehicles, they are adolescent and cheap—a sign of the beginner.

Bedpan
I think there's a lot more genuine fun in bedpan humor than in the other two categories. Body functions and malfunctions are a favorite source of humor because they are generally taboo table conversation and therefore lend themselves to shock appeal. Of all the bedpan comic words, *enema* is the most popular. It has homonym possibilities ("Don't be your own worst enema"), and is a ripe expression for insult humor ("If they ever gave this

country an enema, Detroit is where they'd stick the pipe"). Alan King has an oft-quoted monologue called "An Enema was Mother's Love":

> An enema was a family affair. When you came from a large family, when you saw that enema bag coming. . .and you knew you weren't the recipient . . . "Yeahhhhh! Give 'em an enema!" It was your mother's hand—you had to get well. What do doctors tell you now? Give yourself a Fleet. What the hell is a Fleet? A disposable. You go . . . keeeet! You can't clean out a chicken with a Fleet. I showed it to my mother. She said, "It must be a mouthwash!" My mother had a bone [*demonstrates size*] that went from the tip of my finger all the way to my elbow. That was just the bone. When she inserted it, it cleared out your nostrils, the sinuses, the wax from your ears.

As a result, the list of bedpan words is one of the largest categories of funny words. Here is just a sampler:

hernia	circumcision
urinalysis	diarrhea
specimen	zipper
enema	chamber pot
vasectomy	fart
herpes	gynecologist
guts	urination
hemorrhoids	latrine
prostate	underwear
diaphragm	coma
proctologist	diapers
puberty	feces
dung	belly
pee	toupee
navel	

THE WILD KINGDOM

Certain pets also convey funny images. Puppies, cats, mice, and rabbits all have double entendre associations.

> Zsa Zsa Gabor went on the *Tonight Show* carrying one of her prized felines. As she was sitting there, she suddenly turned to

Johnny Carson and asked, "Would you like to pet my pussy?" "Sure," said Carson, "but first move the cat."

A little girl and her mother came to the doctor's office. Following the girl was a little dog. "Does your dog bite?" asked the doctor. The girl shook her head. As the doctor bent down to pet the dog, the dog sank his teeth deep into the doctor's hand. The doctor yelled in pain, "I thought you said your dog doesn't bite." And the girl said, "This one ain't mine."

The word *beast* is the only term used by women that can both insult and praise a man. And even insects, like bees and cockroaches, are funny humor sources.

A German professor was addressing a Westchester ladies club on the life of the porcupine. "And would you believe it, ladies," he said, "that the porcupine has a prick that is ten inches long?" There were gasps all over the room, and the MC hastily whispered in the professor's ear. "Oh, my dear ladies," he said, "I have made a terrible mistake in English. What I should have said is that the quill of the porcupine is ten inches long. As a matter of fact, the prick is only one inch long."

NUMBERS

Even some numbers are funnier than others, and we're not just talking about *three* or *sixty-nine*.

In humor, the economy of words is almost fanatical. There is one exception and that is when numbers are used. If they're essential in the joke, when we want to give them extra power, they must sound or look important. The number 1,500 should be pronounced (or written) as *one thousand, five hundred*. The time of 8:15 should be pronounced (or written) as *a quarter after eight*. The height of 6'2" should be pronounced (or written) *six-foot, two inches tall*. Every syllable must be an atom of meaning as well as information.

In addition, the following numbers (or expressions), by sound or imagery, tend to stimulate humorous responses:

zero	thirteen
zip	twenty
a zillion	a nickel

three	fifty
a fiver	a deuce
goose egg	a million
ninety-nine	ten
a grand	

A billion dollars here, a billion dollars there. Pretty soon, it adds up to a lot of money.　　　　　　—Everett Dirksen

"Thanks, buddy. Most guys wouldn't have done that for a transvestite."

CHAPTER 10

To Tell the Truth: Exaggerated and Understated Realism

When a thing is funny,
search it for a hidden truth.

—George Bernard Shaw

HUMOR ONLY APPEARS TO BE FREE FORM. Most often it is carefully structured and predictable. "A good deal of humor is observation on everyday life twisted into absurd shapes," said Patrick J. Sweeney. Nowhere is this more evident than in the interaction of realism and exaggeration, two of the six ingredients in the THREES formula. In humor they balance each other like equal weights on a scale. Sometimes the scales may tip, but the variation is always small—and *that's* no exaggeration.

Since humor analyzes our view of the world around us, realism is essential in order for the audience to approve of our hostility toward the target. "Comedy is just truth with a curlicue," said Sid Caesar. On the other side of the scale, facts and conclusions are exaggerated to attract attention. This is a standard theatrical device, granted by dramatic license, to portray objects and events as "bigger than life." In ancient Greek theater, actors wore leather phalli as part of their costumes. "Then, as now," said Joy Lindskold, "men seemed to have a need to exaggerate small things."

THE STRETCH-BAND THEORY

Humor comes out of the unexpected: no surprise, no laugh. In a series, the first two lines are usually straight lines (realism). The third line is the twist—logical but unexpected. Realism is the setup, exaggeration is the joke. "Get your facts first," wrote Mark Twain, "and then you can distort them as much as you please." Thus humor is like a rubber band; the more it can be stretched, the more useful it is. I call it the stretch-band theory.

When the rubber band is stretched to capacity, several things happen at once.

1. The shape of the band (realism) is altered.
2. The rubber band can be pulled (exaggeration) in different directions (overstatement and understatement).
3. Audience tension increases proportionally, up to the breaking point.
4. The sound of the vibrations (emotion) along the length of the band may vacillate frequently.

Realism sets up the joke, as the audience mentally nods in agreement with the introduction, then the joke is sprung loose by the exaggeration. But finding the proper balance between realism and exaggeration is the ultimate test of a comedy writer's skill. Humor comes when the exaggeration is logical. Simply being ludicrous is not a skill.

The Walled-Off Astoria

Starting with realism, the humor writer tries to determine how far in any direction the truth can be exaggerated without destroying credibility. It's called "good, better, best." A story about a prisoner who calls his companion a "cellmate" is good, calling him a "bedroom mate" is better, and calling him a "suite mate" is comedically the best of all. Realism is frequently funniest when it's exaggerated to the most extreme possibility. In math, $1 + 1 = 2$. In humor, $1 + 1 = 11$. This can be done by either overstatement (also known as hyperbole and exaggeration) or understatement. Here are some examples.

Overstatement

CEO to members of the board: "There you have it, gentlemen. The upside potential is tremendous, but the downside risk is jail."
                                        —Robert Mankoff

If I had all the money in the world, I'd pay off my debts—as far as it went.

The scarecrow scared the crows so badly that they brought back the corn they had stolen two years before.   —Fred Allen

Understatement

He jumped out the window. As room 18 was on the fifth floor,
you can imagine his surprise.   —Ring Lardner

Hostess to guests at mammoth reception: "Glorious Food
Caterers did the buffet, but Willy designed the traffic flow
himself."

A scoutmaster is shielding a young scout from an irate and totally disheveled old lady ready to swing her umbrella. He says,
"Don't be upset, madam. He just felt that if taking you across a
street was a good deed, taking you across the eight-lane turn-
pike would be even better."

How far can you go with exaggeration? Generally, the more your punch
line exaggerates the introductory realism, the better the result.

Girls are much more psychic than guys. They're the first to
know if you're going to get laid.   —Paul Rodriquez

What appears to be exaggeration one day may not be the next.

One small town citizen to another: "Those terrorist hijackings
are getting serious. First they were in Beirut, then Cairo,
Athens, Rome. They're getting closer to Ottumwa every day."

It seems logical and obvious, but it isn't easy. Many of today's novice
stand-up comedians have trouble with it. They'll start with some realistic
premise like the way women dress, picking up girls in a singles bar, out-
smarting the police, or advertising slogans, but then they'll shift into fifth
gear with a wild display of ludicrous fantasy that's not connected well to
the initial premises. Their material has a success rate of only one out of four
or five because they make the same mistake over and over. They consistently disrupt the balance of realism and exaggeration.

REALISM

Realism is a big reason for the success of the *Bill Cosby Show*. "My one
rule is to be true rather than funny," says Cosby. The more realistic we
make the humor piece seem, the more our audience identifies with it.

My way of joking is to tell the truth. It is the funniest joke in
the world.   —George Bernard Shaw

Truth (realism) involves the audience. People want to know the latest
news. When we meet each other we ask, "What's new?" The most influ-
ential words in advertising are *free*, *sale*, and *new*. We care more about current events when they affect us directly. The key word is *us*, the audience,
not *you*, the writer. Remember how bored you get when people dwell at
length on their recent business or domestic problems. The classic line is:

He's the kind of bore who, when you meet him on the street
and say, "Hello! How are you?" he stops and tells you.

Fifty percent of the time we don't care about your problems, and the other
fifty percent of the time we're glad you're getting what you deserve.

A customer in a bar is talking to the man seated next to him.
"Strange, isn't it? Normally, I'm a very caring person, but in your
case, for some reason, I don't give a damn."

"I gave up pastries, too many calories. I gave up red meat, too
much cholesterol. I gave up Cokes, too much caffeine."
"Hey, that's great. How do you feel?"
"Hungry!"

The vice president called up the president, "How are you feeling today, Mr. President?"
The president paused and then said, "You *really* care, don't
you?"

A Catholic friend had eight children. We asked him what he
thinks about when it comes to college education. His answer:
"Thirty-two years!"

The importance of realism might seem to run counter to our feelings that
humor should be fictional. After all, we surmise, if everyone knows from
the beginning of a joke that "any resemblance to anyone living or dead is
purely coincidental," isn't there less resistance to laugh at the fool's misfortune? No harm. No enemies. Unfortunately, no laughs either. Here's an
example:

I know a man who teethed on a set of alphabet blocks when he was a baby. He finally tired of them when he was fifteen.

This story is simple enough. We have some realism: babies do teethe on building blocks. We have exaggeration with the age fifteen. We smile at the insult, but there's no *big* laugh, because nobody cares about "a man."

Yet, if we could find someone whose public reputation indicates limited intellectual abilities, and that person is an authority figure or some celebrity who irritates us, then realism helps make it much stronger:

Sylvester Stallone's mother reported he learned to read by teething on a set of alphabet blocks, and he's been swallowing his letters ever since.

Unrealistic Humor

In show business, the key word is honesty. And once you've learned to fake that, you're in.   —George Burns

Many believe that failed humor is most often the result of too much exaggeration. That isn't true. Most often it results from too little realism.

Here are a few simple examples of humor that's unrealistic. It doesn't mean they're not funny. It does mean they have to work harder (through performance) than those that are realistic. The following anecdote works realism too hard:

Tommy came home from school very dejected. "I had an awful day," he told his mother. "I couldn't remember an answer and it was embarrassing." "Forgetting one answer is nothing to be embarrassed about," soothed his mother. And the boy said, "During roll call?"   —Dick Shebelski

Here's the same structure that *could* have happened, at least to a college student:

"They threw me out of my hotel in Fort Lauderdale this spring break for pissing in the pool."
"How could they do that? Lots of kids piss in the pool."
"From the fourteenth floor?"

Unrealistic

The bushman remarked, "I'd like to get a new boomerang, but I can't get rid of the old one."

Realistic

Even my daughter doesn't give me any respect. I put her to bed and tried to kiss her and she said, "Not tonight, Daddy, I've got a terrible headache."   —Rodney Dangerfield

OVERSTATEMENT

Turning realism into exaggeration is easier to understand if we think of it as a transition from sense to nonsense. Bert Williams, one of the first black comedians, used this as his stock story on racial discrimination:

A black fish-peddler climbs up a seven-thousand-foot mountain to sell fish to white folks. One day, after he gets to the top a white man says, "No, we don't want no fresh fish today."
So the black man goes down the steep mountain, nearly losing his life in a landslide. He no sooner gets to the bottom when he spots the same white guy beckoning him. He thinks to himself, "Praise God, that white man changed his mind."
So he climbs back up the rugged mountain, gets to the top and the white man is standing there. He waits until the peddler gets real close and then he clears his throat and says, "And we don't want none tomorrow either."

Exaggeration is embellishing that which you've seen or heard. It isn't only theatrical, it's almost instinctive. We learned as children that we could get attention by lying. We also learned we can get in a lot of trouble. But if we told stories in the form of a joke, we not only got away with it, we got appreciative laughter.

In grade school I was such a hit with my exaggerated mimicking and clowning that the teacher was charging a four dollar cover and a two-drink minimum.   —Billy Crystal

Every installment of *I Love Lucy* began with a logical premise: Lucy wanted to be a singer in Ricky's band, or she was suspicious he might be philandering. Only after a plausible foundation had been established was the element of absurdity introduced. Then exaggeration continued to inflate the plot until the inevitable physical slapstick climax was reached.

We are so influenced by the hyperbole of media, theater, and advertising, which use superlatives to gain attention, that we fall into the habit of believing that certain events and people are extraordinary. This inflated posturing is the balloon humorists aim to prick.

Cartoons and film animation provide endless examples of humor exaggeration: animals talk and take on human attributes, while people get into impossible situations. Janet Flanner, *New Yorker* columnist, said her favorite cartoon was of a lady on the porch of a colonial hut whose husband is obviously inside a boa constrictor hanging from the beam beside her. Without a sidewise glance, she says, "Oh speak up, George, stop rambling."

"This is a perfect example," Flanner wrote, "of our realism, sadism, and also the state of improbability we put into drawings, which take the truth out of the conception so that the spectator cannot be really frightened."

Since audience acceptance of comedy encourages them to set aside disbelief, humorists should take advantage of every opportunity to stretch the truth. In other circumstances, unmitigated exaggeration would be castigated. With humor, exaggeration signals folly and harmless hyperbole.

D. L. Stewart, popular syndicated columnist of the *Dayton Journal-Herald,* asked me during an interview how much exaggeration is acceptable. Newspaper editors disdain any suggestion of misrepresentation. As an example, I pointed out to Stewart that in his new book, *Fathers are People Too!* he had written:

> When you're an only child, you never have anybody to blame. When I was 14 my father came into my room and asked me who had been smoking his cigarettes. I had to tell him it was the dog.

This idea is funny, but by exaggerating and building tension, the last line can be even funnier with the addition of just two words—and an important pause.

> . . . [He] asked me who had been smoking his cigarettes. I had to tell him *the truth*—it was the dog.

Exaggerated Numbers
Math is logic, but when there's a lapse in logic, it's ludicrous.

I want to live to be a hundred, because you rarely read any obituaries about people over a hundred years old.

—George Burns

If there's anything instinctive about humor writing, it's being able to answer the constant questions: "When is exaggeration excessive, and what's the right balance of reality and distortion?" It's the same instinct news editors use daily to determine "what is news?" Their answer: "I know it when I see it."

Exaggerated numbers are a common part of humor writing. They signal to the audience that this is a fictional story, they dramatize the ludicrousness of the plot, and they make a point by shock as well as surprise.

A graduating senior went to the board of health and asked for two thousand cockroaches. He said he promised his landlord he would leave his apartment exactly the way he found it.

The college course bulletin had a misprint in the listing for Advanced Public Relations. It read Advanced *Pubic* Relations. The registration was one thousand five hundred. And those were only the faculty wives.

In these two examples the exaggerations are obvious. In the first story, would fifty cockroaches have been an acceptable number? Although that might be more realistic, the mental image of two thousand roaches is more graphic and therefore more hilarious. On the other hand, what about fifty thousand cockroaches? It could be argued that such an overwhelming number creates an image straight out of Hollywood's chamber of horrors and might change fun to fear. The number two thousand is easy to say (compared to two thousand five hundred) and easy to remember. It sounds right.

In the second joke, the impact is made by a number that's totally inconceivable. Isn't one thousand five hundred too much? Well, we should always test other numbers. Would a registration of seventy-five provide much of a jolt? Maybe to the bursar, but not to an audience, because it's too realistic. How about two hundred? Sounds better! As we go up the scale, we find the impact grows as the numbers grow. Where we stop is an arbitrary decision. Yet in this case, somehow different from the first story, dragging out the number by slowly saying "one thousand five hundred" seems to heighten the impact. It's also the subtle timing, the personal delivery, and the musical cadence that makes the difference.

"What do you expect to be when you graduate?"
"Forty!"

TV quizmaster to dull contestant: "Well, I could go on talking to you for seconds!"

Pick the Right Number

The selection of the best number is a basic skill. And here's a chance to test yours. Each of the following jokes uses a number as the surprise element. After you read each one, select a wide variety of numbers—from the highest conceivable to the lowest. Constantly ask yourself if the humor is strengthened by altering the number in any way:

The average man speaks twenty-five thousand words a day. The average woman says thirty-thousand words a day. Unfortunately, when I get home at night, I've spoken my twenty-five thousand, but my wife doesn't start hers until we get into bed.
—Michael Collins

One evening a Washington street vendor came home with over a thousand dollars. "Where'd you get all that money?" asked his wife. "Selling hot dogs for fifty times their regular price." "Who'd pay that?" asked the wife. "Lots of people. They all work in the Pentagon." —*National Enquirer*

Pete Rose on smashing Ty Cobb's record: "In his lifetime, Cobb had 4,190 hits and batted 367. If he were alive today, he'd probably be batting only 304. . . . Of course, he'd be ninety-four years old."

UNDERSTATEMENT

Subtle humor isn't underrated, it's just understated—an effective humor device because it encourages the audience to participate. The British believe that the underclass overstates and the upper class understates. Humor writers are classless; they use both techniques. Understatement's most famous practitioner today is Woody Allen, whose own humor was influenced by S. J. Perelman, a master of the art. Allen's understatements start out very realistically and are frequently non sequiturs.

If there's a God, why are there such things as famine and day-
time TV?

I don't really believe in the afterlife, but I am taking a change
of underwear.

Understatement is an excellent technique for self-deprecating humor. The
audience feels more comfortable with authority figures who have a modest
attitude toward their accomplishments.

People always ask me if I get stage fright. Believe me, it's not
the stage that frightens me; it's the whole audience that scares
the hell out of me.   —Robert Orben

Editor to writer: "That article wasn't bad."
Writer: "It wasn't meant to be."   —Fred Allen

Hostess to actress: "Darling, what an absolutely sensational
    outfit you're wearing."
Actress: "This old thing? I've had it since two o'clock this after-
    noon."

Understated Numbers
On the other end of the numerical scale, understated numbers are an
equally effective technique:

A newspaper editor was honored at a testimonial dinner by the
governor as one of the great leaders of his community. Flushed
with pride, he asked his wife on the way home, "I wonder just
how many great leaders our city has?" The wife said, "One less
than you think."

I have three children—one of each.   —Rodney Dangerfield

When *New Yorker* editor Harold Ross was once asked why he
printed the cartoons of James Thurber, a fourth-class illustrator,
Ross said, "I don't think he's fourth-class—maybe second-
class!"

Like most humor, the pause before the surprise word effectively builds tension. When a reporter asked David Brenner what he thought of the remo-

deled Catch a Rising Star nightclub, he said, "It's beautiful, impressive. Must have poured three hundred and fifty . . . dollars into this place."

Here's an example of an exaggerated number that would work better if it were more realistic:

> A Hollywood producer, to impress his aged mother on her birthday, bought a bird for $50,000 that could speak ten languages. He sent it to New York. A week later, he called her and asked, "How did you like the bird?" She replied, "Delicious!"

The reaction to that number is, "Jerk. If he spent that kind of money, he deserved what he got." But if the bird cost five hundred dollars, the humor is switched to the little old mother. Then there's more sympathy and more laughter.

THE RIGHT BALANCE

Take an incident that really happened and make it bigger than life. But be careful. Just because your work is outrageous doesn't mean it's creative.

Consider this description by Laurence Shames of a "silly walk" sketch, in which John Cleese portrays a very ordinary Englishman on his way to work at a government office. "Suited, hatted, carrying briefcase and cane, the Silly Walker faultlessly conforms to the type of the proper civil servant. Except that something is very wrong with the way he moves. He suddenly swoops down from his enormous height like some primeval, featherless bird; now he dodges, his spine contorts, his feet perform a going-nowhere shuffle; now his knees buckle so that, apelike, his hands are nearly dragging on the ground. So far, so good—in terms of sheer physical funniness, the sketch is virtuosic, it can have you rolling on the floor. But the kicker is the Silly Walker's face. It is expressionless, implacable, smug. The fellow is a self-respecting Briton on his way to his perfectly acceptable job, and never in a zillion years would it occur to him that he's ridiculous."

The following examples contain an equal balance of realism and exaggeration to reinforce the surprise. By carefully examining them you should clearly see the formula: a cliché opening statement and an exaggerated take-off reply. But note that reality is never overwhelmed. You must continually be on guard not to overload both elements:

> At my age, sex is sensational. Especially the one in the winter.
> —Milton Berle

Prof to class: "Good morning students. And to those of you on speed, good afternoon!"

A waiter, his uniform badly torn, his hands scratched and bleeding, walks up to seated guests: "I hate to inconvenience you, sir, but would you kindly pick out a different lobster from the tank?"   —Arnie Levin

Let's take a realistic situation. Many married adults are ambivalent about taking elderly parents into their homes for care. Their guilt, when personal comfort gets in the way of tender loving care, contains all the elements for realistic humor:

Wife: "Well, your father is playing basketball again. He's dribbling all over the house."

Son to aged father: "Hey, pop, we're having company tonight. Do you mind staying out in the garage?"

One of the writing modes that maintains realism when attempting the explosive release of exaggerated humor is the movie or play review. Critics feel compelled to display their own rapier wit when slicing up the bodies of others, and excerpts from reviews are in every comedic library.

When Mr. Wilbur calls his play *Halfway to Hell* he underestimates the distance.   —Brooks Atkinson

In *King Lear* last night, the lead played the king as though under a momentary apprehension that someone else was about to play the ace.   —Eugene Field

In a review of Cecil B. DeMille's movie *Samson and Delilah:* "Saw the movie. Loved the book."   —John Steinbeck

Humor is most often written backwards. Once you have the punch line of the joke, it's easy to write the opening. In this case, we write setups that permit funny answers to common questions, as "What do I do now?" or "Where do I go next?" or "What do I say then?"

Orson Welles was shopping for a sports shirt at Saks but found the largest size they carried was still much too snug. "Where

do I go from here?" he asked the clerk. "To the gym," she replied.   —*San Diego Tribune*

The aged father moved from New York to Los Angeles to spend
his last months with his son. As his father lay on his deathbed,
the son whispered, "Dad, I know you have a Masonic plot in
Brooklyn and you know I have a family plot here. Tell me,
which one would you like to be buried in?" The old man
looked at the son for a second and then said, "Surprise me."

A priest got on the Fifth Avenue bus and asked, "Does this bus
go straight up?" The driver said, "Tell you what, Father. I can
drop you at St. Patrick's Cathedral and then you're on your
own."

"Ol' Charlie is famous. He was the first to discover you don't need two to tango."

CHAPTER 11

Surprise 'em or Shock 'em: Nihilistic Humor and Language

A walking path bordered the golf course. One afternoon a tee shot nearly smashed into a little old lady. She screamed, "Why didn't you yell fore?"

"I didn't have time," said the golfer.

"Oh, no?" said the woman, "Then how come you had time to yell 'Oh, shit!' "

If we laughed at this story, it wasn't just the element of surprise alone, but a combination of surprise and shock. The vulgarity—so unexpected, so unfettered—delights us, like watching a friend take a classic banana peel fall. We laugh uproariously, then realize that perhaps we shouldn't have.

But just how vulgar is it? What other words could the writer have used to end this story? What if the language were upgraded? Would it still be funny? For instance, "You had time to yell 'Oh, darn,' " said the little old lady."

The answer is obvious. The story would lose a lot in translation. The surprise trip wire may still be there, but the electric shock system is unplugged. "Humor is like guerrilla warfare," wrote Dwight MacDonald. "Success (and survival) depends on traveling light, striking unexpectedly and getting away fast." The original sin may have been nothing more than a bad pun Eve made about Adam's apple.

Lenny Bruce once called George Carlin his comedic heir. Both used the most shocking language possible to enliven their material—and call attention to themselves.

"Isn't it amazing," wrote Carlin, "that most of the women who are against abortion are women you wouldn't want to fuck anyway?" Carlin had other word choices, like "get pregnant," but the vulgarity, because it is a shock, gives the line its flash and power. Carlin added, "If that word shocks you, it's your problem."

Since humor is disguised hostility, violent language can be a device to communicate true feelings.

No Pryor Restraint

Obscenity is partly in the eye (or ear) of the beholder. To get mass attention in public concerts, Richard Pryor and Eddie Murphy deliberately use material guaranteed to offend everybody by challenging the established order. Pryor's language and persona reflect everyday black conversation. He is as much in tune with their attitudes as any black political leader, and he's a lot more fun to listen to.

According to Professor William Chisholm of Cleveland State University, obscene language is now so prevalent and commonplace in our society that nobody is really shocked or disgusted anymore. Therefore, said the professor, if you're going to shock people, you shouldn't use shocking language. Fact is, there are no strong words left anymore. George Carlin's list of "unmentionables on TV" is down to seven, and even that number is dependent on how you use them.

> In TV today, you can say I pricked my finger, but you can't say
> it the other way around.   —George Carlin

Nothing is more pestiferous in contemporary comedy than the growing use of unexpurgated language and the emphasis on bed to bidet humor. But, as much as many may not like it for themselves, the widespread use of obscene words is closely braided into the fabric of contemporary comic material.

> It's easy to get a laugh using sick sex jokes with hardcore
> words—so let's get started.

Crazy Like a Foxx

Obscene language and graphic descriptions of all bodily activities are popping up everywhere—books, films, cable TV, records, magazines, advertising. Editors no longer cross out an expletive if they feel it's germane to the story. In the 1984 presidential election campaign, one public interest group headlined their ad with the word "Bullshit!"

Blue vocabulary isn't shocking to young urban blacks and Hispanics because it's their street language. It could be said (colorfully) that the blue language of Redd Foxx and many of his colleagues is intended mainly to shock whites and unite blacks.

> People tell me that they're disgusted with my kind of language. So I ask if I can take 'em out to the parking lot and slam a car door on their hand. Then, they'll say both "shit" and "mother-fucker."
> —Redd Foxx

Foxx needn't be so selective. You can hear the same language on a golf course when you pick up the wrong ball.

There's straightforward logic for using obscenities, when appropriate. Humor doesn't lead society—it follows. Humor pokes fun at human antics and that includes our language. In everyday life, we use shock words to get attention, so while obscenity isn't synonymous with humor, it's certainly an important ingredient.

A lot of humor serves as communion among members of a specific social, political, or ethnic group. It reinforces group solidarity. If the audience is prejudiced, so is the performer's humor. For instance, the speaker at a segregationist society who announces:

> I am currently devoid of prejudice. In fact, I'm giving a speech about some of my famous black friends—athletes, entertainers and statesmen. The title is "Niggers I've Known."

SHOCK THERAPY

The frenzy of modern communications makes it more and more difficult to get attention. Advertising research claims nearly one thousand ads vie for our attention each day, so our attention span gets shorter. When future generations open today's buried time capsules, they'll think every major decision in our lives was made in thirty seconds. They could be right.

If Moses brought down the Ten Commandments today, Dan Rather would probably broadcast the news this way: "Today, in the Middle East, Moses carried God's Ten Commandments down from Mount Sinai. We'll be back with the three most important after this message from Bartles and Jaymes."

Writers must have a remarkably perceptive ear and insightful eye for the incongruity of language, written or verbal. Their material must be edited down from the short story to the small story. And, as the classic joke goes, to get the jackass's attention, first you have to hit him on the head with a baseball bat. So a great deal of humor language shocks first, surprises second.

Most comedy comes from a climate of rebellion, which results in nihilistic humor. Comedy may question anything that's said or done, nothing is off-limits, nothing so sacrosanct as to be beyond criticism—the Pope, the rabbi, God (God may still be respected, but is not to be feared), the President, mother (who may be put on a pedestal but only as a sacred cow), handicapped children, and debilitating social diseases.

If you kiss him and his lips are on fire and he trembles in your arms—watch out! He probably has AIDS.

Blast-Phony
Today, irreverence is a salable commodity, and humorists could care less about being in hot holy water. Three of those most famous for antireligious material are Lenny Bruce and Woody Allen (Jewish), and George Carlin (Catholic).

A reform congregation member asks his rabbi, "Tell me, Rabbi, is there a God or not?" The rabbi said, "What cheek! To ask this in a temple. We're not here to talk of God, we're here to sell bonds for Israel."   —Lenny Bruce

If only God would give me a clear sign, like making a large deposit in my name at a Swiss bank.

If I could only see one miracle, just one miracle. Like a burning bush, or the seas part, or my Uncle Sasha pick up a check.
                    —Woody Allen

They cancelled Easter this year. They found the body.

I think we should all treat each other like Christians. I will not, however, be responsible for the consequences.—George Carlin

Something Old, Something New, Something Borrowed, Something Blue

On the other hand, there are many people, more demure, who would question whether shock language is humorous in any context, or if it's just a verbal example of adolescent exhibitionism. Successful writers should be lauded for the hard work that goes into creative art and not for outrageous acts. Too often, they claim, blue humor doesn't make us laugh, it makes us blush.

And why, critics ask, must humor concentrate on the negative aspects of life: drug and alcohol-related problems, sexual inadequacy, perversion, and communicable diseases?

In the theater, it's been that way since ancient Greece. In *The Frogs*, Aristophanes tells of a character farting his way across the River Styx. And the theater's oldest running gag is an actor who drops his pants to get laughs. As far back as 1100 A.D. it was a favorite device of the Lenten Players in Kent, England.

Permissiveness has grown rapidly—perhaps too rapidly. Fifty years ago, Clark Gable shocked the nation in *Gone With the Wind* with his closing line: "Frankly, my dear, I don't give a damn!" Today, shock value has diminished. There are no longer any unmentionables. Meryl Streep is winning movie awards saying words that got Lenny Bruce arrested a few years ago.

Is There "Mor-Ass" in the Future?

While there's a difference between being rude and being funny, obscenities are sometimes the perfect words. And when they are, they should be used. I'm *not* advocating hard-core humor for the vicarious thrill of using shock words. That's too easy a laugh! I am suggesting that a word is not just a sound or a random combination of printed letters. Each word in humor is a carefully designed missile calculated to penetrate the mind and leave a very specific impact. The perfect word is not easily interchangeable, despite an unabridged thesaurus. Consider this story:

A few days before Christmas a postman is greeted at the door of a suburban house by a beautiful, curvaceous wife in a see-through negligee. "I've got your Christmas present upstairs," she says, grabs the man's hand and leads him to the bedroom. In seconds she is making passionate love to him.

Finished, she takes him back to the kitchen for a cup of coffee.

"I gotta tell you, Mrs. Martin," says the postman, "I've fantasized this moment since you moved into the neighborhood a few months ago. That was quite a present."

"Oh, and that's not all," says the woman. "Here's five dollars."

"What the hell is this for?" asks the mailman.

"Well, if you must know," said the wife, "I asked my husband last night what we should give you for Christmas, and he said, "Screw him. Give him five dollars."

The following two examples are the same joke told with and without profanity. Which do you think is more powerful?

First Version

Two chickens are talking. One says, "My farmer gets sixty cents a dozen for my eggs. Laying eggs is easy." The other hen says, "Not for me, it isn't. I grunt and groan, but my eggs are bigger and my farmer gets sixty-five cents a dozen." The first hen replied, "For five cents a dozen, it doesn't pay to strain yourself."

Second Version

Same opening. The first hen gets sixty cents a dozen, the second sixty-five cents a dozen. The first hen says to her companion, "What! I should bust my ass for a nickel?"

Audiences appreciate clever word play, such as paired phrases without immediate regard for a statement's logic. There's a similar illogical reaction to off-color words. Here's an example:

Toastmaster: "Please be patient with Milton. He's having trouble with his pacemaker. Everytime he farts, his garage door goes up."

Why do we laugh? The jokes don't even make sense. And that's the point. It wasn't the joke, it was the language.

Writers search for the perfect word as composers search for the perfect note; both are searching for the perfect sound. And when it's found, it shouldn't be cast aside because of fear or priggish morality. As we discussed in Chapter 9, *fart* is a funny word. Even when we're forewarned, the word makes us laugh.

> The new ambassador was introduced to the Queen. As they stood talking informally, at the reception which followed, Her Highness asked him if he could get her a glass of wine.
> "Certainly," he said, "Would you like port or sherry?"
> "Sherry by all means. To me sherry is the nectar of the gods. Just watching sherry shimmer in its decanter fills me with an otherworldly glow. Its sweet bouquet lifts me on wings of ecstasy. One sniff and a thousand violins throb in my inner ear; one taste and a symphony of pleasure explodes in me. On the other hand," continued the Queen, "port makes me fart!"
> —*Playboy*

> I'm in a restaurant and I'm eating and someone says, "Mind if I smoke?" and I say, "Uh, no. Mind if I fart?"   —Steve Martin

Humor, to be *most* effective, must use the authentic colloquial language of its subject and the audience—and, of course, it must be appropriate to the persona of the performer.

> A visitor to Harvard asks a prof, "Excuse me, but would you be good enough to tell me where the Harvard Library is at?"
> "Sir," said the sneering reply, "at Harvard we do not end a sentence with a preposition."
> "Well, in that case, forgive me," said the visitor. "Permit me to rephrase my question. Would you be good enough to tell me where the Harvard Library is at, jackass?" —Charles Osgood

Encouraging humor writers not to shrink from carefully selected risqué language and situations may incur severe criticism from Bible thumpers and English purists. Fortunately, humor is as Constitutionally guaranteed as any free speech—sometimes courts have held that satire is the freest of free speech—and shouldn't be precensored, especially by its own writers.

This story tests the use of acceptable obscene language. Without profanity, there's no point.

> A young man walked into a bank and said to the teller, "I want to open a fuckin' checkin' account."

The young lady gasped. "I beg your pardon, but we don't tolerate that language in this bank."

"Get your fuckin' supervisor!" the man said. In a few moments the supervisor came up. "What's the problem?" "I just won ten million in the lottery, and I want to open a fuckin' checkin' account!" The manager said, "I see. And this bitch is giving you a hard time." —*Playboy*

People who rail the loudest against tastelessness are often the most hypocritical. What magazine in the country could be more conservative and apple pie than the *Reader's Digest?* Yet, the humor of *Reader's Digest* is 50 percent jokes on brassieres, girdles, toilets, breasts, and sexual innuendo. I know from personal experience. This anecdote, by Hy Gardner, was reprinted in the *Digest* in August of 1964:

Advertising director Mel Helitzer flew to the coast to discuss a TV show starring Jose Ferrer. The actor apologized for the absence of his wife, Rosemary Clooney, explaining that she was upstairs caring for their five children. "What ages?" asked Helitzer. "Five, four, three, two, and one," smiled Ferrer. "Say," commented the advertising executive, "I hope I'm not keeping you from anything!"

I teach humor writing at Ohio University's School of Journalism, so I'm a strong advocate of free speech. I never censor language. For some students this means, unfortunately, tacit approval to use obscenities. One prissy English professor once asked why I permit students to use the word "shit" in performances. I had to tell her the truth—they're just too old to say "doo-doo."

Transposition

The question is not whether shock words should be used, but when. The borderline of good taste in humor is as subjective as sex between consenting adults. However, humor has so many forms, it's easy to avoid words that might offend the audience. There are as many euphemisms for hard-core words as there are for a man's penis ("I call mine by it's God-given name: 'Vesuvius,' " remarks Robert Wohl). Another device is transposition, as illustrated by the following story:

One doctor to another: "I've got to get rid of my nurse. She's constantly getting things balled up." Just then, with a blood

curdling scream, one of the male patients ran wildly down the hall pursued by a nurse holding a pot of scalding water. "See what I mean?" said the doctor, "I distinctly told her to prick his boil."
                                                    —George Carlin

There is a comedic axiom: insult only ugly people or ignoramuses. Who's going to come up and complain "Hey, man, *I'm* an ignoramus"? The axiom also holds for taboo material. It should be appropriate for the specific audiences.

Audiences send out reaction signals. Experienced performers test the limits of their racier subjects by purposely inserting trial material up front. If the reaction is negative, they respect the signals immediately, because humor can never be forced.

UNDERSTATEMENT: TAKING YOUR TALE FROM BETWEEN YOUR LEGS

There is an alternative to obscene language. It's called understatement. This is one of the higher techniques of humor writing because it's so difficult to carry off effectively, without the point being lost in subtlety. Both understated realism and understated shock material cater to the audience's imagination and intelligence, encouraging them to complete the script using their own words. Then, who can complain?

Saw this commercial on TV for Ex-Lax, it says, "Works while you sleep." That scares me.   —Steve Mendoza

"Doc, my girlfriend has a problem. She thinks she's a rabbit."
"Okay, bring her in. I'll talk to her."
"Thanks, doc, but whatever you do, don't cure her!"

Understating is a sign of confidence as well as maturity. Just as in real life, the rich and the very successful understate. The insecure or nouveau riche overstate.

Soon after I arrived in Athens, our gardener invited me to go fishing. At the end of the day, I said, "I don't understand it. I've got better gear than you. I use better bait. I'm in the same boat. And I haven't caught a thing and you've caught the whole lake." The man said, "I fish by hunches. When I get up in the morning to go fishing, if my wife is sleeping on her right side,

then I fish off the right side of the boat. If she's sleeping on
her left side, then I fish off the left side of the boat." "And if
she's on her back?" I asked. "Then, I don't go fishing."

Everyone is familiar with Thurber's cartoon showing two dueling
men. One of them slashes his foil across the neck of his opponent, decapi-
tating him, and shouts, "Touché!" That's shocking, but it has lived for fifty years as a classic example of understatement.

My mother said, "Why don't you wear your grandfather's nice
dress slacks?" So I grabbed the shovel. . . .

I knew psychology as a child. I had a lemonade stand and I
gave the first glass of lemonade away free. On the second glass
I charged five dollars—it had the antidote.   —Emo Philips

One of George S. Kaufman's most famous quotes came from a letter to his
daughter:

Try everything in life except incest and square dancing.

That's shocking enough, but someone added a reverse that really throws
your imagination into high gear:

. . . so you can see that Kaufman's humor comes from the fact
that he is ridiculing something increasingly popular, lots of
fun and American as farm apple pie. Now, as for square
dancing. . . .

Outrageous Humor Needn't be Obscene

Reforming words is an easy way to be shocking. It takes no great talent. The talent comes from suggesting hard-core humor, but never actually
stating it.

A sexually frustrated young girl sat on Pinochio's nose and said,
"Now lie to me. Now tell me the truth. Now lie to me. Now tell
me the truth."   —Paul Krassner

Everytime I look at what I have to pay in taxes, it scares me
shirtless.   —Robert Orben

Gilda Radner, on *Saturday Night Live,* loved to use malaprops like "endangered feces." When Ron Nessen, a former presidential assistant, guest hosted the show, Alan Zeibel wrote a skit which reformed "presidential elections" to "presidential erections." That could have been a cheap laugh and probably wouldn't have been acceptable to NBC censors, but Zeibel finessed that by referring to buildings and monuments. The audience got the point immediately, and the laughter was even louder because the implicit joke made them feel more comfortable.

> The Lone Ranger was about to be hung by outlaws. He was granted a last wish—a few hours to pray to the god of fire. He used the opportunity to send smoke signals to Tonto. They were just about to string the Lone Ranger up a tree when suddenly, over the hill, came Tonto with six beautiful, nude women. The Lone Ranger turned to one outlaw and said, "That dumb Indian never could learn to spell *posse.*"

THE SHOCK EXCHANGE

Moving beyond the morass of obscenity, another way to achieve shock is to use names of celebrities—national or local—in your humor. As stated previously, they're excellent targets. "Trading gossip," wrote Daisy Brown, "is the shock exchange."

It may seem like a cheap shot, but celebrities are usually happy to be used and misused in humor stories—it's called free publicity. The "People" columns in entertainment and most major consumer magazines are based on press agents' abilities to write humorous anecdotes about their clients. Woody Allen got his start writing humor that way. The "just spell the name right" psychology seems exploitative, but the fallacious intrigue works—it daily reminds the gullible public that they should go see Brooke Shields's movies and buy Joan Collins's cosmetics.

> Frank Sinatra once admitted that if he had as many love affairs as his publicist, Henry Rogers, had given him credit for, he'd be in a jar in the Harvard Medical School.

Joan Rivers brazenly targets England's Royal Family, Elizabeth Taylor, even blind pianist Stevie Wonder.

> How fat is Elizabeth Taylor? Well, she has more chins than a Chinese phone directory.

Can we talk? I think the Royal Family's a bunch of dogs. That's right, a bunch of dogs. Just go out on the street and shout: "Queenie, Duke, and Prince," and see what shows up.

Rules for Playing the VIP Game

There are five basic rules for lampooning celebrities:

1. The person must be well known.
2. The person should be controversial. Those who do the most—good or bad—are humor's "who's who." People like Howard Cosell, Jesse Jackson, Elizabeth Taylor, Henry Kissinger, and Princess Diana (who plays "Dallas at the Palace") are just a few examples of a long list of personalities whose activities inflame large groups of supporters and opponents.

An empty cab drove up and Madonna got out!

3. The audience feels you personally know the individual, so your humor has the ring of inside gossip.

When Sinatra was elected Abbot (president) of the Friars' Club, Milton Berle said, "I wish they had elected him Pope. Then I'd only have to kiss his ring."

4. The humor must be based upon a realistic premise (i.e., once Elizabeth Taylor lost weight, the fat jokes stopped).
5. What you say sounds so impermissible that it creates tension. Humor aimed at a specific target packs a punch, sometimes too literally. Shecky Greene used to kid Frank Sinatra unmercifully in his nightclub act when they were both playing Las Vegas. He got big laughs. One day he showed up badly bruised. "I was almost killed by three thugs last night," Shecky said, "but Sinatra saved my life. He said, 'Okay boys, that's enough!' "

The same five rules apply to local names. It seems easier to get tacit approval from the mayor, the police chief, the bank president, and the football coach, but even then be sure your black belt in karate didn't come solely from a written test.

I once told students, "Be suggestive because you must reach a broad market. Reach out for the satire of George Bernard Shaw, the wit of Oscar Wilde. What I'm trying to tell you, students, is to up your standards."

And they shouted back, "Up yours!"

CHAPTER 12

Stay in Character: Speak Softly But Carry a Big Shtick

A comedian says funny things.
A comic says things funny.
Tonight, I will prove that I
—am a juggler!

—Michael Davis

JUST AS YOU'RE OBLIGATED TO KNOW your audience before you write material, it's just as obligatory to know your client (speaker, stand-up, skit performer—or juggler) and his or her character. That's because humor doesn't go *into* a character, it comes *out* of a character. A character needs a trademark, a predictable point of view which does not change. If a performer doesn't have an individual style (sometimes called a hook or shtick), the writer (frequently a writer/director like Jane Wagner who works with Lily Tomlin) shares the burden to find one that fits. Without a shtick, the performer is just a reciter of jokes. With it, a comic can get laughs even with mistakes, because, in a way, the performer is the joke.

WHAT'S WITH THIS CRAZY SHTICK?

It's unusual for a famous performer to have more than one character—it's also dangerous, because audiences like to stereotype humorists. Stereotypes are a shortcut to thinking and the audience gets confused if a performer changes characterization in mid-act. Rarely do established comedians, in films or theater, play characters that are opposite to their personas. The most successful movie comedians (Bob Hope, Eddie Murphy, Rodney Dangerfield, Jerry Lewis) are those who play every part the same. Woody Allen tried to alter his character in several of his films and, painfully, those were the ones which failed financially and artistically.

With few exceptions every successful performer in comedy has developed at least one basic and memorable character. Not only does the audience feel comfortable with this, but the material is easier to write.

Professional humor writers are known for two reliability constants: material that has a consistent quality and material that is consistently on target. A rejection slip which reads "I don't do that kind of material" is damaging because it indicates that the humor writer didn't know the market. He not only wasted his time but that of the performer as well. Only neophytes get that kind of rejection. Pros do their homework, which means performer research. That takes time: reading previously published material, attending their performances, and listening to their tapes.

While comedy is more adventurous and unpredictable than ever, Eric Allen wrote, "Basically every joke's been done, so you get laughs out of looks, gestures, and catch phrases" ("Make my day," "Well, excuuuuse me," and "You look mahhvelous"). The voice must be as elastic as the face.

The writer must instinctively know whether the material is right for the character. A little voice inside says, "This isn't right" or "Hey, this works!"

Ed Hercer, editor of *The Comedy Roundtable,* is also an actor. "I was playing a dumb Congressman who said, 'The trouble with these other countries is—they're all being run by foreigners.' The director wanted me to deliver the line and then laugh heartily at my own joke. My contention was if I was really a dumb Congressman, I wouldn't have recognized the humor. The audience didn't laugh hard because they didn't sympathize with a dumb Congressman. So when the line was delivered without the actor laughing, the audience howled because the joke was on him. It was his character they were laughing at, not the material."

THE TWENTY MASKS OF COMEDY

He was born with the gift of laughter and a sense that the
world was mad.   —Raphael Sabatini

Theater began in Greece with one actor in a variety of masks playing all parts. In humor, there are approximately twenty major and distinctive character masks. But each comedian can have only one. The paradox is that it must be a perfect characterization of an imperfect character. The character can be anything from an erudite scholar to a simpleton, a suburban yuppie, even a dope addict, a sexual deviate, a braggart, a tightwad, a drunk, or a coward (and that should take in every friend you've got).

Each of the following twenty choices is broad enough to have a number of variations; there is also a great deal of overlapping.

The twenty basic stock characters are categorized into three basic groups: *the single, the team,* and *the artist* (with props). While sometimes the character was found first and fiction became fact, in the majority of cases the character fit the personality of the performer, complementing physical appearance and speech ability as well as talent. The foundation was honed; it was not fabricated.

The Twenty Masks of Comedy

The Single

1. The Stand-up
2. The Aggressor
3. The Sad Sack
4. The Druggie Rebel
5. The Student
6. The Political and Social Satirist
7. The Storyteller
8. The Rube
9. The Old Timer
10. The Ethnic Type
11. The Immigrant

The Team

12. Partners
13. The Sketch Performer
14. The Ventriloquist

The Actor

15. The Impersonator
16. The Clown
17. The Artists, Musicians, and Cartoonists
18. The Vaudevillian
19. The Improvisers
20. The Bumbler

THE SINGLE

1. The Stand-up

The most popular comedic character is the stand-up comedian, sometimes called a jester, a wag, a wisecracker, or a quipster. The most successful personalities dress neatly, in anything from sport jackets to striped formals. Women wear evening gowns, bejeweled or feathery. The material is a series of one-liners and short comments on the contemporary scene. There are hundreds who could be listed in this category, but some examples are Johnny Carson, Dick Cavett, and Bob Hope. According to Milton Berle, the reason Henny Youngman does one-liners is that he can't remember two.

> A girl goes into a clothing store and asks the salesman, "Can I try on that bikini in the window?" The salesman said, "Go ahead, lady, it might help business."

2. The Aggressor

For years, comedian Jack E. Leonard had an arsenal of below-the-belt insults which he machine-gunned at celebrities, especially if they were in his audience. After Leonard's death, Don Rickles became show business's merchant of venom. Here are three of his little digs that went to market:

> *To Frank Sinatra:* "Come right in, Frank. Make yourself at home. Hit somebody."

> *To Dean Martin:* "You're Italian, right? What the hell do we need Italians for? Oh, yeah, to keep the cops busy."

> *To Sammy Davis:* "You should be proud of your race. A great Negro, Emerson Johnson Jones, once said in Mobile, Alabama, 'All aboarrrd!' "

3. The Sad Sack

> I went to my psychiatrist. I said, "Doc, I have this terrible feeling that everyone is trying to take advantage of me." He said, "Relax. Everyone thinks somebody else is trying to take advantage of them." "Gee, thanks, Doc. How much do I owe you?" "How much have you got?"

Rodney Dangerfield practically owns this character at present, but it has been a comedy standard for hundreds of years. The comic plays the insecure, timid Milquetoast, always seeking approval, confused by women, unable to get dates or make any relationship work.

> I took my girl to a drive-in movie and she said, "Do you want to get in the back seat?" And I said, "No. I want to stay up here with you."

The audience delights in laughing at the plight of others. This is one of the easiest characters to use when you're a neophyte performer trying to get your first laughs. The trick is to get the audience to like you immediately; otherwise they have no sympathy and are happy to see you get what you deserve. Thus the opening joke is far more important here than in most other categories.

Garry Shandling and Jackie Gleason are just two practitioners of this style of humor which might be called "seeing the world through woes-colored glasses." Every joke is self-deprecating:

> I'm dating a girl now . . . who's unaware of it, evidently.
> —Garry Shandling

Because it fits his physical appearance, Gleason does a lot of fat jokes:

> I do fat humor because sex for a fat man is much ado about puffing.

4. The Drug Rebel

During prohibition in the 1920s, the comedic performer who assumed a drunk posture was a popular nightclub, film, and campus entertainer. W. C. Fields was one of the first; then came others like Joe E. Lewis (who was the town drunk and he lived in Chicago!), and Robert Benchley. They frequently went on stage with drinks in their hands or would appear to borrow one from a ringside table.

> Benchley once came out of the Waldorf Astoria hotel very loaded. He said to a man in uniform, "Call me a taxi." And the man said, "I am not the doorman. I am an admiral." To which Benchley replied, "Okay, then call me a battleship."

When prohibition ended, so did fascination with alcoholic clowns. The drunk delivery frequently covered up a minor comedic talent; this tech-nique has helped Dean Martin remain commercial as a singer for the past twenty years. The classic line is that he couldn't hear the heckling because of all the boos.

Today, the alcoholic character of twenty-five years ago has turned in-to the druggie. This eccentric counterculture weirdo is a delight to college students and a disgust to current knights of middle age.

Lenny Bruce was the guru of drug humor. Robert Klein says every modern comedian owes Bruce some debt of gratitude. Bruce claimed he entered the arena of sex and scatology to make a philosophical point. Don't believe it. He got in the smoking ring because it separated him from more erudite satirists, like Mort Sahl.

Typical of Bruce's humor were the following "social" comments to a judge:

> *Bruce:* Your honor, it was my mother-in-law who broke up my marriage. One day my wife came home early and found us in bed together.
> *Judge:* Don't you think that's perversion?
> *Bruce:* Perversion? What perversion? It was her mother, not mine!

> *Judge:* Mr. Bruce, the officer's report states that you used the word "cocksucker" on stage.
> *Bruce:* That's right, your Honor.
> *Judge:* He said it was the most disgusting show he ever saw.
> *Bruce:* I don't know why, your honor. I *said* it. I wasn't *doing* it!

Bruce's legacy was picked up by George Carlin, a true counterculture comedian. "The population segment I appeal to is the one that feels there is no hope for the human race," he says. Carlin uses dazzling word play as he viciously ridicules all parts of the Establishment. His essential themes are drugs and rebellion, and he uses hardcore words and ideas to shock his stunned audience to attention. He is a favorite of college pupils. (The rea-son I call them pupils is because by ten in the morning their eyes are still di-lating.)

Another drug humorist is Emo Philips, who spent nine years develop-ing his spaced-out character and now looks like he hasn't eaten for five of those nine years.

5. The Intellectual

The most successful erudite character in contemporary humor is Woody Allen. He carefully dressed and looked like a student—even with a tie and jacket he would purposely wear running shoes.

Allen played the mascot of the intellectuals for twenty years. His humor is based on the incongruity of his appearance and his material: the mousy physical look that ridicules a secret sexual prowess, the very antithesis of aggressive dominance that is the character of Shecky Greene, Jan Murray, and Jack Carter.

> I told my sexual experiences to Parker Brothers, and they made it into a game. —Woody Allen

Today, there are hundreds of stand-up comics playing the worldly observer in blue jeans and sneakers. Steven Wright's persona was influenced by Woody Allen's analytical style. Wright attempts abstract surrealism—illogical logic based upon literal interpretation. His onstage costume is always the same: jeans, work shirt, rolled up sleeves, tennis shoes, frizzy hair, and a sullen face that never laughs. It gives him the appearance of an iconoclastic drifter.

> I got up this morning, I couldn't find my socks. So I called information. I said, "Information? I can't find my socks." She said, "They're behind the couch" . . . and they were. . . . I went to the cinema box office. It said "Adults five dollars. Children two-fifty." I said, "Okay, give me two boys and a girl. . . . I went to a restaurant. It said, "Breakfast anytime." So I ordered French toast during the Renaissance. . . . I've never seen electricity. That's why I don't pay for it. I write right on the bill, "Sorry, I haven't seen it all month." . . . Yesterday I saw a subliminal advertising executive—just for a second. . . . I put instant coffee into a microwave oven. I almost went back in time.

Another of this genre is NBC's late night mop-up man, David Letterman, whose character is hip and sarcastic, with a frosting of sadistic hostility. His overnight bag of humor contains "inside jokes" that belittle guests, especially if they're celebrities, like Mariel Hemingway cleaning fish or Tom Selleck sticking his head in a tub of water and doing motorboat impressions. Letterman was influenced by Steve Allen, but he admits to being easily embarrassed by watching his own routines. He seems stuck with his goofy character, a mean-spirited yuppie in a suit and tie, surrounded by Joe College silliness.

6. The Political and Social Satirist

Satire is a humor maverick. Like topical humor, it has a life no longer than that of a fly, and one of the most famous satirical stylists, Mort Sahl, used to carry a rolled-up newspaper on stage as if he were ready to swat that fly. Satire reflects who and what are in the news at the very time a joke is being told. Next week the same material may be too old.

Satire attacks social and political targets and, therefore, is very controversial for large, mixed audiences. Satirist Will Rogers felt that if he could score a 50 percent "laugh rate" he was doing well. Mark Russell is the only political satirist on TV, and then only on Public Broadcasting. The public feels more tolerant toward print satirists, like Art Buchwald, Russell Baker, and Ellen Goodman, who appear on the Op Ed pages of newspapers. Perhaps that's because, in performance, there's a second when the audience is thinking—not laughing. And for a performer, even thoughtful silence can be deadly.

7. The Storyteller

There's a lot of characterization in this shtick. The story line is not a potpourri of one-gag anecdotes, but is confined to one unique theme, with heavy use of strong critical comment strung out for as much as ten minutes. Eventually it has a point. These jokesters don't flip from gag to gag as much as they share a universal experience and irritation. Like actors, they carefully rehearse and dramatize their stories. As a result, their material tends to stay away from topical current events and concentrate on standbys like family, business, and social situations.

Before broadcast humor, tellers of tall folk tales were the staples of frontier humor. They went with the territory—a world of yokels and rustics where everything was tall. They had joke-telling contests, story-telling contests, and even awards for the biggest liars. Imagination was encouraged and humor opportunities were limited only by the boundaries of the individual's mind. The antecedents of these Western homespun fables were George Ades and Mark Twain at the beginning of the twentieth century.

Among those who fit into this category today are Danny Thomas, Buddy Hackett, and Alan King. Currently, the two most popular storytellers are Garrison Keillor and Bill Cosby.

Keillor's radio program *A Prairie Home Companion* uses myth and exaggeration as its only story line; it emanates from fictional Lake Wobegon, "a small town that time forgot," located in a state of mind. It's a love poem to America's small towns, a universal birthplace for those who once lived west of the Hudson and like to go home for a few hours each week. The audience warms to Keillor's mythical folk humor about overstocked hardware stores, soda fountains that serve giant sundaes, and schools where all the children are above average.

Bill Cosby started with "one of the boys" routines on neighborhood characters (Fat Albert, Weird Harold, Dumb Donald, etc.). Now, he's so confident in his own material that he breaks the first commandment of comedy—"push for a first, big laugh." He's a stand-up comic who prefers being a sit-down storyteller, almost chatting with his audience about a common problem, a facsimile of his family life. He calls it building a rapport. He creates a stock situation first, then follows with exaggerations. He builds animated cartoons with words, not jokes. In story telling the big benefit is that if the audience doesn't laugh at what was supposed to be a funny line, it doesn't seem to matter unless it's the last line.

It's unfortunate that this delightful form of oral humor is a dying art. One reason may be that the seemingly extemporaneous style of story telling requires a talented actor with exquisite timing and accent that can only be accomplished by years of careful character honing. Many young performers don't want to practice that hard. Another reason may be that in our frenzied tempo of communication, we just don't take the time to listen to long stories. It's a product of our credit card mentality, where every hour today must be devoted to paying for the excesses of yesterday. Humor, like decisions in commercials, is judged in thirty seconds.

8. The Rube

This country boy humorist, tipping back in a cane bottom rocker on the front porch of the general store with a hound dog at his feet, is a consistent hit with rural audiences. They feel comfortable laughing at some yokel less intelligent than they are. There have been few costume changes in a hundred years, except that the wide-brimmed farm hat has been replaced by a tractor cap and the fiddle's been replaced by a harmonica.

Patricia Leimbach, at sixty, is to the farm belt what Joan Rivers is to the borscht belt. She wears grandma spectacles and a "Hogs are beautiful" button. Her audiences are farm conferences and her material is strictly outhouse: "What's the difference between a pigeon and a farmer? Well, a pigeon can always make a small deposit on a tractor." She plays to the insecurity of her audience by making them feel farm smart.

City slicker to Farmer Brown: "You must be a farmer. I saw the manure on your boots." "Yup. And you must be from Harvard. I saw your ring when you picked your nose."

The Amish character plays up to the Pennsylvania Dutch faithful with this kind of material:

> *Amish farmer to stubborn mule:* "Mule, thou realize that be-
> cause of my religion I cannot beat thee, or curse thee, or abuse
> thee in any way. But, mule, what thou do not realize is that I
> can sell thee to a Southern Baptist."

In advertising, the two most successful commercial spokespersons are two comedians with distinctive characters. Bill Cosby is well-known for his national spots for Coca-Cola and Jell-O pudding. But in hundreds of local markets, with three thousand different TV spots for over 200 different sponsors, the most famous and, paradoxically, the most obnoxious character on commercial TV is Ernest P. Worrel, a gangly redneck with a cavern mouth created by actor Jim Varney. Ernest utters an overbearing fountain of unsolicited advice. He looks like the consummate Appalachian rube intrusively advising you how to fix the world. Ernie gives his advice to his unseen friend ("Hey, Vern"), but then to give the viewer superiority and revenge, he reduces his "Know what I mean, Vern" smugness to self-ridicule by going berserk and doing something incredibly stupid, like slamming a tailgate on his hand or electrocuting himself: "Shall I carve, Vern? What'll it be, light or dark?" Then, he takes a chainsaw from behind his back and, giblets flying in all directions, saws through the turkey, the plate, and the table.

9. The Old Timer

When he was ninety years old, George Burns said, "At my age, I don't even buy green bananas." Consistently deprecating his physical functions, this easygoing, hesitant style plays to the sympathy of the audience.

> The only time I have a sexual experience now is when I get
> frisked at airports.

It's the most honest character in humor. "You've got to be your age in humor. You can't be any younger than you're supposed to be, nor any older," said George Burns, a man who gets a standing ovation just for standing. Asked what he thought of younger comedians, Burns said, "You mean Milton Berle and Danny Thomas? They'll make it one day." But Berle and Thomas aren't waiting; a high percentage of their material is based upon age and impotency:

The only time I get a laugh from my wife is when we're in bed.
I don't think it's fair of her to laugh and point at the same time.

10. The Ethnic Type

One step up from the gag is the ethnic and folk anecdote. This material is a collection of rambling tales—short, short stories that end with a raunchy one-line climax. The performer spins the story in dialect; Irish, Scotch, Italian, and Jewish have always been favorite caricature stereotypes. Today, the dialects are often black or Hispanic.

Jewish visual humor has its model in Chaplin's tolerant tramp—the sweet smile of a person "longing for belonging," who accepts failure with a shrug of resignation, then disappears down the road.

According to Barry Gross, Jewish performers have played characters which made Gentile audiences feel safe: self-deprecating, self-effacing, nervous, neurotic, timid, and awkward. Verbally, traditional Jewish humor emerges from an outsider's poverty and pain. Its strength is its intellect, generating laughter at the expense of less-educated authority figures: religious zealots and goyim in general. A *goyisher kop* is synonomous with stupidity. The Jewish comedian's philosophy is pervasive skepticism against the status quo and what Theodore Reik called "explosive truths," or what Joseph Dorinson called "the two-sided weapon of gallows humor." With wit, Jews try to keep the bullies at bay. "If they're laughing," asked Mel Brooks, "how can they bludgeon you to death?"

Unlike Jewish humor, which is based upon life on earth, Irish humor is based upon fear of purgatory, an almost preordained condition of devout Catholic upbringing. Their humor evaluates sin—drinking, carousing, and political deviousness. They claim the three-day wake just makes sure the corpse is dead, not dead drunk.

An Irishman lies in his coffin with a big smile on his face. "I didn't dare wipe it off," the widow said. "You see, he died in his sleep, dreaming about something he was doing while he was alive. I'm afraid, if he wakes up and finds out he's dead, the shock will kill him."

11. The Immigrant

To make the audience feel comfortable, performers from foreign countries, from their opening sentence, denigrate their own nationality by playing off positive American stereotypes of life.

I'm a comedian from Russia. I like American women. They do

things sexually Russian girls would never dream of doing—like
showering.   —Yakov Smirnoff

I'm a comedian from Korea. Actually, I'm half Korean, half Japanese. I'm known as Kojap.   —Johnny Yune

American men always want to take you right back to their
apartment and make love. They don't even want to buy you a
cup of tea. In Australia, where I come from, making love is
something rich and beautiful. It's worth a cup of tea.
                                                       —Maureen Murphy

THE TEAM

This combo consists of one stooge and a straight man. They used to team
three or four comedians at one time (the Marx Brothers, the Three Stooges,
and the Ritz Brothers), but nowadays group humor is exclusively the prov-
ince of improv comedy, like Second City.

12. Partners

Comedy partnerships like the Smothers Brothers, Bob and Ray,
Smith and Dale, Laurel and Hardy, Abbott and Costello, Martin and
Lewis, Amos and Andy, as well as husband and wife teams—Stiller and
Meara, Burns and Allen, Fibber McGee and Molly—are rare today. No
one seems to be able to explain why. There may be a unique opportunity
here for two new comedians to team up and fill this void.

The original purpose of team humor was to permit the audience to
laugh at a schlemiel (fall guy). It may have been just a coincidence, but the
first name on a team billing was generally the straight man and the last
name got the laughs.

13. The Sketch Performer

Specialists in slapstick and burlesque humor, these performers are
not so much word illusionists as facial contortionists. They convey ideas
physically, with a rubber face and exaggerated body language, and squeeze
out every drop of the humor through repetition. The sketch performer is an
effective actor who can make an audience see a fly buzzing around a soup
plate or an old man crossing the street.

The comic must make the audience believe he's an irate husband, a
doorman, a German professor, a turtle, a baby, or Napoleon. One of the
most talented was Phil Silvers, whose Sergeant Bilko character was popu-

lar on TV for years. The audience identified with this noncom with brass balls and a love of gambling.

Voice quality is extremely important. A good sketch may combine pantomine, mimicry, and accurate impersonation. A Jewish accent gooses the humor out of the interview skit perfected by Mel Brooks and Carl Reiner in their *2,000 Year Old Man* album. Reiner acted as a reporter questioning Brooks, playing an old man who claimed to be a firsthand observer of history. The performance tension was contagious, because Reiner appeared to be throwing out impromptu questions. Brooks loved it: "The best time for humor is the first time it's performed. There's something in the voice, the excitement, the fighting for your life when somebody challenges you."

> *Reiner:* Tell me sir, what was the means of locomotion two
>   thousand years ago?
> *Brooks:* What d'ya mean, locomotion?
> *Reiner:* What was it that got you to move quickly from one
>   place to another?
> *Brooks:* Fear.

The success of Jackie Gleason's *Honeymooners* skits was based upon characters the audience could feel superior to: Ralph Kramden was a bus driver and his friend, Ed Norton, worked in a sewer.

Skits, the heart of burlesque and review comedy, have become rare comedic meat. They are in only a few TV formats, like take-offs on quiz shows, news broadcasts, and interview shows on *Saturday Night Live* and *Not Necessarily the News*. Benny Hill, typecast as a middle-aged chaser of well-endowed girls, uses escalation skits with soft-core double entendres. Carol Burnett got her start as a skit performer, and the greatest of all was Sid Caesar on *Your Show of Shows*.

A list of just a few other artists in this category would include Mickey Rooney, Red Buttons, John Belushi, Jack Gilford, Chevy Chase, and Alan Arkin.

14. The Ventriloquist

This classification also generally includes the monologists who work with an unseen partner on the telephone. Archie (of *Duffy's Tavern*) and George Jessel established the telephone skit, Shelly Berman and Lily Tomlin perfected it.

The orthodox ventriloquist act—performers like Edgar Bergen, Shari Lewis, Paul Winchell, and Ronn Lucas—seems to have lost its appeal to contemporary audiences, although there are scores of excellent artists still playing lounges and small clubs. The basic format hasn't changed; the performer plays a straight man and sets up lines. The dummy or puppet (called a character) is a brat and a wise ass but gets all the laughs. If the laughs don't come, the comic has a basic saver. The dummy turns to his master and says, "Hey! Don't complain. You're doing all the talking."

Again, the audience isn't intimidated by a wooden dummy. The humor would never work if the lines were transposed.

THE ACTOR

15. The Impersonator

This character is an expert dialectician who impersonates in stories, songs, and patter the mannerisms, accents and material of famous people. Also known as impressionists, impersonators work mainly on voice and a few exaggerated mannerisms. There is very little acting or skit situations; a few lines are sufficient to get audience appreciation. Impressionists get more applause than laughs for their skill.

As children, impersonations were one of our earliest introductions to parody. We loved to imitate the voices and idiosyncrasies of neighborhood characters, school faculty, and often our own parents. Maurice La Marche, who can do over a hundred different voices, was voted by his senior class as "most likely to be someone else."

Mimicry is generally a fast way for performers to get public attention. All profess to use impersonations solely as a starting point for creating their own, more original material. They lie!

The current master of impressionists is Rich Little, who is famous for his impersonations of Jimmy Stewart, Ronald Reagan, and Richard Nixon ("I didn't do it, and I promise never to do it again!"). Actors who can imitate even one voice to perfection have made millions. Vaughn Meader's claim to fame was his impersonation of the Kennedy voices. His act died in a Dallas motorcade. Joe Piscopo probably will be best remembered for his Frank Sinatra impressions. One of the most talented of all was Larry Storch.

16. The Clown

This category also includes mimes and zanies. In the tradition of the circus, clowns wear greasepaint. But in comedy, makeup is secondary to a mobile face—innocent pop-eyes, bulbous nose, electrified hair, or bald head—frequently on top of a short, tubby body (or a tall, thin one). If an artist drew a police caricature of that description, you'd end up with a male who looked like Zero Mostel and a female like Lucille Ball.

Their shtick is triumph over failure and humiliation. They are rarely as adept at creating funny situations as at executing them. Material for clowns still has to be written.

Clown material should play in all languages. Starting with the walk, clown comics are more physical than verbal. Props include "lean shoes" so heavily weighted that the performer can lean forward, like an Olympic ski-jumper just before take-off, and still not topple over. They wear over-size clothes, a bizarre hat, wig, or hair piece, horn-rim glasses and, not infrequently, white finger gloves. It isn't necessary to look funny before you perform funny, but this generation of normal looking comedians, who rarely resort to funny faces, has to work harder.

In addition, the comic clown must be a communicative mime, an eccentric dancer, an elasticized gymnast, an accomplished juggler and, above all, an expert actor of broad comedy. Clowns must constantly win our sympathies, not our annoyance, as they become confused by life's obstacles.

In developing a clown act, as in conventional humor, the ending is resolved first and then the beginning is improvised until the best route to the finish line is discovered. The basic scenario is that of an innocent simpleton trying to get on with his ordinary life but constantly suffering from the interference of others. Clowns are indefatigable in their persistence, because just as one problem starts to become solvable, a new dilemma is introduced.

A clown standard, perfected by George Carl, is getting entangled in different objects—like a microphone. First the comic finds the mike has stuck to his hand; then trying to pull himself loose, he becomes entwined in the cord which, in turn, becomes twisted in his suspenders, jacket, and shirttail.

Of all comedians, the comic clown has the most leeway to exaggerate life. But the audience must still identify with a realistic dilemma, then find personal recognition in the solution.

The quintessential clowns in comedy were Ed Wynn, Harpo Marx, and Bert Lahr. They called Charlie Chaplin a clown, but that's an oversimplification, because Chaplin's theme was pathos, so delicately tuned it created laughter instead of sorrow.

The most talented of the current crop is Bill Irwin, whose polished comic routines have delighted audiences from the circus to Broadway. According to Mel Gussow in a *New Yorker* profile, Irwin's most famous routine, now a standard, is putting his foot under a curtain and pretending he is suddenly being pulled offstage by a mysterious vacuum. No matter how

Irwin struggles, his foot, then his whole body, and finally his flailing arms get sucked under the curtain, like Jonah going down the mouth of an invisible whale.

17. The Artists, Musicians, and Cartoonists

Many comedians use musical instruments as character props, because a number got their start in show business by climbing the musical staff. Many claim there is a metric beat in comedy as there is in music. If the performer has the talent—and it need not be virtuoso—instruments make excellent counterpoints, provide some relief from the barrage of comic hostility, accompany satirical songs, and permit strong opening and closing mood numbers.

Piano comedy is a signature of Victor Borge, and some of his nonsensical tinkling was inspired by the finger-pointing punctuation notes of Chico Marx. Mark Russell, Steve Allen, Dale Gonier, and Abe Burrows are others whose ability at the piano helped distinguish their early careers, and many still combine music and comedy in their acts today. Jimmy Durante's act was to destroy the piano, which was more fun than hearing him play it.

The violin, whose first stringers were Jack Benny and Henny Youngman, seems dated as a musical prop, as is the cello, used by Morey Amsterdam. The guitar has taken their place and a number of performers such as Dick Smothers and, formerly, George Gobel and Tennessee Ernie Ford, among others, find humor and folksinging perfect companions.

Sid Caesar started out in show business as a saxophonist; Peter Sellers began as a drummer for dance orchestras. Johnny Carson, Joe Piscopo, and Mickey Rooney sometimes still play drums in public performances, but telling jokes and punctuating them with drum rolls isn't an acceptable format. Other musical instruments that make good humor props are harmonicas and accordions; Spike Jones used everything from whistles to washboards.

It is Steve Allen's theory that their musical talent was never that great or they would never have switched to comedy.

18. The Vaudevillian

This category includes jugglers, magicians, and acrobats.

Vaudeville started in Italy in the fifteenth century as *commedia del l'arte;* its American obituary was written in the 1940s. But today, magicians and jugglers have found that vaudeville may have been buried prematurely.

Humor is the vehicle that's propelling a new vaudeville. Humor integrated into specialty acts was first introduced by tap dancers. Then Will

Rogers combined it with rope twirling. W. C. Fields started out as a juggler. Today, comic clowns must invent a specialty—part physical, part comedy—that makes them memorable as well as admired for their talent. The Flying Karamazov Brothers are jugglers, Penn and Teller are magicians, and Bruce D. Schwartz wears a puppet body.

One current example is Michael Davis, an improv actor turned juggler because, he said "jugglers don't get a lot of respect outside a circus sideshow . . . most people think there's just one juggler who runs all over the country. If people see me just juggle, they think I must be that guy." So Davis added deadpan (and some bedpan) wit. As he tosses one ball in the air, "I have an unusual philosophy about juggling. It's not important to me how many." Then he takes out five balls and adds, "You've got to admire a man with five balls." As he juggles knives, axes, and meat cleavers he adds lines like "I could hurt myself at your expense." To Davis, comedy takes top priority: "If people are applauding and not laughing, then I'm failing."

Two pegs up from magic and juggling humor is comic basketball, as practiced by the Harlem Globetrotters, and even comic ballet, as performed by men in drag for the Ballet Trocadero de Monte Carlo.

19. The Improvisors

These are the newest and most exciting characterizations to hit comedy in hundreds of years. They still have one character but they have dozens of voices.

This group includes the most imaginative comedians in show business: Lily Tomlin, Jonathan Winters, and his disciple, Robin Williams—all of whom are breathtaking in their versatility.

Robin Williams has been called the poet laureate of the eighties. His rock-and-roll comedy has spawned a new generation of fast-talking, inexhaustible comics whose wild antics both dazzle and fatigue the audience. Williams is an uninhibited child, uncensored, unedited, and always testing the limits of audience tolerance. His comedy is based on speed; that's his pace, not the drug. But heavy drugs are a generous portion of the material he spews out in short takes. One of his characters is a black outfielder who stares longingly at the long white line going from the outfield to home plate. "Wait," he yells, "don't steal home. Share it!" There are not many great one liners, although "Cocaine is God's way of telling you you've got too much money," became a national slogan.

A comic doesn't fail—he dies. And improvisation ups the ante.

20. The Bumbler

This category includes the buffoon, the bungler, the scatterbrain, and the shlemiel. Here's another standard characterization that's going out of fashion.

The bumbler is sometimes part of a comic team (Gracie Allen) where the straight man (George Burns) sets up the gags. The fall guy becomes the humor target who not only can't do anything right, but whose language often takes on the color (or drunken odor) of a misfit. The bumbler can be a dullard or a plain tightwad. Where there's weakness there is comic strength.

Some of the most famous examples are Peter Sellers as Inspector Clouseau; Irwin Corey, the absentminded professor; and Robert Benchley, whose major accomplishment each day was to get out of bed without a mishap. They are the comedic opposite of the stand-up—they fall down.

THE JOKERS ARE WILD

Characterization can also be accomplished in any one or combination of the following four ways:

1. Costume
2. Props
3. Voice
4. Physical appearance

Costume

A farcical costume is certainly one of the most visual ways to signal the audience that the performance is nonthreatening. It's the first thing we notice—that is, after we note whether the performer's male or female, and that's getting harder to tell every year.

In the Middle Ages, jesters wore floppy, belled caps, scalloped shirt and trousers, large, pointy-toed shoes, and carried a wand or scepter so as to appear silly and nonthreatening. Even today, baggy pants signal a comic character. Only a fool dresses like one.

A scout is a boy who dresses like a schmuck. A scoutmaster is a schmuck who dresses like a boy.

Today, the same harlequin tradition is carried by clowns, just as on stage or street corners, mimes have an established costume of top hat, grease-painted face of stark white with red lips, black leotards and soft black shoes. Their costume is so traditional you can spot them a quarter of a mile off: "Caution—Mimes Ahead!"

The outlandishness of Charlie Chaplin's tramp, who sported a tooth-brush moustache, wore a bowler, enormous trousers, gigantic shoes, and always carrying a slender walking stick, was "a totemic figure of such deceptive simplicity that it can be imaginatively interpreted by everyone," wrote Luc Sante. Chaplin took several years to develop a character that was hapless, yet graceful; mischievous, yet chivalrous. In many respects, the tramp is a descendent of Peter Pan. He played for tears as well as laughs.

The impact of a large black moustache was a comic symbol in the slapstick films of Ben Blue among others, and the painted moustache was the comic trademark of Groucho Marx.

In contemporary comedy, costumes of some nature are important parts of the performance of such artists as Pee Wee Herman, whose infantile, wacky character is reminiscent of the arrested development of Jerry Lewis. Herman wears his costume on and off the stage. Even in public, he's unmistakable in a shrunken checked suit, white shoes, and starched white shirt topped by a bright red bow tie.

Steve Martin, after being a gag writer for the Smothers Brothers for several seasons, decided to go on stage himself. He played the jerk originally, but he struck out on the adult comedy circuit the first two years. Only after he went from witticisms to put-down humor as a wild and crazy show-off, in a contrasting pure white three-piece suit, white shoes, and arrow through his head, did he find his audience with fifteen to thirty-year-old college kids.

Robin Williams's trademark is a printed Hawaiian shirt. Lily Tomlin always wears black trousers and color-splashed blouses. Her characters—militant feminists looking for intelligent life ("I'm against war, but if it weren't for Army surplus I'd have nothing to wear")—wouldn't permit her to wear dresses or frilly anything.

Props

Hats are effective props (Bob Hope, Pinky Lee, and Red Skelton), as are drinking glass (Joe E. Lewis and Jackie Gleason), food, such as donuts and teacup (Red Skelton), bag of silly magic tricks (Harry Anderson and Howie Mandel), chair (Bill Cosby), a watermelon and a mallet (Gallagher), and a cigar (George Burns and Ernie Kovaks). Today, Groucho Marx's cigar, nose, moustache, and glasses are more often used as the symbol of comedy than the traditional clown mask.

Groucho to TV quiz contestant: "Tell me, Mrs. O'Leary, how many children do you have?"

"I have fourteen, Groucho."

"How come so many?"

"Well, I love my husband."

"I love my cigar, too, but I take it out of my mouth once in a while."

George Burns comments: "I use my cigar for timing purposes. If I tell a joke, I smoke as long as they laugh. When they stop laughing, I take the cigar out of my mouth and start my next joke." Other effective props include canes, golf clubs, balloons, pipes, and uniforms, such as military and sports gear.

Voice

Voice is certainly the most obvious physical instrument for conveying character. In some scripts the words are written on music bars with pitch notes. The right tone can portray people of innocence and ignorance (as used by Gracie Allen and Lou Costello), the angry man (Alan King), the disciplinarian (Bill Cosby), the yuppie sophisticate (Bob Newhart), and most often it is used to set up an ethnic or regional character.

There are five major regional American accents: New York, New England, Southern, Appalachian, and Western. In addition, this country is rich in ethnic voices, such as black, Yiddish, Hispanic, Italian, and Indian.

And finally, there is the personal character voice: the homosexual, the redneck, the gangster, and scores of others. While heavy dialect humor, on the national level, is becoming rare, character humor using regional accents, pauses, and grammatical levels is as popular as ever.

Voice inflection, from malicious cackling to nasal whines, indicates personal characteristics not physically evident: parsimoniousness (Jack Benny), hostility (Richard Pryor), egotism (Johnny Carson and Jack Paar), viciousness (Don Rickles), sadism (David Letterman), and innocence (Jack Lemmon).

With his voice, Bob Hope can become a ladies' man—an inept braggart full of false bravado. Hope bombed in his early years with three other formats, including a slow Jack Benny character, before discovering his "Rapid Fire Hope" dialogue style that challenges the audience to keep up.

Humor helped keep Bing Crosby, Perry Como, and Dean Martin popular for many years beyond their peak as vocalists. Shecky Greene is the most famous comedian to use singing in his act, but the day (or night) of satirical composers like Allen Sherman, Abe Burrows, and Tom Lehrer seems to have faded.

Appearance

Some comedians like Buddy Hackett ("the face that launched a thousand quips") have such comic looks that you're laughing just watching them screw up their faces. Durante played off his Cyrano nose, and Rickles rushes to be the first to kid about his bald head. Ben Turpin's crossed eyes were such an important trademark that he had Lloyds of London insure them against accidentally getting straightened out. Buster Keaton, "the great stone face," learned at an early age that audiences enjoyed him more if he acted passively about every slapstick trick the heavy played on him.

But cosmetic pride has killed off a lot of humor. Phyllis Diller for years ridiculed her face; her hair purposely looked as if she'd stuck her finger in an electrical socket. She could have played the witch in *The Wizard of Oz* without makeup. One day she had a facelift and now has to concentrate on exaggerated gown colors. She was funnier when she looked funnier. Jack E. Leonard was so big he was known as "Fat Jack," then one year he went on a crash diet and lost one hundred and fifty pounds. This killed his act—his material had disappeared.

Billy Elmer, a Pittsburgh comic, weighs three hundred pounds and gets a lot of laughs at his own expense. He lets people introduce him as "a really big man in show business." Elmer wears a T-shirt with the motto "Just tell us the jokes, fat boy." It's merely stating the obvious. "I let the audience know I can make fun of myself; it cuts down their attack because my jokes are funnier." The first twelve minutes of his act are all fat jokes.

> Yeah, I'm overweight. Actually, it's due to water retention.
> Right now, I'm retaining Lake Erie. Once I laid down on a
> beach. I got harpooned twice and fourteen guys tried to drag
> me back into the water. I buy Hefty designer jeans, not at The
> Gap, at the Gorge.   —Billy Elmer

If your client has big eyes, make them work for you as Marty Feldman and Carol Channing did in the seventies and Eddie Cantor did in the thirties. Woody Allen has made his eyeglasses a part of his act, particularly in films.

The performer must be honest as well as comfortable with the character. Makeup and lights can change looks. Props and costumes can emphasize ethnic characterizations. But many things are almost impossible to change: age, color, height, and whether you're male, female, or both. Therefore, over the long haul, personality must coexist with character.

Beginning performers are well advised to try several characters before they settle on one. And that's when the real work begins.

PERFORMANCE SECRETS

The performer must immediately communicate the following information
to an audience:

1. Establish an identifiable character.
2. Let the audience feel superior.
3. Make the audience care.

   1. If the character isn't instantly recognizable, the performance is off
to a risky start. Generally, there's no time to build a hidden character the
first time the audience meets you. Comedy demands that you get laughs
within the first few paragraphs or within the first thirty seconds.
   2. To make the audience feel secure, the performer must eliminate
any threat of intimidation. The nebbish look of a Woody Allen, the weirdo
clothing of an Emo Philips, and the squeaky voice of a Pee Wee Herman,
Jerry Lewis, or Pinky Lee are all carefully designed to let the audience feel
superior. Just imagine the difference in perception if Steven Wright raced
through his material in Henny Youngman fashion.
   3. Since we tend to feel sympathetic with the underdog, performers
often try to extract caring through a discourse on their misfortunes. But
there's always the danger that no respect can lead to disrespect.
   Once you find your character, you must stay in character. During one
of the annual San Francisco International Stand-Up Comedy competitions,
Jon Fox, a coproducer, reported that after Charles Cozart won a number of
preliminary rounds with a take-off on a militant black, several of his competitors implied he wasn't versatile enough to do any other material. Cozart rose to the challenge and in the next round did a completely different
set. Unfortunately, they were right. He went down in flames, finishing
dead last.
   The big difference between performers and their alter egos, the comedy writers, is not ability but conceit.

> Comedians as a group are a neurotic bunch. Most are imma-
> ture and self-centered, insecure, and (at one time) at least
> three of the funniest were certifiably emotionally unbal-
> anced.   —Steve Allen

The performer seizes every opportunity to stand in the front of the room. The writer prefers to sit at the back of the room, without the sense of belonging but thereby more able to notice the inconsistencies and incongruities of life.

The Romans had an interesting practice. When they finished building an arch, the architect was ordered to stand beneath it when the scaffolding was removed. Humor writers should be forced to take this test, too. Before selling your material to someone else, you should stand underneath an audience's "scaffold" by trying your own material in some public or group arena. If it doesn't stand up, you'll be the first to know. This is for your own protection. If the performer bombs, you bomb with him. The comic may not be killed, but you certainly will.

Part 2

The Markets

Unaccustomed as I am to public speaking . . .

CHAPTER 13

Testing—One, Two, Three—Writing Humor for Speeches

THE CLOSEST MOST PEOPLE COME TO HUMOR PERFORMANCE is when they're called upon to deliver a speech. David Brinkley commented that we may be reaching the point where there are more people willing to give luncheon speeches than are willing to listen to them.

But that's only a joke. The fact is that speechmaking continues to be more popular than ever. In this electronic society, where so much information comes to us via radio, television, newspapers, and specialized newsletters, office computer, telephone, and direct mail, there still seems to be a need to get out from behind our desks and communicate with groups of other people person to person.

We make the time for it. The number of luncheon clubs, service clubs, and a myriad of social, political, and religious organizations—all looking for speakers—continues to grow. Activities coordinators still think of speeches first when they're assigned to schedule entertainment.

I feel very much more at ease speaking here than I did at the last luncheon. They had a sign there which read: "Do not photograph speakers while they are speaking. Shoot them as they approach the platform."

The saying goes that all of us are ignorant, just about different subjects.

Translated to speechmaking, each of us is an expert about something—at
least we know more than the other people in the room—so we're qualified
to talk about it. But that's only half the story. Speakers are selected as much
for their ability to know *how* to say things as they know *what* to say.

Whatever the reasons, humor speechwriters for politicians, business-
men, newspaper editors, and entertainers are in such tremendous demand
that there are not enough qualified to fill the demand. A ghostwriter with
humor material has become a businessman's status symbol, like a chauf-
feur. For full-time business employment, the salary runs high. Consider
that Lee Iacocca hired one for $90,000 per year.

Few modern politicians write their own speeches. The President has a
team of twelve speechwriters and one is a specialist in gag writing.

> When President Lyndon Johnson was in office, reporters had a
> difficult time knowing when this Texan was telling the truth.
> Then they figured it out. They learned that when he pulled his
> ear, he was telling the truth. And when he rubbed the bridge
> of his nose, he was telling the truth. And when he took off his
> glasses, he was telling the truth. But when he opened his
> mouth. . . .   —Robert Orben

Speechwriters for important executives, like the President, work in teams.
This is sometimes hard on humor, because it's so subjective. ("If a committee had written the Gettysburg Address," wrote columnist Mike
Royko, " 'four score and seven years ago' would have to be written as
eighty-seven or rounded off to ninety for fear the less sophisticated would
think that scoring has something to do with sexual prowess. And 'our fathers brought forth on this continent a new nation' would have had to be re-
worded because it left out women.") Despite the fear of creating camels instead of horses, humor collaboration is highly recommended.

Since there are many excellent books on public speaking techniques,
we'll concentrate here on the humor ingredient. (See Appendix A for a list
of books for a humor writer's library.) Speeches are a good place to test
comedy material, and many humor writers will accept small speaking en-
gagements just to test public reaction to material before it's presented to
their clients. In any speech, there are six special areas where humor is important.

1. *Preparation:* "Getting ready, getting set."
2. *Title:* "Getting 'em into the hall."
3. *Introduction of speaker:* "Hold on to your seats, folks."

4. *Introductory remarks:* "Relax, this'll be great."
5. *The speech:* "Everybody's entitled to my opinion."
6. *Getting off stage:* "Exit lines that will earn a standing ovation."

PREPARING THE SPEECH, THE SPEAKER, AND THE SPEAKEASY

The strongest advice I can give is that the speechwriter must work directly with the presenter and not get the assignment from a third party. Writing and thinking are interwoven. You can't have one without the other. Writers must know the client's philosophy intimately in order to organize, fine-tune, and clarify "executive thinking."

> I asked my secretary to find some good "quotable quotes" that packed some solid advice in them for today's speech and she came back with this little memo: "Dear Boss: The only good quotes I could find are these few from Socrates, who also went around giving people advice, and—unless you've forgotten—they poisoned him."

A good speechwriter is aurally oriented. There is a major difference between language for the ear and language for the eye; the way a speaker phrases humor is as important as what's written. "Write a speech with your mouth," recommends Ed McMahon. So speechwriters must practice with the client, because only you know the "sound," the appropriate phrasing, of the words you wrote.

Speakers should rehearse their speech at least twice. The second rehearsal should be recorded on audio cassette and, if possible, on video cassette. Speakers are in show business, whether they admit it or not (and because they like the sound of it, they admit it). Even seated at the head table they're on stage. If they look bored, talk to their neighbors when others are speaking, or bury their heads making last-second changes in your speech, they may think they're invisible—but not to a critical audience.

The speechwriter is also a director, a detail man, and a publicist. Here are just a few of the details a speechwriter is responsible for, and a few tricks of the trade. (Such as never telling anybody you're in comedy. They may demand proof on the spot.)

Be Prepared

Rehearse, rehearse, rehearse! If you are going to deliver a speech, play back the audio cassettes over and over. Many speakers sincerely believe that one run-through is sufficient before going onstage. But once is not enough in comedy or any other art, business, or sport. And it's particularly not easy with humor, where timing is so critical. The pros just make it *look* easy.

> Nobody realizes that I woik eighteen hours a day for a
> solid month to make that TV hour look like it's never been
> rehoised.   —Jimmy Durante

Early Birds
You and your client should get to the hall early. You must check the mikes, the podium height, whether all audiovisual systems are cued up and the lighting system is organized. While you're doing all that, the client should be shaking hands with as many members of the audience as possible, calling them by their first names as soon as they're introduced (or read their name tags). The speaker should circulate quickly, not staying in any one place for too long. The object is to make "friends," since we laugh more easily with friends.

> Theater critic John Mason Brown was a famous lecturer, partic-
> ularly with women's clubs. As he was circulating around the
> room before the speech, a little white-haired lady, holding a
> cane, approached him and said, "I'm so looking forward to
> your speech, sir, because I've heard that you just love old
> ladies." Quick as a flash, Brown said, "I certainly do, but I also
> love them your age, too."

The More the Merrier
Try to jam-pack the hall. Better fifty standees than fifty empty seats. Also, the smaller the room, the better laughter sounds. Laughter is contagious. Everyone wants to know, while they're laughing, that this experience is being shared by the group, so they can enjoy even taboo material without being ridiculed.

There is something else unique about laughing out loud. We rarely laugh out loud when we're alone. In order to encourage the individual TV viewer to laugh out loud and, thus, to appreciate the show more, sitcom producers have refined the electronic laugh track. Even when action takes place in a combat zone operating room (as in *M*A*S*H*), the home audience enjoyed the show more when an amplified laugh track was added. It gave them permission to laugh.

Loud and Clear

Goose the sound system above normal. At best, the client is competing with normal crowd movement, whispers, and paper or plate rustle. At worst, a speaker may need to overcome competition from those who are telling their companions how your joke ends two seconds before the punch line. And don't attempt humor outdoors. The vastness of any outdoor arena dissipates even enthusiastic laughter.

THE TITLE

The speech title is far more important than most writers at first believe. The title not only indicates the subject, but attracts attention when listed in advance publicity; sometimes it can even prompt press coverage. Then, announced by the MC at the meeting, the title sets the mood for the audience. They are ever hopeful that the next speech they hear will be far better than the last one. We may be speaking more, but audiences are enjoying it less.

> The last time I made a speech, the program chairman asked me to talk about sex in the classroom (about which I am highly qualified). But my wife doesn't think so, so I told her I was going to talk about the problems with too much air travel. Well, the sex speech got a pretty good reception. And the next day, the wife of a member of the audience met my wife in the supermarket and said, "I heard Bill made a very good speech last night. He must be an expert on the subject." And my wife said, "Oh, no. He's only tried it twice. The first time, he lost his bag, and the second time he got sick to his stomach."

Even if the speech is on a serious topic—politics, the economy, business, education, nuclear energy—it's still possible to consider a humor twist that will increase interest and attendance.

For example, there's nothing more deadly than sales training speeches, but consider the reaction to these titles:

- "Yogi Berra Was Right—It Ain't Over 'til It's Over"
- "Where Have You Gone Alex Bell, or What D'ya Mean My Three Minutes Are Up?"
- "Caterpillars and Other Special People"
- "What They Never Dared Tell You About PR"

THE SPEAKER'S INTRODUCTION

A humorous introduction humanizes your client, and it's your responsibility to see that it's done properly. Don't let some inept MC start the speech off on the wrong footnotes. Who remembers any facts when a detailed bio is lifted from *Who's Who?*

The right way is for you to write your own client's clever introduction. A day or two in advance ask the MC if there's one already written, but even if there is, suggest that yours may contain some ideas that will help make the introduction more fun. MCs always respond positively to that suggestion, since they're on stage, too. Don't be timid. You and the MC will be the only ones who'll know who wrote it.

After your flattering introduction, your client can charm the audience with acknowledgments like this pairing:

> I'm sorry my father and mother aren't here. My father would have loved it and my mother would have believed it.

INTRODUCTORY REMARKS

Nothing helps you to be a better listener than knowing you're going to be the next one called to the podium. And then a little humility helps:

> I was flattered by our toastmaster's introduction. The hardest thing for a speaker to remember is not to nod his head in agreement when the toastmaster praises him.

But not too much humility. The audience gets suspicious of those too pious. Golda Meir once said to a colleague after an introduction: "Don't be so humble. You're not *that* great."

Even an accomplished professional suffers from stage fright. A certain amount of anxiety is natural and even desirable because it pumps adrenalin into the system and primes performers—including speakers—to do their best. If you find your client gets nervous, plan some put-down openers. "It's one of the most effective devices an executive can use to open a speech," said Robert O. Skovgard. A few humorous lines can get the speaker off to a popular start, and the first audience barrier, skepticism, will have been overcome.

> I must admit I am more comfortable behind a desk than I am behind a podium lectern. Let me give you an example. As I was coming into the building today, I decided to go to the wash-

room and freshen up. I heard a voice behind me ask, "Mr.
Wells? Do you always get nervous before a speech?" "Why,
no," I said, "not really. Why do you ask?" And the voice said,
"I was just wondering what you were doing in the ladies'
room!"

Here's a line so overused as a dinner speech opening that it's become a cliché (and was even the basis for the title of a Broadway musical): "A funny
thing happened on my way here tonight." It would be easy to recommend
that it never be used again. Yet, like so many other rules, there are exceptions. Here's one of the best:

I had a terrible day. This morning my collar button fell off. On
my way here, the handle of my briefcase fell off. You know, I'm
afraid to go to the men's room!   —Larry Wilde

Comic relief is a good idea, but only for old, poor comedians. A speaker
should never be asked to include more than three pieces of humorous material during the introductory remarks. Don't try to imitate a Bob Hope
routine. The comparison rarely comes out favorably.

As I look out over this auditorium, I realize that this graduating
class represents the results of the finest minds and talent this
university can muster. So I thought it was very apropos when
Reverend Martinson opened up with a prayer for our country.

And a speaker should never try to act like a pro comic or brag like Johnny
Carson, who gets away with it because *that* is his character. The following
opener puts a small smile on the lips and a large pain in the stomach:

One thing I can guarantee you. You may not be a great deal
wiser from my talk today, but you will be a great deal older.

THE SPEECH

Usually, the easier something reads, the harder it was to write. Public
speaking is like writing. It comes more easily if you have something to say.

Never lose sight of the reason your client was given prime time.
Speechwriters who spend their time putting funny words into a speaker's
mouth would be better off if they put in a few important ideas. Wit is the
salt of conversation, not the meat.

There are a number of truisms about after-dinner speaking:

> The recipe for being a successful after-dinner speaker includes using plenty of shortening.

> A good speaker is one who rises to the occasion and then promptly sits down.

The speech, including introductory material, should never take more than twenty minutes. At the normal speaking rate of two words per second that means the speech should be a maximum of 2,500 words. That's President Reagan's favorite time frame, and his motto is that an immortal speech should not be eternal.

Shake the idea that scholarly words and long sentences make a good speech. Sentences in speeches *must* be shorter than written sentences because the audience has no chance to reread something they haven't comprehended. The best length for a sentence in a speech is approximately fourteen words. Sentence length should vary to avoid monotony, but this is a good rule to remember.

> During a recent election campaign in the backwoods of Kentucky, a Huey Long type state senator was running against the president of a small college. He would begin his speeches with "Now, you all know me. But what do you know about my opponent? Did you know his college is a den of iniquity? Why, in his college, male and female students use the same curriculum. Not only that, but they sometimes secretly show each other their theses. And if that isn't bad enough, folks, he even lets these young people matriculate together."

A speaker's humor must have all three of the following ingredients:

- It must be funny.
- It must be comfortable for the speaker.
- It must be comfortable for the audience.

Funny Business
It must be funny, and not just funny on paper, but performable. Some humor takes a long buildup (that's out), some requires a dialect (that's out), and some reformed clichés (puns) contain homonyms that work only on paper (*red, read* or *night, nite, knight*). The following puns would be next to impossible to pull off aloud:

Once a knight, always a knight, But once a night is always enough.

In my day, the little red schoolhouse was very common. Today, however, it's the little-read schoolboy who's too common.

Jokes and anecdotes should *not* be read but told looking out at the audience. If there's anything a speaker needs to memorize, it's the humor. Not only must it be delivered confidently, but memorizing it will encourage a more accurate rendition.

Personalize the humor whenever possible, even though many in the audience will know it's fabricated. Humor, as we've already seen, permits the audience to set aside disbelief. No one will stand up and challenge you. Use words like "I" and "last week"; mention local names and places.

I thought I was a good drinker, but I'm nothing compared to Mike. He doesn't drink when he's driving, not only because it's dangerous but because he might spill some. Just before lunch he went up to the bartender and said, "A martini, very dry. In fact, make it about twenty to one." The bartender asked, "Shall I put in a twist of lemon?" And Mike said, "Listen, when I want lemonade, I'll order lemonade."

All speechwriters must develop tolerance—that's the ability to listen to a client louse up one of your best jokes. Instruct your client not to try and finish a joke that's been stumbled over. The joke has been killed, so take the loss right away. Recommend (and write) savers, those little disclaimer lines that help save face when a joke gets messed up or bombs.

Now you know why my husband says, "Unaccustomed as you are to public speaking, you still do it!"

My wife says I have a wonderful way of making a long story short. I forget the punch line.

By letting the voice rise on the last word, the speaker can "punch the punch line." It's usually the most important word, and it's a sin to bury anything that's alive. And speaking of dead, the words *dejected, appraisingly,* and *sarcastically* read better than they sound, and should be deleted.

Never apologize. "Here's something I just dashed off. This may not be very funny, but. . . ." Also, don't explain. "See, the guy was an atheist, and. . . ."

Don't hesitate to give credit to other professional humorists when using their material. It's not only courtesy, it shows you're well read and aren't afraid to surround yourself with brilliance. And don't be afraid to write in a story you've heard or even one you've used before. You can never satisfy 100 percent of an audience with any material, so if you've got surefire material, don't hesitate to reuse it. The only old joke Robert Orben says he knows is the one told by the previous speaker.

> One day I went to a trial of a guy accused of trying to rob a warehouse, but the police grabbed him trying to get away. I was seated next to a little old lady in the back of the room who was weeping and wailing "My son. My son." Being a parent, I felt sorry for her so I tried to comfort her. She turned and said, "If he had only listened to his mother. How I begged him. How I pleaded with him. 'Get the getaway car overhauled.' But, they never listen."

At Ease

The humor must be comfortable for the speaker and every joke must make a relevant point. Gene Perret describes what he calls the sandwich technique. The top line tells the audience the point you wish to make. Then, in the middle, a humorous one-liner or juicy anecdote is added which illustrates the point. Finally, the bottom line is reached by summarizing the point in different words.

Here are just a few do's and don'ts.

Your client must believe in the importance of your material, because this chemistry affects the audience. If the speaker doesn't care, why should they? Encourage your client to go slowly, but not so slowly it drags. Pauses make the speech sound more impromptu.

If you can, have the speaker tell a story on himself. The audience will appreciate that, despite his title, age, or reputation, he's still "a regular guy." That's what people mean when they say "He's got a sense of humor."

> I certainly appreciate your inviting me to speak today. I sort of feel like Raquel Welch's new husband on their wedding night. I know what's expected of me. I'm just not sure I've got the ability to make it interesting.

Perret frequently tells stories in which one of his children's remarks gets the big laugh. Then, he ends up with a delightful humanizing comment, "As a comedy writer, I hate kids who get bigger laughs than their fathers."

Use a prop if it aids communication. Funny props work well, like charts, books, pictures, and posters. The prop also serves as a security blanket. And don't be afraid to let the speaker ham it up, but only if it fits her persona. For example, when a joke bombs, encourage her to take a file card off the podium and dramatically fling it back over her shoulder. In reverse, if a joke gets a big laugh, she should pick up a card, obviously give it a big kiss, then put it in her pocket and pat it fondly.

"Make Yourself at Home"

The humor must be comfortable for the audience. Find out from your host, long before the speaking date, as much as possible about the composition of the audience. Stag or mixed, young or old, and with political, racial, and religious differences, audiences require tailored material.

For instance, this joke might lay a big egg if you cracked it in a meeting of Bible-thumping fundamentalists:

> As one tropical fish said to another, "Okay wise guy. If there's no God, just answer me one question. Who changes the water in the tank every day?"

According to Ed Hercer, audiences want the speaker to succeed. If the speaker is enthusiastic, they'll be on his side, encouraging him with laughter. After all, they want their "just desserts."

But here are a few warnings. E. B. White once wrote, "Nothing becomes funny by being labeled so." Therefore, don't predict or fanfare humor. ("Hey, here's something funny!" The audience will be thinking, "Just tell us the joke. We'll decide.")

When you do humor, hecklers are encouraged to join in. In addition, technical difficulties are a constant hazard, so you might as well prepare your client for what can go wrong.

Hecklers may get involved with lines like "to make a long story short," yelling, "Toooo late!" And don't every say, "I just threw that in," because a heckler will shout, "Well, you should have thrown it out." If the mike goes dead and the speaker yells, "Can you hear me in the back?" and someone says, "No!" then the heckler will stand up and shout, "Well, I can hear and I'll change places with you."

During the question-and-answer period, discourage talking back to hecklers with loaded questions. First of all, they'll be getting the attention they want. More important, if you start with one there may be fifty of them, each with one good line. They always outnumber you.

Advise your client not to try and ad-lib with another comedian in the audience, because the pro will be faster on the draw. Besides, the comedian is probably there to watch your client speak (a compliment) and not to gratuitously take part in someone else's act. If you want to use the pro, pay him!

According to Fred Ebel, humor in front of a small audience—ten or twenty people—is very hard to bring off because each individual is afraid to laugh for fear of being conspicuous. The speaker should try to find the one person who's got a booming laugh, look at him and even wink at him once or twice. His laughter may be the catalyst that starts the audience laughing. Also, the client should get as friendly as possible with the senior official of the group. People will frequently "follow the leader." If the boss laughs heartily, it gives them permission to break out.

> Let me tell you how I got elected. I was campaigning against the former incumbent and we were asked to speak at a farm festival. My opponent went first, but just as he was really getting going the rain started. Most of us ran and stood under a tree. But not him. He just kept talking to a few die-hard supporters who were left. Finally, a farmer walked over to me and said, "You certainly proved you're the smartest. None of us are ever going to vote for anybody who's too dumb to come in out of the rain."

GETTING OFFSTAGE

Any speaker can rise to the occasion, but few know when to sit down. The best speeches are those that have a good beginning and a good ending—close together!

> During my last speech, I noticed a little old man in a wheelchair. After I stepped down from the podium, I went over to him and thanked him for coming. I said, "And I hope you get better real soon." And he said, "After listening to you, I hope you get better, too!"

Never speak at length at the tail end of a long program. No matter how you may try to avoid it, it sometimes happens. When it does, and unless your client is the featured speaker, cut the speech in half, and end with lines like these:

It has been my responsibility to speak and yours to listen. I am delighted that we've finished our responsibilities at the same time.

Always thank the audience. There is no better exit line.

If I've held your interest this is a good place to stop. And if it's been a bad speech, then this is a very good place to stop. Thank you.

In conclusion, say "In conclusion." Next to "I'll take the check," these are a dinner audience's favorite words.

In conclusion, I have had a very difficult task. The food has been good, the drinks plentiful, and you have been a wonderful audience. I feel like the preacher who noticed a small boy sitting in the front pew alongside his father who was nodding off. "Billy," he said, "wake up your father." And the boy said, "Wake him up yourself. You put him to sleep."

A good salesman always ends a pitch by asking for the order, and that's not a bad idea for speakers. Tell the audience what you want them to do: buy a product, donate to a cause, vote for a person or issue, etc. You can do it with humor, too.

Young boy to family: "I'm going up to say my prayers. Anybody want anything?"

SPECIALIZED OPPORTUNITIES

Roasts

Roasts are very popular but difficult to bring off. They require a lot of organization, including a number of different speakers, all of whom must agree not to take more than two minutes.

Roasts are intended to be fun at the expense of the guest of honor, so even though he claims to have a thick skin and a good sense of humor, don't take anything for granted. Clue him in advance as to the type of material, the names of the roasters and warn him that the audience will be watching him at the end of each line—funny or not. If he doesn't laugh first, they won't laugh last. He must be as much an actor on stage as anybody.

Also encourage him to let you write a short rebuttal, perhaps taking one verbal swing at each presenter. In that way, he'll feel more of a participant and less of a sitting target. Even then, the odds are that a few jabs will bruise for a long time. That's why the best time to run a roast is when the guest is retiring or departing the locale—forever.

Stag roasts work best. Once a woman executive was retiring. One of her male friends said, "I'm delighted to see Agnes being roasted. It's the first time in six years she's been in heat!"

The best lines aren't just put-downs but help make the person feel he was doing his job enthusiastically.

> If Martians ever appear on this campus, the only one who would pay attention would be our bursar, Charlie. He would swing into action and immediately bill them for out-of-state tuition.

Humor for Business

Besides speechwriting, humor material can be effectively used in business in the following areas:

1. Interviews, where it encourages both parties to relax. 2. Training sessions, which begin with humor references. 3. Sales meetings, because attention starts to wane after five minutes. 4. Bulletin board signs, which boost employee morale.

> In order to continue to produce the highest quality work possible, all company executives will be trained in our new Special High Intensity Training (S.H.I.T.) program. We will be giving our executives and supervisors more S.H.I.T. than any other company in this area. If you feel, as an employee, that you would like to participate in this program, please ask your supervisor to place your name on his S.H.I.T. list.
>
> —The Management

5. Interdepartmental memos, where humor gets them read first. 6. Compliment letters, which are saved and passed around. 7. Sales letters to long time customers, where it can help to deflate hostile criticism.

Humor is a powerful aid in building a team spirit.

FINAL NOTES

A well-researched, well-written speech takes a full week to compose. Writers' rates vary, but prices just for the humor material range from $100 to $500 per double-spaced page.

There are two reference resources for speechwriters that are highly recommended. *The Executive Speaker,* Dayton, Ohio, is an invaluable monthly publication. It gives hints on speechwriting techniques with illustrations from dozens of important speeches delivered by business and government executives.

The dean of humor speechwriters is Robert Orben, former chief speechwriter for President Gerald Ford. Orben is a prolific author of over twenty books of advice and material for humor speechwriters; he also gives workshops all over the country. You'll see his byline frequently on material printed in the "Pepper and Salt" column in the *Wall Street Journal,* and his newsletter, called *Orben's Current Comedy,* is sold to hundreds of top speakers, disc jockeys, and newspapers.

"Back with news, sports, and in keeping with tradition, a wise-ass comedian doing the weather."

CHAPTER 14

Stand-Up or Sit Down: Humor for Live Entertainers

THE NEED FOR HUMOR WRITING SEEMS INEXHAUSTIBLE because every professional performer needs fresh material: they need it when they're getting started, and they need it even more when they're on top, because that's when they're the most fearful.

David Letterman says, "Now that my ratings are good, I have a different kind of fear. It's like a tap on the shoulder from an ominous unknown force. That's the position you don't want to find yourself in, the one you can't sustain. It's like a warning that I've got to do better, and keep doing better, or the ratings will go down and I'll be left a lonely broken shell of a human—like I am now."

Next to drops of water on a hot frying pan, nothing evaporates faster than the value of a topical joke on TV. Comedians are constantly being interviewed and their best quotes are reprinted. That's why jokes the pros use for the freebies (press publicity interviews) are different from their act material.

But no matter how they try to contain it, comics cannot resist overdoing everything—they can turn a simple interview into one long comedy routine. But what's even more frustrating to their writers is that reviews are often illustrated with examples of their best lines. The result is that the best material has the best chance of being dated first.

Many have said that there is a correlation between humor and math.

Well, there is when you plot out material for a show.

Bob Hope has seven writers. In his typical TV monologue of eight minutes, he covers twelve topics, such as the latest Presidential exploits, an earthquake, the Miss America pageant. Each topic will last approximately forty seconds at the rate of about four to five jokes per topic; that averages one joke every eight to ten seconds including a predictable amount of laugh time. According to Phil Lasker, each writer must provide twenty gags on each topic, and that (7x20) equals 140 jokes from which Hope and his chief writer will select the best five.

Breaking In

It isn't a waste of time to send your material to big-name entertainers through the mail. Only a fool would refuse to look at new material. But some entertainers are afraid that unknowns may not be sending in original material, and they don't need more aggravation. So until they get to trust you, we have a Catch 22 situation. One way to promote this trust is to be sure you don't waste the performer's time by submitting unusable material.

On the other side, neophyte writers are afraid of being ripped off. Sometimes they are, but not as often as they fear. There are several reasons for this. Performers are anxious to develop reliable sources of material, not steal one joke. They are looking for consistency as well as quality, writers who can produce today, tomorrow, and next week.

Gene Perret, in his book *How To Write and Sell [Your Sense of] Humor,* offers this advice: Start locally. Find out where comics are performing and offer them material (hint: have it typed up, with name, address, and phone number, and ask a waiter or usher to take it backstage) so you can start out your careers together. Once you have a few names, you may find local comics listed in the phone book—you can call or write them. Payment may not be much at first, but the experience will be invaluable.

But don't hesitate to contact the big names in the business. How do you reach them? Don't fight the crowd trying to go through their agents or reach them at home. Instead, find out where they're performing and send them a letter there—a collection of gags or routines, not just a single item. Again, make sure you enclose all information needed to contact you if they like what they see. You can find out where they're performing by looking at the current issue of *Variety,* which has listings of who's appearing where. They might even be coming to your home town. But don't try to corner them on an elevator: submit material in writing. The professionals know what funny is and what jokes will be right for them. If they like your material, they'll get in touch with you.

A final hint: Whether a comic is just starting out or established, he or she will probably be a member of the American Guild of Variety Artists (AGVA). If there's a chapter where you live, they may be willing to put you in touch with a particular performer you'd like to offer material to. AGVA headquarters is at 184 Fifth Avenue, New York, New York 10010 (212) 675-1003; by calling or writing, you can find out the location of the chapter nearest you.

There are a number of topflight comedians who are willing to look at an unknown's material. And they're not just being friendly. They include Joan Rivers, Phyllis Diller, and Rodney Dangerfield, among many others. If they read something they like, they'll try to test it before purchase. A joke that's never tested cannot be called funny; it can only be called a *bit*. If it works, it's called a funny bit.

COMEDIANS DO IT STANDING UP

Comedians have unusual opportunities to test material that print writers never have. They can do jokes in small speeches and they can try out their monologue bits in small comedy clubs.

There are more than 300 comedy clubs in the U.S. and Canada. These clubs and performers are tracked monthly by the trade newspaper *Just For Laughs*, 22 Miller Avenue, Suite G, Mill Valley, CA 94941. These comedy clubs are rehearsal halls for many of the big names. Crowds at clubs like the Comedy Store (Los Angeles), the Improv, and Caroline's (New York) are frequently delighted by surprise appearances of such high-priced talent as Eddie Murphy, Robin Williams, and Billy Crystal.

Even though Rodney Dangerfield has his own Manhattan nightclub, Dangerfield's, every few nights he'll walk over to the Catch a Rising Star comedy club, amble on stage and unemotionally read new jokes to the audience. That's right—read—he doesn't even try to perform them. He wants to know how strong they are without the talent element factored in. If he gets a strong reaction, he'll nod to his manager and a check will be in the mail within a few days. Only then does he start to rework the joke into his routine.

Before his concerts were filmed for *Live on Sunset Strip*, Richard Pryor practiced night after night for nine months at a small comedy club in Los Angeles. It took him that long before he was confident enough of his material to go before the cameras and the live audiences—and even then it took three separate concerts to be able to edit enough winners into the final film.

Lily Tomlin has one of the most carefully choreographed acts in comedy. Before her big openings in New York or Los Angeles, Tomlin and her writer will move across the country putting on "work shows," where a small door charge entitles audiences to put up with half-acted, half-read material onstage.

Comedy is written word by word, as a football team grinds out touchdowns yard by yard. Jay Leno describes his technique this way: "If I sat down and wrote ten jokes, maybe one of them would be funny. So, I don't try out new material in bulk. In an hour show I'll try out only ten seconds of new material—one or two lines. If they work, the next night they stay in the act and I'll try out something else. At the end of a week, I'll have done sixteen shows, and I might have another solid minute and a half of material. Then, I feel I've been working at it."

The comedy clubs are a good place for beginning writers to talk to active comics and hand them some material. Once club owners know why you're hanging out there, you won't be thrown out as a drifter. Of course, if your material is bad . . . !

THE DJs—THE TALKERS AND THE HAWKERS

A stand-up comedian does ten to fifteen minutes of material regularly. When she's headlining a show, she may do up to an hour. No matter how much she needs new material, she's entertaining a new audience every show, so her material is mostly repeats.

Not so the DJ. He's on live radio four to six hours for five days a week and his audience is fairly loyal. With humor, a DJ changes from a voice-over announcer to a personality. The memorable DJs of the past ten years (like Larry Lujack, Howard Stern, Charlie Tuna, Don Imus, and Gary Owens) all made their reputation through the humor they presented, not the records they played. No one needs a more constant supply of fresh humor material.

Joke-Writing Services

A joke can be used by hundreds of local disc jockeys all across the nation, even if they all broadcast on the same day. "Most jocks need all the help they can get," according to Andy Goodman. "On the air, they're short order cooks. They spin the music, read the news, spit out sports statistics, give the odds on the weather, and try to interpret traffic reports."

During radio drive time, humor is a welcome companion and helps to relieve road frustrations. But imagine how difficult it is for those who are paid to be good and funny on mornings when they're feeling good and lousy. They need a lot of material. According to Julie Skur Hill, stations that do use humor will insert funny bits three to four times an hour.

This has been a test of your emergency broadcast system. We repeat, this has been a test. If this had been a real emergency, you can bet your ass that I wouldn't be here now!

To help, hundreds of DJs use a joke-writing service that sends out a weekly batch of mimeographed humor material to clients on an exclusive market basis. For those who want gags on today's headlines, there's a high-tech joke service, The Comedy Writer. Roger Wilko writes his material every morning on his computer in Venice, California, and within seconds after he's finished gags like "Remember the gool ol' days, when kids took the teacher an apple instead of driving her bananas?" radio stations all over the country with a telephone modem and their exclusive password can screen his jokes on their own PCs, print off what they want, and be on the air with humor material that's related to today's news. Humorous current events unite the audience, because news is what they have in common.

There are about twenty companies selling laughs, but since there are more than twenty AM and FM stations in each big league city, there still aren't enough heavy humor hitters to touch all the bases. And most of these DJ comedy services are one-person operations, so they welcome freelance submissions.

The American Comedy Network produces audio tapes ready to be plugged into a DJ's program with scripts so the DJ can interact with the material and eliminate the canned effect. In Texas, Lone Star offers a joke-writing service customized to the DJ's request for humor on a local topic. "All they have to do is ask," claims publisher Lauren Barnett Scharf.

There's tough competition among the stations to provide material that attracts the right demographic audience. That's why the humor is targeted for stations catering to chart-oriented Top 40 music. Jokes that are timeless enough to be used in the year 2000 are obviously valuable to those who get their material through the mail. You know the mail these days!

DJs have notoriously strong egos; many won't use anybody else's material verbatim. Although they have to pay for their material, they'll subscribe to a number of different services and rewrite material to fit their own persona. They don't want jokes, they want ideas.

And that's where the local gag writer has an advantage over the syndicated service. Your knowledge of local events, names of local celebrities, and popular gathering places becomes invaluable. Most joke services must send their material with generic references, so the DJ has to fill in the blanks with local names.

Besides one-liners and pretaped skits, the humor material DJs desire most include mock telephone calls to celebrities using impersonations, "on the street" interviews of the famous and the infamous, and "on this date" history items.

Long anecdotes can be dangerous, because there's only one laugh in the time it might take to deliver four or five one-liners. The longer the story, the more the audience anticipates a big ending. If it fizzles, everything goes flat.

Advertising Parodies: "Honest, I Was Only Kidding"

There is a great debate in broadcasting about advertising parodies. Some agencies feel that a spoof degrades the real spot. Others, more sophisticated about humor, are flattered and claim the listener will pay more attention to all commercial spots, not knowing which ones are supposed to trigger a laugh. Unfortunately, many real commercials do that even when they're trying to be serious.

Matt Neuman specializes in advertising satire and has written ad parodies for a number of network comedy shows. His comedy spots mirror the style and texture of the original ad. One of his favorites is a spot for the product "Same," which has only one redeeming benefit: it leaves the consumer completely unchanged. His take-offs have also included a nun doing a testimonial for a "genuflect cross-your-heart bra," a spot for "Porn Flakes," one for a car called "The Vulva," and one for Washington's Watergate apartments, "where you are never alone and there are copy machines on every floor."

Faithful rendering is the key to effective parody. The best take-offs sound so real, using the calculating copy of the advertisers, that listeners don't know until the pay-off line that they're being twitted.

VJs DO IT ON CAMERA

The newest category of DJ is the host of video music programs that promote records and musical events by playing video trailers. The most famous VJ service is the MTV network. To develop a distinctive on-air personality, many VJs use humor. Their material includes sight gags, classical slapstick humor, clips of old films with new off-camera commentary, newsreels with new dialogue, and "man in the street" interviews taken out of context.

TALK SHOW HOSTS—THE MOUTH THAT ROARS

Johnny Carson has been a role model to everyone in the business since 1962, and he continues to be the best. His irreverent, tongue-in-cheek attitude disguises a lot of hard work by Carson, his twelve writers, and his production staff. His gags on current events keep his show fresh and keep his writers among the best-read magazine and newspaper subscribers in the world.

Talk shows in general have fallen on hard times. Many of the hosts not known for humor have been cancelled in the past few years: Merv Griffin, John Davidson, Mike Douglas, Dick Cavett, and Tom Snyder. The public gets tired of too many talk shows, featuring the same VIPs, promoting the same films, books, and records. The host is the only variety, and comedy helps keep the audience entertained during an interview with the author of a diet book for Japanese Sumo wrestlers.

Staff writers carefully interview the guests days in advance so they can prepare bright questions and, more important, funny ad-libs for their star. And they work six days a week—including Sundays, if the show is on Monday.

A talk show gag writer's tenure generally runs in thirteen week cycles. At the end of each period, the producer exercises the contract's option renewal clause, which means if you haven't gagged enough during the previous three month period, you'll gag that day.

Even Phil Donahue, who deals most often with serious topics, still counterbalances his show with carefully scripted comic relief. When he does have a chance for an ad-lib and he isn't prepared, he regrets it for years. So do his writers.

The term "staircase humor" refers to the great lines we all wish we'd said, but we thought of only on the way out of a meeting—or two weeks later! Donahue remembers an opportunity when a very attractive young woman stood up to ask a question. She was carrying an infant whose face was covered with a checkered bandana. Impulsively, Donahue pulled back. the kerchief and exposed on camera not only the child's beautiful face but the beautiful breast she was nursing on. The audience exploded with laughter and Donahue was speechless. To this day he thinks of staircase lines like, "Anything in there for me?" or "Well, you can see this young lady keeps abreast of the times!"

For over ten years, the most consistently popular financial program has been *Wall Street Week*. One of the reasons is the outrageous puns and witticisms of host Louis Rukeyser. Even money can be funny.

Be My Guest

People who have something to promote—authors, recording artists, actors, show promoters, athletes, and even zookeepers—are expected to be entertaining as well as informative. The funnier they are the more often they're invited back to Johnny's couch.

As a result, they frequently hire freelance humor writers to help them prepare for their media tour, which may take them to a dozen cities in two weeks.

Nurse of diet expert to patient: "Sorry, the doctor is booked up for three months—and that's just the talk shows."

—Schwadron

Topical humor subjects are a major problem. Writers always prepare humor material with knowledge of the program's air date. Live shows, like the morning interview programs, are no problem. But roughly 25 percent of Carson's programs are repeated up to a year later. Other talk shows are taped and syndicated so they actually run on a six-week delay. In addition, many syndicated shows run at all hours of the day. Some humor works better when the audience is in the bedroom than it does when they're in the kitchen.

Advise your client to save the funny material for the air. Once Merv Griffin had Olivia de Havilland on his show. They met backstage and she told Griffin a hilarious joke. When they got on camera, he asked her to repeat it. "But I just told you," she said. When he insisted, she did it half-heartedly. It had suddenly become an old joke. That's why Johnny Carson never meets guests before shows.

QUIZ SHOW MCs

Quiz show MCs have a longer tenure than any other stars on TV. Some have been doing the same show for twenty years, and the ones who last are experts at humor. Many of them started as comedians, like Groucho Marx, Jan Murray, and Richard Dawson.

"What they all have," says Mark Goodson, "is a sense of assurance in dealing with contestants, skill as a technician, intelligence, and the ability to say the right thing, make the right quip." They are expected to be funny.

Like talk show guests, carefully screened quiz contestants are interviewed days in advance by a staff writer. It's the writer's responsibility to ferret out the best guests. "Aunt Charlotte may be funny at home," says Jack Barry, "but we have to be sure she's funny this Monday in Studio 33." Questions that will elicit clever answers from contestants are carefully scripted. And since the MC must appear to be glib, "ad-libs" are also scripted.

Quiz Show Guests

A number of quiz programs invite celebrities to team up with members of the audience. Stars are used for their name value, but they're also good for spouting a few one-liners.

Comedian Paul Lynde became famous as a regular quiz show guest on "Hollywood Squares" for thirteen years. His distinctive laugh and his quick "ad-libs" were actually carefully prepared answers to the MC's questions.

Host: Why do motorcyclists wear black leather?
Lynde: Because chiffon wrinkles too easily.

Host: What do they call a college advisor?
Lynde: An obstetrician.

Host: In England, they're called solicitors. What are they called here?
Lynde: In Los Angeles, they're called models.

Host: Is spanking legal in this country?
Lynde: Yes, but only between consenting adults.

NEWSCASTERS, SPORTSCASTERS, AND WEATHER FORECASTERS

Newscasters are always seeking humor, because TV news is constantly under attack for presenting too much violence and tragedy and not enough good news. Reporters who know how to utilize humor find their segments generally make the exit story for the evening news.

Successful sportscasters have to be loud, knowledgeable, accurate and carry a big shtick. Some, like Joe Garagiola and Bob Uecker, make more money off-the-air as speakers and TV guests than by announcing play-by-play action. Since they don't have sex appeal and lots of teeth, humor keeps them in the public eye and gives them the nod on choice sports assignments. Even local sportscasters, like Glenn Brenner in Washington, DC and Warner Wolf in New York, use a steady beat of quips to build their reputations and bank accounts. They look for help from humor writers with specialized knowledge of sports. Some of the best one-liners are also printed (and paid for) by *Sports Illustrated* and other jock publications.

Another news area where humor pays dividends for writer and performer is weather—but if one more forecaster uses the line "weather or not," I'll scream! Few do humor better than Willard Scott of NBC's *Today Show,* and his delivery and material are worth studying.

DIAL-A-JOKE

Some people claim they can't wake up entirely until they've had their morning coffee. Others claim they need their morning laugh. As a result, phone companies are offering dial-a-joke services, along with those for sports scores, time, weather, movie reviews, and astrology predictions.

These services need lots of jokes, at least a new one every day. Conservative phone systems shy away from blue, ethnic, and put-down material, but they delight in localized humor. While there are national services that provide dial-a-joke material, and they need writers, too, local writers may get assignments by calling the phone company's ad agency and asking for contact information.

CHAPTER 15

Saw the Picture, Loved the Gag: Humor for Cartoons and Comics

MOST HUMOR HISTORIANS AGREE THAT THE ADVENT of *The New Yorker*, in 1925, most influenced the development of the gag cartoon. This magazine made cartoons respectable, and, according to M. Thomas Inge, it also "established the standard against which the works of all modern cartoonists are measured."

Prior to *The New Yorker* style, humor cartoons primarily consisted of illustrations indicating a dialogue between two people, both of whom were identified by pronouns, names, or titles as if the caption were a play script.

> *Gentleman caller to maid:* "You might ask your mistress if she is at home?"
> *Maid:* It's no use, sir. She saw you coming."

Drawings were stylized and not intended to add much to the comedic impact. The narrative was expected to carry the full load.

Today, the formula is the same, but the style is different. The humor copy is shorter—pithy and specialized. Because of the influence of *The New Yorker,* the two-person dialogue has practically disappeared in favor of the one-line gag caption. The subject matter, however, now includes the entire range of human experience. Today's *New Yorker* satirical cartoons demand an audience that's sophisticated and literate enough to be comfortable with the eccentricities of metropolitan life.

In print, the humor writer can sell material to the following cartoon markets:

1. Humor cartoonists
2. Political cartoonists
3. Artists who do humor (not adventure) comic strips

There are three basic opportunities for cartoon humor: *verbal, visual,* and *in combination*. The combination is the easiest to understand because the picture and the caption work together simultaneously. But the verbal is used most frequently.

SINGLE PANEL CARTOONS: VERBALS

The Last Word

If there is any one question cartoonists are asked every day it's "Where do you get your ideas?" One cartoonist who tried to answer is Dana Fradon, a *New Yorker* cartoonist for over thirty years. He told Lenore Skenazy of *Advertising Age,* that "the ideas come when I'm sitting behind a desk, usually with a *New York Times* in front of me, a piece of 17x24-inch paper, and I just start free-associating."

"I'm skeptical. I'm not a cynic, but I am pessimistic." Fradon loves to pounce upon the hypocrisy of the power elite like a hunting dog upon a rabbit. For instance, one morning he read in the paper the cliché "wave of compassion." He asked himself, "Now who's overcome by this wave?" Then, he supplied his own answer, "It can only be someone who's rich and not thinking about the poor most of the time."

The cliché phrase somersaults in his brain. He's not sure how to serve this hot dog up with proper relish. He visualizes the line in a variety of settings: Who's saying it? Where? When? How? How about a baseball field? Not funny! How about a corporate suite? The strobe lights in his brain start flashing. He writes the caption, then rewrites it many times. The final result:

A swooning executive is reassuring two lackeys who have
rushed to his side: "I'll be all right. I was suddenly overcome
by a wave of compassion for the poor."

Only after he's satisfied with the caption does he turn to the artwork. He takes just a minute or two to draw a sketch of the scene. This is only one of twenty light humor ideas he'll submit that week to his editor at *The New Yorker*. They select only one of the twenty—and that's not a bad average. Only after being given an assignment does he return to the drawing board for the final artwork.

The Basic One-Liner

If you had a hundred different professional cartoonists and you gave each the same caption: "Why such a long fez, Abdul?," you'd get one hundred different illustrations, but not one would be any funnier than the other. In fact, readers could do almost as well visualizing this cartoon for themselves—it would have two Turks, one with a regular fez and the second wearing an extra long hat. What else is needed?

In single-panel illustrations and comic strips, the one-liner is still the meat and potatoes of cartoon humor. Such gags combine a stereotype setup with a surprise caption. Since the caption carries its own weight without the need for a distinctive graphic, it can be successfully quoted in reprint publications like *Reader's Digest* without any artwork at all.

> *Girl introducing one beau to another:* "Albert, this is Edward. Edward, this is goodbye." —Leo Garel

> *Wife, opening present, to husband:* "It's just what I always wanted. Did you keep the sales slip?" —Gamel

> *Employer to girl:* "Sexist? Don't be ridiculous. We hire plenty of broads." —Dole

The verbal humor techniques most frequently used in print cartoons are exaggeration, reverses, and double entendres.

Exaggeration

As indicated in the THREES formula, exaggeration is part of all humor. The visual cartoon element just provides more opportunities.

> *Secretary to visitor:* "Mr. Rafferty has been kicked upstairs. You'll find him on the roof." —Cole

> *Man to office staff examining broken computer:* "Anybody here remember arithmetic?" —Odehek

The Reverse

The illustration is straight, but the caption is a twist on a cliché.

Doctor, pointing to the X ray of a beautiful girl: "What's a joint like this doing in a nice girl like you?"

More often, the caption is a reverse of a train of thought.

Husband, watching TV, to wife at door: "A walk in the moonlight? Sounds like a great idea. Take the dog with you."

—Hagerman

Tricks of the Trade
Inside trade talk of every profession or business encourages double entendres. They are especially valuable for trade magazines looking for customized humor.

Waitress to executives in studio commissary: "Our super-duper colossal lunch today consists of a gargantuan salad, a stupendous soup, and a four-star super-gigantic double-feature entree surrounded by a galaxy of scintillating vegetables. 'Excellent,' says Dribinger of *The Times*. 'Solid, with a touch of pure whimsy,' says Blobington of *The Tribune*."

Bookseller, staggering under the load of a large, flat stone covered with hieroglyphics, to customer: "Here's that first edition you wanted."

Man to garage mechanic: "Your estimate of 'in the neighborhood of $500' sounds like a neighborhood where a guy could get mugged."

—Polston

Judge to jury: "I trust that the court's indiscriminate use of the phrase 'scum of the earth' will not unduly influence the jury in reaching a decision."

Transfers of Language, Habits, and Customs
Current habits and customs can be humorous when spoofed by super-sophisticated children, super-sprightly elders, Martians, and implausible animals.

Two children, looking at a bent nail: "I think it's called a dammit."

—Burbank

Old lady to cowboy on a bucking horse: "That could be you and me in the bunkhouse tonight, sugar."   —Buck Brown

VISUALS

The ability to produce visual humor without captions or dialogue is a very rare talent. It's the ultimate skill in graphic humor. Otto Soglow, who draws "The Little King" strip, has this talent, as does Charles Addams. One of Addams's cartoons has remained a perfect model of illustrated humor for more than forty-five years. In the cartoon, a skier looks in amazement at the tracks of another skier who has mysteriously maneuvered one ski around the right side of a tree and the other ski around the left side—and is still on his feet skiing down the hill.

For the most part, however, visual humor in single-panel cartoons still draws heavily on slapstick. The cartoon isn't intended to create a complex situation, so the visual must take only a second to absorb, and there's very little space for more than a punch line. The situation must immediately be within the readers' intellectual grasp. If they must pause to figure it out, too many will just skip to the next cartoon.

There are about forty different setups that are used and reused. Most cartoonists have their own favorite settings; Fradon's, for example, are baseball fields, corporate board rooms, the nightly news, road signs, heaven, hell, and court. Most of the time there are two characters, but only one does the talking. Other basic illustrations range from one central character talking on the phone to cartoons showing small groups of three or four easily identifiable characters. The caption is about the only thing that surprises.

Two chorus girls: "I think a girl should marry for love. I'm going to fall in love with the first millionaire I meet."

This is Balloony

Humor copy can be written in balloons above the speaker's head or as a caption underneath the illustration. The balloon doesn't even have to contain copy, as in Randall Harrison's cartoon which shows a man with an empty balloon above his head, while the balloon above the woman reads: "Richard, you're always so thoughtless."

Humor copy can appear in a wide variety of other forms and places. Here are just a few:

- buttons
- store window signs
- posters
- graffiti on walls
- movie billboards
- outdoor ad billboards
- flags
- T-shirts
- placards
- newspaper headlines
- office desk signs
- book titles
- banners
- tombstones

The sign, which must be very short, is frequently a reformed cliché:

Man tunes piano as assistant stands by wearing a T-shirt that
reads: "Tuner Helper."   —Estes

But by far, the most frequent use of sign copy is as a setup for a take-off remark:

Tourist reading sign on castle: Begun 1072. Completed 1250.
"Must have been the same contractor who's remodeling our
bathroom."

Devil to associate hanging up sign: All hope abandon, ye who
enter here. "It just occurred to me that it would be even more
hellish if we left them just a little bit more hope."   —Lorenz

As new technology is introduced, so are new opportunities for placing humor copy.

Writer reading message on computer screen: "This is a terrible
story. I refuse to take part."   —David Jacobson

For maximum sales opportunities, the site must be timeless—kitchens, business offices, classrooms, street corner conversations, etc. Some locales are too topical and may be rejected on that basis alone. Scenarios like a hippy commune, a gas station with energy crisis jokes, or a submarine investigating the *Titanic* site are dated and unsalable now.

Even the characters in the cartoon must fit stereotyped perceptions. For example, business-types are all predictable (and the images aren't very flattering): the big boss is bald and corpulent, the administrative employees are thin, timid, and bifocaled, the secretaries are well-endowed females, and the factory workers wear hard hats.

Eileen Hoover's research indicated that cartoon humor in mass magazines is not yet comfortable with women in executive positions, or as doctors, lawyers, psychiatrists, and politicians. Unfortunately, the occupation roles of women in most cartoons continue to be secretary, salesclerk, maid, waitress, teacher, nurse, and chorus girl. As homemakers, they can thread a needle but can't park the car in a narrow garage. They continue to henpeck their husbands and burn the chicken, although a number of them would rather reverse that procedure.

Cartoon stereotyping follows the current lifestyle. When a majority of cartoons reflect new roles, then history can more accurately record that these roles are widely acceptable in our society. For example, husbands are now much more involved in housekeeping. The following cartoon caption reflected the sixties but wouldn't be as funny in the eighties:

Husband to wife in hospital bed holding newborn infant: "The house is just as you left it—a mess!"

Two common difficulties that beginning artists have result from carelessly drawn illustrations. Since the artwork appears fairly primitive, they frequently forget the need to make it clear in the drawing which of the characters is speaking. Also, the integrity between the text and the illustration is often lacking—many just don't seem to fit well together.

The Hidden Element

The basic gag in this illustration is that something is hidden from one of the characters. Everyone else, including the reader, knows what's taking place. For example—a scuba diver doesn't see what's coming up behind him, or a wife, looking out into the jungle, keeps talking to her husband, who's being swallowed by a python. Incongruity is fundamental in humor and this type of cartoon is a perfect example of the superiority theory. We laugh because we know somebody else is about to become, in more ways than one, a fall guy.

Understatement

This is a combination of verbal understatement combined with an exaggerated visual happening. Generally, the action indicates turmoil and great excitement involving many people. Then the main character says a word or a sentence that indicates innocence, naïveté, or general stupidity.

The theater is on fire and a man on stage reads prepared notes to the seated audience: "The management has asked me to make the following announcement."

The patient in the dentist's office has smashed through the ceiling as evidenced by a large jagged hole in the plaster. The dentist, standing on the chair and looking through the hole, asks: "Did I hit a nerve?"   —Al Johns

A movie director, sitting on a camera boom looking down at thousands of extras all groping around on the ground, yells: "Well, it's a hell of a time to lose a contact lens!"—Donald Reilly

Department store information clerk to flasher who has opened his raincoat: "Boys department. Third floor center."

Woman to lover in bed: "If this bed could talk, it would have nothing to say."   —Zahn

Overstatement
This is a reverse of the previous technique. In both cases, however, the formula is throwing the scene out of balance with an audacious comment by one character. In overstatement, you have an exaggerated verbal reaction occurring in a commonplace setting.

Woman to department store clerk: "What do you suggest as a gift for my husband who gave me a new septic tank for *my* birthday?"

Woman with baby in her arms outside of apartment house door: "It's not the kind of message I can slide under the door."

Caveman to friend playing golf: "I feel safe in saying that this game we've invented will be a calming and soothing influence on mankind for all time to come."   —Bernhardt

Transformations
In mythology, when human characteristics in language and thought are attributed to an animal, it's called anthropomorphic. In humor, it is called transformation. It is a favorite cartoon device and has been around since the caveman. A current practitioner is Gary Larson, creator of the widely-syndicated "The Far Side." An example of Larson's style of humor shows a lady crouching down to feed squirrels. One squirrel says to the other, "Oh I can't stand it! They're so cute when they sit like that!"

Here are some other cartoonists' beastly visions:

A kangaroo mowing the lawn with a power engine catches the clippings in his pouch.

A giraffe bends his neck down to ape's ear: *"Now,* can you hear me?"   —Zetterberg

One forest ranger to another as bear drives off in jeep: "I warned you about leaving the key in the ignition."

Nowadays, transformations take place almost as frequently with machines.

A baby computer crawls up to a big computer and says, "Data."

Change of Time Frame

When today's customs, habits, or word usage are juxtaposed with those of another era, you have an opportunity for understated or overstated incongruity. Charles Addams's scene of a space rocket ready for launch being boarded by a long trail of animals, two by two, works visually and needs no further caption.

The Reverse

This technique, so popular in other forms of humor writing, surprises us when we take a topsy-turvy look at the world. This can work either as a visual, as a verbal, or as a combination of both. As a visual, an example would be two horses playing horseshoes with a set of human shoes. As a verbal it's a standard scene:

Woman talking to friend: "I like sex in the morning—right after Bill goes to work."

As a combination, the reverse works like this:

MC introducing beautiful girl to reunion dinner party: "And now for the award to our former classmate who's changed the most since graduation. You may remember her better as Ed Furgeson."   —V. M. Yels

A frequent reverse formula is to take a verbal cliché and apply new visual interruptions. "Darling, they're playing our song" is a straight line when it's a caption under a picture of a couple dancing. It becomes a reverse when the illustration shows a stout couple on a luxury liner hearing the steward strike the dinner bell. It also works (without the word *darling*) when one mechanic shouts it to another as two cars smash into each other just outside of their garage.

COMIC STRIP HUMOR: THE PLOT NEVER THICKENS

Here are some of the basic rules regarding humor strip (not adventure) comics which vary from the single-panel cartoon.

1. *Keep the spotlight on the star.* The focus of humor is always on your lead character. This is also true in sitcoms and in sketch comedy. The cast is there to support the central character, that's why there are never more than three main characters in any one panel.

2. *A character is a constant.* The star doesn't change, but always looks the same, wears the same basic expressions—and not too many of those, either. This character's actions are predictable.

3. *There is no plot.* The first frames are only the setup and background for a simple line of logic or illogic. Running gags are popular. Popeye's spinach and Dagwood's super sandwich are still working after fifty years.

4. *Dialogue is always sparse.* Sentences run four or five words. There's a great use of exclamations. The key words are repeated.

Panel One. Two kids sitting on steps watch Charlie Brown approach. Boy says to girl: "Well! Here comes ol' Charlie Brown."
Panel Two. Charlie is next to them: "Good ol' Charlie Brown . . . Yes, sir!"
Panel Three. Charlie has just passed: "Good ol' Charlie Brown . . ."
Panel Four. Charlie is out of sight: "How I hate him!"
—Charles Schulz

POLITICAL CARTOONS—WHERE EVERYTHING'S BLACK AND WHITE

Political cartooning is the best example of the use of hostility in humor. The artist is the reader's surrogate attorney, while the cartoonist represents the reader's outlet for bitches and gripes. Cartoons offer a chance to blow off steam, a chance to say, "Yeah! Give it to 'em." A cartoon's value is as an irritant, a lightning rod, a catalyst.

According to Alan Westin, in his portfolio of political cartoons, *Getting Angry Six Times a Week,* political cartooning has a long stormy history that probably began when the first critic scratched an irreverent caricature of a tribal chief on a cave wall. Practitioners have been a powerful intellectual and political force. Benjamin Franklin drew the famous "Join or Die" cartoon that showed the colonies as separate pieces of a serpent. Thomas Nast created the Democratic donkey and the Republican elephant, and helped drive Boss Tweed and his Tammany crowd from power in New York in the 1870s. Clifford Berryman's drawing of Teddy Roosevelt refusing to shoot a cub bear was the inspiration for doll manufacturers to create "Teddy's bear."

Until World War II the center of gravity of American political cartooning was profoundly conservative. But then the granddad of today's political cartoonists, Bill Mauldin, focused on the irreverence of the American GI, even as another hero, Herb Block—known as Herblock—focused on the hypocrisy of American political figures. Political cartooning has never been the same since.

Today's cartoonists were the children of the turbulent sixties. They cut their opinionated liberal teeth on the excesses of the McCarthy era, the agony of Korea, then Vietnam, and the student protest movement which resulted in tragedies like Kent State.

Since then, racial segregation and civil rights, women's lib and abortion, antiwar sentiment, Nixon and Watergate, the FBI and the CIA, police abuse, freedom of the press, treatment of the elderly, pornography, busing, capital punishment, terrorism, and affirmative action have provided the grist for a steady diet of cartoon barbs.

Today, we are in the golden age of political cartooning. There are more than 150 full-time editorial cartoonists lampooning the dominant social and political attitudes of our day. They are growing in number and prestige in counterproportion to that of their India-ink cousins, the sports cartoonists, who are dwindling so quickly they may soon be endangered species.

"Even those editors who don't have the guts to hire their own political cartoonist," says Tony Auth, "can subscribe to four or five syndicated cartoonists and take their pick without having to hassle someone with a strong mind."

The newspaper political cartoon is an offensive weapon in a negative medium. You'll rarely see a good cartoon about anything positive. And cartoons are rarely, if ever, ambiguous. They're strong, biased, and opinionated. The dream is to make the opposition gag on their breakfast.

According to Jules Feiffer, "Outside of basic intelligence, there is nothing more important to a good political cartoonist than ill will. Cartoons are more likely to be effective when the artist's attitude is hostile, to be even better when his attitude is rage, and when he reaches hate, then he can really get going."

Cartoonists delight in their self-perception as the champion of the common man. "The worst you can do to a cartoonist," says Doug Marlette, "is to deprive him of his suffering." Only secretly do they sometimes wonder what gives them the right to take advantage of editorial power and shoot from the hip so often. Occasional tastelessness and even unfairness go with the territory.

"Cartooning is not a fair art," says Mike Peters. "You can never treat anyone justly. Most cartoonists like me—who like to attack—are like loaded guns. Every morning we start looking through the newspaper for a target to blast. That's our function. If you're trying to be fair, whatever you're putting across is going to be watered down."

Cartoonists aren't happy or positive they're getting their message across unless they're besieged with obscene mail, threatening phone calls, and petitions urging they be reassigned to the unemployment line. "The dream of every editorial cartoonist is to get picketed. It's got to be," says Peters.

The only option an incensed target has that seriously troubles cartoonists and their distributors is a lawsuit. Not because the lawsuit can't be won, but because they're so expensive and time-consuming.

The paramount element political cartoons have in common is that they're devastatingly funny. Political cartoonists would like to be feared for their anger, but they also want to be loved. Their caricatures and situations raise smiles, laughs, whoops, and the desire to repeat the message to your associates. Increasingly editorial cartoons not only expose the emperor's naked body (or thought) but do it humorously.

Why humor? Journalism tends to make all kinds of people and things bigger than themselves. "Humor just reduces them back to their rightful size," says William Hamilton, and it makes the point memorable. In addition, the competition of TV encourages the use of visual jokes. "To maintain an audience, the cartoon has to be entertaining in itself. You have to make an editorial statement, but you need humor and ridicule," says Paul Szep.

Cartoons also have an inherent weakness—you have to do it all in one shot. The visual metaphor must be a well-known subject. "People must really understand what you're talking about before you start communicating," says Hugh Haynie.

Therefore, humor must make a biting point, not just play against the illustration. It can do this by either exaggerating the art or exaggerating the joke.

The real test is coming up with ideas day after day, so while they don't like to advertise it, political cartoonists are ripe markets for freelance humorists who know their style and idiosyncrasies. Just send them the idea. They'll do the drawing.

Exaggerated Art

Artwork for political cartoons is far more important than in single-panel cartoons. For one thing, the ability to caricature famous and recognizable personalities is a must. The best cartoons must hit you squarely in the jaw, so the artists look for personalities that are easy to caricature by taking a distinctive physical feature and exaggerating it. A stout woman is depicted as very fat. A tall man becomes a giant.

The most frequent caricature is that of whoever happens to be President. Nixon, with his dark-shadowed face and beady eyes, was a political cartoonist's favorite target, pounced on with devastating force. "I miss Nixon," said Don Wright, "but I wasn't willing to sacrifice the country just to have an easy subject around."

Another requirement is the use of stereotype symbols, like Uncle Sam, the Russian bear, and religious artifacts. Action is always exaggerated. To some cartoonists, the CIA is a cloaked individual stealthily sneaking around corners. To others, it's Frankenstein's monster breaking down doors and crushing innocents.

Pat Oliphant has a distinctive style that's instantly recognizable. His characters are usually engaged in a burlesque of some current controversy. And always, in the lower corner of the panel is a wisecracking penguin commenting on the action. His style has been so widely copied that it's almost reached the point where many young cartoonists find it obligatory to insert a smart-alec animal of their own in the corner of their drawings.

Exaggerated Joke

Besides physical characteristics, cartoonists jump on names that lend themselves to double entendres. Bill Sanders tells of a municipal court judge by the name of Christ T. Seraphim. Wrote Sanders, "He used to take his first name seriously and the Bill of Rights in vain."

To attack the high cost of health care, Kelley of the *San Diego Union* drew a scene of a patient in a doctor's office falling backwards off his stool after reading his bill. The doctor scribbles on his chart, "Reflexes normal."

There's probably not a happier tribe of scalpers in the world than cartoonists. "What can be better than being able to draw, get pissed at people, and mouth off whenever you want to?" says Mike Peters. "Now I'm getting paid for what I used to get in trouble for when I was in school—drawing in class," says Ben Sargent.

GENERAL MARKETING INFORMATION

For single-panel cartoons, *The New Yorker* is the most prestigious place to be published, but the odds against the freelancer are very high. The editors have first option on the work of forty to fifty contract cartoonists. The editors also supply their artists with gag ideas and sometimes even change the caption after a cartoon has been submitted. Despite this home team advantage, they still look at over 2,500 professional submissions per week. Only twenty cartoons per week are published.

Cartoon humor requires a partnership of an illustrator and a gag writer. But the partnership is not equal. The illustrator gets three times as much money, 75 percent of the fee. If you can do both well you'll get richer a lot faster, but a cartoonist who can both write great humor and draw is as unusual as a major league pitcher who can hit home runs.

In most instances editors contract for the services of the illustrator first. The artist, or his sales rep, comes in with a portfolio of material on spec. If the editor loves it, she'll try to work out some agreement, either exclusive or first option, because each major cartoon market—magazines, newspapers, or syndicates—wants an individual look. You can achieve that in graphics more easily than you can in one-liners.

Once the job is assigned, it's up to the artist to produce the quality of humorous material demonstrated by his portfolio. Buyers don't care how he does it. The artist is the only one paid and how he splits his fee with gag writers is none of the buyer's concern, unless somebody sues.

As a result, the artist hires agents who seek out gag writers. An established artist can work through the mail with a dozen freelance writers on a "pay if used" basis.

In a sense, the cart is more valuable than the horse. Illustrations are not great works of art; most of them are stereotyped setups and, like a greeting card, the fun is in the text. The artwork is cosmetic. The gag writer does most of the creative work, and the artist gets most of the money. It doesn't sound fair, but it's not that different a setup from performers and their gag writers.

Each gag line should be submitted on an individual 3x5-inch file card. Make sure the back of the card includes your name, address, phone number, and the file number you assigned to that gag so it can be referred to in correspondence. Gag ideas are all the artist requires, unless the humor is the result of a unique illustration. Few are.

There's a comprehensive list of agents, artists, and material requested in *Writer's Market,* published and updated annually by Writer's Digest Books, 1507 Dana Avenue, Cincinnati, Ohio 45207. In addition, you'll find helpful information on the publishing process, including syndication fees and creative rights.

Newspaper comic strips, as well as single-panel cartoons, are a serious business. The market is controlled by a handful of syndicators: United Feature Syndicate, the Washington Post Writer's Group, the News America Syndicate, the Universal Press Syndicate, United Media, and the King Features Syndicate.

Each will introduce three or four new strips per year. A winner in the cartoon field is a contract with two hundred newspapers, paying from four dollars to two thousand dollars per week. The average is twenty-five dollars. But as a group, the major syndicates receive more than three thousand proposals annually. That means you can get better odds at the race track. However, the dream of that big payoff, the blockbuster success of Peanuts, Garfield, and Doonesbury, will keep the windmills turning. As they claim in lottery ads, you can't win if you don't play.

Gag Recap Publications (Box 86, E. Meadow, NY 11554) publishes a monthly mimeograph newsletter reprinting the gag lines and description of 500 cartoons that appeared in about fifty different magazines. It also publishes information on names and addresses of artists and gag writers in search of each other, rates, and general news of the cartoon market.

The Cartoon Art Museum (1 Sutter Street, San Francisco, CA 94104) will answer your individual questions about cartoon marketing.

"Do you have a card that says, 'Well, it looked
like an appendix'?"

CHAPTER 16

Proses Are Read:
Humor for Greeting Cards,
T-Shirts, and Bumper Stickers

Roses are red, violets are blue,
Thought I'd let you know,
I miss you.

GREETING CARDS—HUMOR IN THE MAIL

GREAT POETRY AND SENTIMENTS LIKE THIS have been incorporated in American greeting cards since the 1870s. When telephones became popular there was fear in the greeting card industry that such brief missives would be one of Ma Bell's first victims. *Au contraire!* Letter writing is down, but greeting card sales continue to skyrocket. *Forbes* estimated that half of all personal mail is now preprinted greeting cards. "You can't put a phone call on the mantle," says Henry Lowenthal.

There is great debate whether greeting cards represent the decline of American culture. But one thing is certain. On a cost basis, greeting cards are one of the great financial rip-offs of all time.

Most cards are printed on one piece of 6¾x9-inch stock folded once so that it has a front cover (known as the *outside*) that opens to a double spread (known as the *inside*). Including four-color printing, the cost of manufacturing the average fifty cent greeting card, consisting of four lines and a muted sunset, doesn't exceed seven cents, and in quantity (which starts at ten thousand) that price is shaved considerably. Even after adding the usual marketing costs of distribution, sales, advertising, and overhead, the profits from greeting card publishing are enormous.

That's really not important. What is significant for the world of humor writing is that every year seven billion buyers are willing to spend fifty cents and up to have someone else write a clever, mass-produced message for one of their dear relatives or friends. For fifty cents to a dollar you can buy a greeting card with cutesy-poo lettering that consists of only two words: "I'm sorry." You no longer have to screw up your courage to apologize face to face or write and rewrite a letter of apology. Claims Mary Jane Genova, "You can get off the hook for a buck—and look pretty cute while you're at it."

It isn't that cards are a convenience item. It takes a lot more time to drive to a store, park, pick out a card, and mail it than it does to write a personal letter. Its sole value is that it communicates an idea that's funnier and more entertaining than anything the lazy minds who purchase them want to take the time to do. Besides the value of the coin, the only other effort required is to sign your name and make sure the address is correct.

In truth, a personally written message would be far more appreciated and treasured. My intent is not to put Hallmark, American Greetings Corporation, Gibson, and five hundred smaller card publishers out of business. They're a big, booming, 3.5 billion dollar industry sprouting faster than crabgrass in August. My purpose is to identify greeting card companies as a highly desirable market for budding humor writers. If you think receiving a greeting card is heartwarming, think how you'll feel receiving heartwarming checks just for writing them!

They are not all American *kitsch*. They are not all drivel or slurpy sentiment. The popular *alternative* card, formerly called *contemporary* and now sometimes called *risque* or *goofy,* offers something different. These are nothing more than one-line jokes:

> *Outside:* Roses are red, violets are blue,
> *Inside:* I'm schizophrenic and so am I.

The public has been clamoring for cards with more humor, sarcasm, and outright outrageousness. Alternative card publishers, who claim they just reflect society, have been growing faster than the industry in general. Cards have been published for divorces, new car purchases, gays, and even an "all-purpose generic card." Its message: "Whatever."

> *Outside:* I'm thinking of going in for a sex change.
> *Inside:* And I'd like to start having some.

Hallmark recently launched a line of alternative cards under the brand Shoebox greeting cards. Immediately, small card publishers accused Hallmark of ripping off their ideas and using corporate muscle to restrain their sales.

Outside: Hold me tight! Kiss me quick!
Inside: Do any one-syllable thing you want.

The humor is high quality, creative, and very formulized. Best of all, for freelancers, the writing can be done from your own kitchen table.

To a professional gag writer, greeting card humor is no different from cartoons and one-liners—it's a classic cliché gag. The opening (*outside*) is most frequently a cliché. The payoff line (*inside*) is a take-off, often another reformed cliché.

Outside: You're the cat's meow.
Inside: Purrfect in every way.

Or the pay-off may be a paired expression:

Outside: You not only light up my life.
Inside: You light up the whole darned world.

Cards are tested with small print runs in specially selected retail stores. Advertising for any one card is nonexistent, and is confined instead to lines of character cards, like Suzy Homemaker, Holly Hobby, or Peanuts. A card company has cutthroat battles with competitors over shelf space. The only test, therefore, is whether a card sells off the counter display. How many would buy this one?

Outside: Did you know that at your age some people have sex thirty-seven times a week?
Inside: And then, they die!

When You Care to Send the Very Beast

Aggressive cards, under the brand names Anonymously Yours, encourage people to attack their target with a caustic greeting card rather than a broken beer bottle:

I'm sorry I'm late with this Valentine, but if you're looking for admiration and love, if you want respect and affection, if you want to come home at night and find little faces pressed against the glass waiting, then buy yourself an ant farm.

TIPS FOR FREELANCERS

1. Take a field trip
2. Specialize
3. Communicate
4. Energize
5. Once you've cut the mustard, cut the fat
6. Get real

Take a Field Trip

Go to your local card shop and read. It's essential research. Familiarize yourself with the humor already on the market and what styles are currently popular. Read the back of each card to acquaint yourself with the styles of different publishers.

Once you've found a few greeting card companies that publish the kind of material you're comfortable writing, check their addresses in *Writer's Market* (or on the backs of their cards) and write directly to the company for their guidelines, called tip sheets. The editors spell out exactly what type of humor they are currently looking for, what they perceive their market to be, their current idea needs, and information about any of their idiosyncrasies (i.e., whether they return copies of unaccepted work, whether artist's instructions are necessary or acceptable with each card suggested).

The more informed you are about the publisher's needs, the greater your chances of success.

Specialize

Have a specific idea for a specific occasion. As much as our wit would rejoice in put-down humor, market economics dictate that sugar-coated messages account for 80 percent of total sales.

The first problem humor writers must take into consideration is that the vast majority of cards are sent for occasions like New Year's, Christmas, birthdays, births, get well, graduation, engagement, wedding, mother's and father's day, Valentine's day, sympathy, and come-to-my-party.

> Get-well cards have become so humorous that, if you don't get sick, you're missing half the fun.   —Earl Wilson

They may be called holiday and special occasion cards by the general public but they are called *everyday* cards in the industry. The humor category is called the *studio* card. Other major card categories are *mechanical* (pop-up, 3-D, and die-cuts) and *inspirational* (religious).

Communicate

Greeting cards are a form of interpersonal communication. They must convey an intimate thought from the sender to the receiver. Slant the point of view for women because they buy 85 percent of all cards (with the exception of Valentine's Day cards when the male-female ratio is closer to fifty-fifty).

Greeting card companies are aware that when it comes to a wife, mother, sweetheart (girlfriend or boyfriend), we don't want to look cheap. Some recipients habitually look at the back of the card where the retail price is written in easy-to-decipher code. Now you know why the majority of Valentine and Mother's Day cards are much more expensive.

Cards talk to the reader, tell them what they want to hear. They are not just opportunities for you to get a gag off your typewriter. When Peter Stillman began writing greeting cards, his first effort was a photocopy of a dozen dimes on the outside with a picture of a coin-operated laundry dryer, socks spinning around in the window on the inside. The tag line: "These are the dimes that dry men's soles." Funny? Yes. Salable? No!

Energize

Cards don't suddenly materialize. After all the advice and demographics are finished, somebody still has to sit down and write the copy.

What sells a greeting card is the tag line, not the art. True, the art has to be adorable, even cute, to clue the reader that the message is whimsical. But once you've accepted the fact that greeting cards are the biggest zoos for anthropomorphic animals, most illustrations seem trite, sentimental, and borax.

According to researcher Marcy Brown, many card publishers have their writers work in teams to encourage brainstorming. One easy way to encourage the creative process is by association—playing around with home truths or tossing clichés around.

Let's say you have to come up with a birthday card that would be sent from a boss to an associate. Start thinking of what a birthday really means: well, it's once a year, you get older, you get gifts, parties, people are nicer than usual—BINGO! When you hit "people are nicer than usual," an idea flashes. And you may come up with a reverse like this Dale card:

Outside: Enjoy how sweet, how thoughtful, how kind I'm being on your birthday.
Inside: Because tomorrow it's back to the same old shit.

Or you may write a birthday card focusing on fun. Birthdays are parties and fun, but you wouldn't expect too many to buy a card that just said,

"Have a great time" or "Hope you enjoy yourself."

Again, you turn to associations: cake, drinks, hugs and kisses, the morning after—BINGO! The morning after is generally a big letdown. It happens to everybody. Why not exaggerate and make it exceptionally lousy. Like this graphic and text by Hallmark:

> *Outside: Cover art features a woman hiding under her covers, her arms wrapped around her pillow as the one last secure comforting thing in her bleary-eyed, headachy world. Text reads:* The morning after your birthday celebration, pause and ask yourself—
> *Inside:* Who put the little socks on all my teeth and how could I have slept through it?

You can also be creative with clichés. The key point is to have an active mind and to play with cliché expressions. For an all-occasion card which tells someone how great she is, you run through all the appropriate clichés, taking each word apart, doing verbal gymnastics, hoping to find one that's a perpetual firefly. "You are the sunshine of my life . . ." NO! "How much do I love you? Let me count the ways . . ." NO! (Didn't someone else write that?) How about "Mere words can't describe how wonderful you are"? NO! But wait! There's a sound there that suggests a reformed homonym. BINGO! You're inspired, just like someone at Hallmark who got a check for this one:

> *Outside: Three badly dressed men, in plaids, stripes, spectacles scratching their heads and looking obviously confused.*
> *Man One:* You're so . . . uh?
> *Man Two:* No, you're more like . . . ahhh?
> *Man Three:* You have so much . . . uhhh?
> *Inside:* Mere nerds can't describe how wonderful you are.

Once you're on to a good idea, a whole series of cards can be assembled:

> *Outside: Same group of nerd characters.*
> *Inside:* Beware of geeks bearing gifts.
>   Happy birthday.

A good rhyming dictionary and thesaurus are essential, and many of the techniques we've already discussed apply to greeting card humor. Once you know how to write humor, greeting cards are one of the most formalized formats.

Take-off

Outside: Some people might say that I think too highly of you
but—
Inside: I worship the water you walk on.   —Gibson

Reverse

Outside: It's your birthday, so pucker up.
Inside: And kiss another year goodbye.   —Gibson

Triple Reverse

Outside: You're perverted, twisted and sick.
Inside: I like that in a person.   —Dale

Pairs

Outside: You're not losing a hairline,
Inside: You're gaining a waistline.   —Dale

Outside: Happy birthday to a man who has it all,
Inside: From a woman who wants it. —Recycled Paper Products

Family Hostility

Outside: Now that I'm a big success, I couldn't have done it
without my loving wife.
Inside: You wouldn't let me!   —American Greetings

Insult

Outside: Sometimes, we get too smart for our own good.
Inside: But you don't appear to be in any danger at this particular time.   —American Greetings

Reforming Bedpan Words

Outside: Some birthday advice.
Inside: Don't kiss your honey when your nose is runny.
You may think it's funny—but it's snot!   —Dale

Once You've Cut the Mustard, Cut the Fat

Your message must be conveyed clearly and with as much impact as possible.

Outside: I'd like to tell you just how much I love you.
Inside: Have you got all night?

You must go over your copy asking yourself if each word is necessary, and this review must be a continual process. Is there a clearer way to express your thought? What's the rhythm? Do you really need twenty-eight words on the inside? Verbosity is permissible only when you are making fun of it. Consider this birthday card from Dale:

Outside: Goodness gracious, me oh my, and gosh I hope you
   have a swell birthday.
Inside: (This card has been approved by the Moral Majority.)

Most copy can stand tightening. Once you've sharpened a few cards, you'll see the difference. And so will the editors. By the way, don't expect the editors to do your work. If your copy takes too much editing, they'll toss it out. They get hundreds of contributions that are clean, sharp, and creative. Don't be lazy.

Get Real

You have a set of twenty or more ideas you've fallen in love with and now you're ready to mail them off. Before you do, set them aside for a day—or a week—and then put them through a test suggested by Helen Lehrer, editor at Oatmeal Studios:

1. Look at them again. Be honest with yourself. Are they still funny? Or are they just silly?
2. Would you really spend a dollar for each and send them to someone you know?
3. How would you feel if you received them, and how would you feel about the person who sent them?
4. Show them to your friends. Do they laugh? Solidly or politely?
5. Are they true? Is each situation possible? Is there a grain of truth to make the purchaser or receiver relate to them?

If you can't get a resounding positive answer for each question, it's back to the typewriter . . . or the wastebasket.

THE BRASS TACKS

Hallmark, the nation's largest card company, publishes 32,000 different cards and replaces 90 percent of them each year. To fill that reservoir of lush and gush, Hallmark has a creative department of 700 people situated in bullpens on three floors of their Kansas City headquarters. Writers are hired right out of college at a starting salary of $17,000. Staff writers are very competitive; they work long hours and are always on deadline, even though they're writing for occasions twelve months ahead. The best writers are in great demand, so, in order to keep the best ones, Hallmark now prints writer/art director credits on cards and pays royalties on best-selling cards.

You don't have to be an artist. Card companies have a full stable of in-house artists. They need humorous prose and verse. When Hallmark advertises once a year for freelance help, their ads beg for humorous ability:

ARE YOU FUNNY OR WHAT?

Well, if you can channel your sense of humor into the creation of brilliantly funny greeting cards, we have a place for you at Hallmark. . . .Just write ten funny greeting card ideas on a single sheet of paper and send them along with your resume to Hallmark. . . .

If you apply, Hallmark will ask to see your portfolio. To help you develop one, they suggest a number of exercises to work on: puns, choosing which one of a variety of copy ideas is most appropriate for a wedding day card, topical ideas for cards, samples of sentimental copy, insult humor (called slam cards), and a new product idea in which you also demographically identify the intended market.

American Greetings, in Cleveland, Ohio, has a similar quiz for staff prospects, but they also test for scansion (a device to determine the rhythmic quality of a verse), how well you can spot intentional errors in verses, and ability to use alliteration. Applicants who send in ideas that spark are invited in for personal interviews. The final decisions are based on the applicant's portfolio of ideas, not necessarily on previous experience in the greeting card field.

Freelance Options

The mechanics of sending out freelance material for consideration by greeting card publishers is rather simple. Companies prefer submissions to be sent in batches of ten to twenty card ideas. Each idea should be typed individually on a 3x5 index card. Some will even accept handwritten ideas, but the writer looks amateurish doing it that way. If you want to be respected as a pro, look like one. On the back of each card, put your name, address, phone number, and an ID code number for each idea for quick reference.

The codes help organize your files, because you'll have a lot of submissions going out all over the country at one time. But be forewarned, simultaneous submission of the same ideas to different companies is a major mistake! Can you imagine how thrilled they'd be if two bought the idea and published it? You might need a lawyer. Because of the long time delay, however, you can't write just twenty ideas, send them out and wait for an answer. You'll need to contact other publishers with additional ideas you didn't send to the first. The sales price runs anywhere from $25 up per acceptance, so you'll need volume to make even postage and mailing costs.

Keep your submissions moving. Don't get discouraged after a few rejections and toss them in the attic. Persistence is the name of the game. And just because you're new in the business, stop fearing that a company will copy your ideas before sending them back with a canned rejection letter. They're looking for reliable sources. And if you're close to the mark, they might send along a rejection letter with some helpful advice—and encouragement.

If they give you advice, take it. But more often they will return your batch with no personal note, even though their rejection may be for no better reason than they're overflowing with birthday messages to grandma, and that's what you sent. You'll never know, and they won't answer your calls or letters to explain why. Even asking them is unprofessional.

These days, greeting card publishers are more leery of unknown writers than ever. What they fear most is a lawsuit from some amateur who spots a published card with an idea similar to one he claims he submitted four years previously—and he's screaming "thief" from his lawyer's office. It's hard to prove or disprove these claims. Most of all, it's expensive. Many lawyers instruct their publishing clients to return all unsolicited material unopened. Sounds logical, until you try to figure out how anyone can be sure what's inside an unopened envelope. Solicited material results from a favorable reply to your original query letter by a specific editor who will give you a name and sometimes a box number for submissions.

BUMPER SNICKERS—HUMOR ON THE MOVE

Bumper stickers publicly indicate the way we feel about ourselves and mirror our contemporary lifestyle. They are for adults what T-shirt humor is for adolescents. They are more popular than buttons and more socially acceptable than painted graffiti.

Their form is very structured:

1. *They must be short, rarely more than eight words.*

Honey lovers stick together.

2. *They are usually a POW—play on words.*

Archaeologists do it with any old thing.

Old mailmen never die, they just lose their zip.

3. *Paired words are encouraged.*

To make America work, Americans worked.

4. *They frequently refer to a local situation.*

I is a college student.

5. *They are frequently nihilistic.*

Get a taste of religion. Bite a preacher.

6. *They include a lot of put-down humor or insults.*

Watch out for the nut behind me.

Pass with care. Driver chews tobacco.

They are marketed like greeting cards. There are published lists of printers who specialize in bumper stickers. The cost of getting into business, however, is so low that many print shops are local, small, undercapitalized, and slow to pay. Even though royalty fees are lower, it's better to work with the majors, who have national sales forces and marketing know-how.

T-SHIRTS—PUTTING UP A GOOD FRONT

If there was ever a cottage industry in humorland, it's the T-shirt business. You not only can write the gags from your own kitchen, you can be in business in less time than it takes to marinate a steak. Typical of the success stories is Dan Gray, a high school dropout from Cleveland, who went into business with an investment of $600 and five years later was grossing six million dollars in sales under the name of "Daffy Dan T-Shirts."

T-shirt humor is written from the point of view of adolescents who discover that body language is the next step up from sticking out their tongues to win attention. The humor is mostly "in-jokes" brazenly poking fun at some local happening: a current news event, sports event, or a success story ("I survived . . ." is the most popular copy legend).

The writing technique uses mostly double entendres or reformed clichés. The only other requirement is that the copy be short and accompanied by a cartoon illustration. T-shirt manufacturers must get in and out of fads quickly because the humor is topical and very shortlived; three weeks is average and a fad that lasts three months is a big winner. As a result, they welcome ideas and suggestions offered "on spec" (payment only if accepted, with no guarantee of acceptance). The only value, in this case, of a "spec" presentation, is that a meeting may result in an assignment from the manufacturer to focus on a specific event or future happening. Copy sales run $50 to $100 and you sell all rights.

T-shirts are popular premium giveaways for commercial firms who are also open for tie-in copy ideas. Even dentists award child patients with T-shirts that read "I got drilled by Dr. Allen."

Sex teasers are one of the biggest commercial successes and coeds will wear T-shirts with suggestions they wouldn't dare say out loud: "Consume now before I'm all used up," "You can't win if you don't play," "Feel good all under," and "Help with the fun raising." T-shirt humor, like the T-shirt itself, is quickly dirty.

FORTUNE COOKIES: LEAVE 'EM LAUGHING

The climax of a meal in most Chinese-American restaurants is the award of a free fortune cookie, tiny paper missives inserted into crisp moon-shaped cookies as they were being baked.

The interesting fact is that they are unknown in China, although a few Chinese historians believe they were originated (under the name *Chien Yu Bing*) by revolutionaries during the Ming Dynasty (1368-1644 A.D.) who used the brittle folded cakes to pass secret messages. (No, one of them was not "Help! I'm a hostage in a fortune cookie factory.") Today, they are like the penny prize in the Cracker Jack box, attracting family customers who enjoy reading aloud the exciting predictions and compliments. On request, some restaurants even have pornographic cookies.

They must sound like they were composed by Confucius: "Success is relative. More success, more relatives." In truth, they're written by gag writers who knock off fifty improbable predictions, bits of sage advice, and witticisms a day: "Money not key to happiness, but unlocks interesting doors." Chinese restaurant managers even have their own gag line for customers who complain when the cookie is accidentally empty. Sara Wilson tells the story of the waiter who said to his customer, "Ah, velly lucky. No news is good news."

*"Would you mind holding Buchwald's column up a
little higher?"*

CHAPTER 17

Print Humor:
Columns, Articles, and Fillers

NEWSPAPER HUMOR

Journalists call it the toy department—the editorial page of a newspaper. Reporters dream of getting there and doing their own columns. "If the editorial column is the land of Utopia," wrote Ed Cohen, "then the humor column is its capital city." While the political, medical, business, and fashion columns are respected, studies show that a newspaper's two most popular editorial pieces are both humorous—the editorial cartoon and the humor column, in just that order.

Columns are soapboxes for clever writers to air their views. Humor permits them to take stands on issues of major and minor importance. Some of the most persuasive articles start out as humor pieces.

Bob Greene, a Columbus, Ohio humor columnist (now nationally syndicated), was an avid Coca-Cola drinker. When Coca-Cola broke a ninety-nine year tradition and changed their recipe, Greene wrote an "outrageous" humor column demanding Coke bring back the old formula. He thought his temper in print would have no more sting than the usual political cartoon. Even he was surprised (and delighted) when his article helped snowball a national protest and the public outcry encouraged Coca-Cola to bring back the old formula under the name "Classic Coke."

Most frequently humor columnists are discovered in some other area of the paper shuffling humor into their news articles. Some, like Russell

Baker, were specialists in politics, others in society, lifestyle, food, arts and leisure, and business.

Erma Bombeck started out as an obit writer for the *Dayton Journal Herald*. In 1963 she talked the editors into letting her have her own column, for which she was paid three dollars each. She claimed it was really worth twice that much.

None have a faster road to humor fame than the entertainment columnists who combine humor tidbits with celebrity gossip. They give the blue-collar workers a peek under the carnival tent of show biz, sports, and the underworld. They are the most avid devotees of the celebrity wish-hunt. "I never name-drop myself," wrote Peter DeVries, "as I've said to Babe Ruth, Jack Dempsey, and Bea Lillie."

The two most popular columns, in terms of newspaper subscribers, are the lovelorn columns of "Dear Abby" and "Ann Landers," both of which are read as much for their humor as for their advice. Next in line are the three Bs: Erma Bombeck, the third most popular syndicated feature in the U.S. (with over nine hundred newspapers), followed by Art Buchwald and Russell Baker (each with about five hundred papers). A humor column has a second life. Bombeck's have been the source of seven best-selling books, such as *The Grass is Always Greener Over the Septic Tank*. Buchwald has written almost as many.

Columnists need famous targets. Baker claimed that President Reagan got rid of all the people on his staff who were funny. "I mean now we've lost James Watt. That's a real blow to my business. We've lost Alexander Haig. That was a terrible blow."

The average columnist works under the same daily deadline, but he doesn't have the excuse of general reporters that it was a slow day so there's no column today. On good days or bad days, approximately three times per week, their columns average 450 words, rarely exceeding 600. As a result they frequently concentrate on the beat they know best, themselves.

D. L. Stewart of the *Dayton Daily News and Journal Herald* writes a column, "Off the Beat," about ordinary things that happen at his house. One day his son, as a science project, had to observe the effect constant rock music has on house plants. "They're (the plants) all deaf and two of them are starting to grow zits. And last night our Boston fern's hair caught fire."

Some columnists work in rhyme, and nothing could be verse than that! This four-liner by Don Marquis, entitled "Nothing to It," refers to his humor column:

I do not work in verse or prose,
I merely lay out words in rows.
The household words that Webster penned—
I merely lay them end to end.

Russell Baker once ridiculed the Internal Revenue Service with a "Taxpayer's Prayer" parody in Biblical form:

O mighty Internal Revenue, who turneth the labor of man to ashes, we thank thee for the multitude of thy forms which thou hast set before us and for the infinite confusion of thy commandments which multiplieth the fortunes of lawyer and accountant alike. . .

But verse or prose, column humor comes in only five forms:

1. The anecdote
2. The one-line joke
3. Overstatement
4. Understatement
5. Ironic truth

The Anecdote

Humor in print demands a lighter touch than verbal humor. According to Roy Paul Nelson, in his book *Articles and Features,* a light touch simply means a relaxed writing style, but not so relaxed it ends up cute.

A light touch, for example, means peppering your manuscript with anecdotes, those short, short stories that are rarely more than a paragraph or two. Rejection slips from editors often mention that an article could have used anecdotes to illustrate adjectives like frugal, tough, fast-thinking, and horny. Anecdotes breathe life into any article and can either precede or follow a generalization.

In nonfiction pieces they should be true. But, as in much humor, anecdotes have a unique permission to be fictional. Even though her three children are now all adults, in print Erma Bombeck's beat is still the problems of child raising and that thankless turf between the kitchen sink and the washing machine. "Housework, if you do it right, can kill you," she once wrote, but her children now call her a fiction writer.

It's more important for anecdotes to be believable than to be true. Writers shade facts and edit true stories to save the punch line for last.

When stories are made up, the readers should be clued with lines like "This story may be apocryphal, but. . . ." (Few readers know that word, anyway.)

Some anecdotes are obviously fictional; others may need a disclaimer. But if you start off with "One day, God, Jesus, and Moses were playing golf," don't bother using a disclaimer. Keep 'em guessing.

Nels F. S. Ferre in *God's New Age* offers this anecdote to explain philosophical terms:

> Three baseball umpires were arguing. Said the first, "I call balls and strikes exactly the way they come." (This man was an objectivist.)
>
> Said the second, "I can't do that. I call them balls or strikes the way I see them." (This man was a subjectivist.)
>
> But the third had ideas of his own. "They are neither balls nor strikes until I call them." (He was an existentialist.)

The reader understands that Ferre did not happen upon three real-life umpires engaged in so convenient a conversation.

The Joke

A joke is written differently for the verbal humorist than it would be for the printed page. Bill Cosby's monologues in script form are comparatively lifeless. Art Buchwald's columns could never be performed on stage.

Few do a printed joke better than Erma Bombeck; she was the first to recommend that any husband who watches eight consecutive football games on New Year's weekend should be declared legally dead. Her column "Wits End" is filled with one-liners like:

> I don't think women outlive men, it only seems longer.

Columns and articles still use a high percentage of cliché-inspired aphorisms. The printed page permits more homonym reforming (puns), because they're easy to see in writing.

> A pastor said to his congregation: "To meet our budget deficit, I ask all of you to consider giving 10 percent of your income. Frankly, your church is fit to be tithed."   —Herm Albright

> The Baseball Hall of Fame is known as the Cooperstown (NY) whacks museum.   —Antoni Tabak

You'll find double entendre puns all over the editorial pages. These puns are also a basic tool of newspaper headlines and photo caption writers. Within hours after a humpback whale got lost and mistakenly swam sixty miles up the Sacramento River into the middle of California, editors and T-shirt designers were having "a whale of a time." And when a luxury car fell into a giant pothole in Columbus, Ohio, even the *South China Morning Post* in Hong Kong ran the picture with the caption: "The hole truth—Mercedes bends."

Overstatement—Going for Baroque

Humor writers get more recognition in print than in any other medium. Pulitzer Prizes have been awarded to three syndicated columnists who are outstanding humorists: Russell Baker (1979), Ellen Goodman (1980), and Art Buchwald (1982). Even though there is no humor category, Pulitzer judges properly classify humor under "Criticism or Commentary," and all three writers do both.

Russell Baker is a master of literate humor. He is a natural cynic who sees the world as it is, instead of as it should be. In "An Idea That Must be Unfolded Now," note how Baker used exaggeration to describe an early success of his "National Bumbershoot Academy":

> The pattern is familiar to us all. If you rise on a rainy morning and go to the closet for your umbrella, you find the umbrella gone. Usually it has gone to the office. If you go to the office on a clear morning, and it rains in the afternoon and you go to the closet for your umbrella, what do you find? Your umbrella is gone. Most cases it has gone home.
>
> From this pattern it was child's play to deduce what was happening. When an umbrella at home realized there would be rain by morning it went to the office. When it was loafing around the office and suddenly sensed an afternoon rain impending, it pulled itself together and went home.
>
> The reason for this behavior baffled men for 20 years, until Spitzstein (head of the agency) explained it in his famous First Law of the Umbrella: "Umbrellas don't like to be wet."

Baker, a tough Washington bureau chief for the *New York Times*, used humor to report hard news. He called the White House during President Dwight D. Eisenhower's term, "the tomb of the well-known soldier." In 1962 his first humor column was a widely acclaimed lampoon of President John F. Kennedy. Later, he turned his descriptive skill against President Lyndon Johnson, whom he described as "a big, outsized, outlandish character out of some kind of medieval burlesque, a great bestriding colossus who ran every mood on the emotional gamut.''

Another example of overstatement is Baker's attack on the Super Bowl, the Miss America pageant, and the Academy Awards as three American religious rituals. He called them "utterly boring, meaningless, pointless, and whatever happens doesn't make a goddam bit of difference to anything that is going to happen tomorrow. But when they run, the whole country comes together in some kind of great national town meeting.''

Erma Bombeck also uses a great deal of exaggeration, as when she describes trying to pass her varicose veins off as textured stockings.

Understatement

Art Buchwald's satirical humor is best when it's understated, so ironic that the uninitiated reader thinks Buchwald is deadly serious. In July of 1986, the Attorney General published the report of a commission formed to recommend action against pornography. Here are just a few paragraphs of Buchwald's column:

> The best thing about the report of Attorney General Meese's Commission on Pornography is its call for "Citizen Watch" groups to monitor what types of publications are sold in stores. If, in the view of the group, the material is pornographic, the citizen's group will organize a boycott, and God knows what else, to rid the store of the rot.
>
> . . . I'd like to volunteer my services. One of my greatest fantasies has been to censor magazines and send those who sell them to jail. . . . My qualifications? I've read many of the magazines the pornography commission finds objectionable. Secondly, I know exactly where in the store such reading materials are kept. I have done a lot of dry runs since the report was published. I know how to distinguish between literature with no redeeming value as opposed to magazines which are just trying to give me a cheap thrill.
>
> If you elect me, I promise to go through every store in your neighborhood . . . You can trust me that no page will be left unturned without my stamp of approval. I'm not only talking about nudity, depravity, and sexually obnoxious material, but also other stuff that might not look offensive on the cover, but when you read between the lines can lead to crime too horrendous to mention.
>
> Without wanting to brag, I think I'm the best man for the

job. I've hung around newsstands all my life. I can spot a *Playboy* or *Penthouse* reader a mile away, and I know how to read any magazine sealed together with cellophane.

The Ironic Truth

Erma Bombeck once wrote, "Anybody can bring out your tears. That's a piece of cake. It is twenty times—no make that fifty times—easier to make people cry rather than laugh."

Jim Murray, a columnist with the *Los Angeles Times* for more than thirty years, once wrote that the announcer at the Indy 500 had shouted, "Gentlemen, start your coffins." Murray campaigned for qualified black golfers to be invited to national tournaments. "It would be nice to have a black American at Augusta in something other than a coverall," and finally his observation: "Woody Hayes of Ohio State was a grouch, but Woody was consistent. He was graceless in victory and graceless in defeat."

Art Hoppe of the *San Francisco Chronicle* once wrote, "Writing a humor column beats honest work. It leaves mornings free for other projects, such as writing rare books. In my case, the books are extremely rare."

Humor columnists are introspective and fearful. I doubt there's a columnist who doesn't live in dread of drying up. Consider that Art Buchwald, Russell Baker, and Erma Bombeck are the founders of the American Academy of Humor Columnists. They have a whopping membership of six, and they intend to keep it that way. Said Buchwald, "If a new young humor writer sends along some of his material—no matter how good it is—we write him back and say, 'You don't have it, kid. Go into advertising!' "

MAGAZINE ARTICLES

Magazine editors are demanding more, not less, levity. Even in serious nonfiction pieces, they're anxious to lighten the load with humor. They realize there are few new stories, so they're looking for new ways of telling the old story.

There's a fine distinction between being funny and being humorous. Writing jokes, you just want to be funny. When writing a humorous article, the object is to inform and educate in a humorous way. Humor is appropriate in either of the two following situations:

1. *If the subject matter is a person known for humor, then humor becomes almost mandatory.* The trick is to avoid trying to upstage the subject by forcing your own humor into the article. This is especially risky when you are writing about humor professionals who've spent many years perfecting

their lines, while you've got only a few days to perfect *yours*. You're bound to come off looking second-rate. Make use of the great lines they've created. Don't compete.

2. *If the subject is serious but can be made funny in the phrasing.* For example, you can use out-of-character humor, someone who plays a role completely different from what you'd expect: an old lady who rides a motorcycle or a dog who sings along to rock music. And incongruous situations open up hundreds of possibilities.

Of the two possibilities, it's obviously easier to produce humor when the subject is humorous. The humor for the second subject must be gentle, reassuring, predictable. It celebrates ordinary events in a new way. It brings a smile of recognition rather than a hearty laugh. Its success is based upon genuineness of feeling and clarity of writing. These more serious subjects are researched like a regular piece, but then the humor is added to make it more memorable. Don't take extraneous jokes and try to bend them to fit the subject. Humor must come out of reality.

The key to a sale is the perfect marriage of quality humor with the magazine's special interest and audience. One team of comedy writers, Stef and Mary Kaiser Donev, sells regularly to regional medical journals with small pieces like: "Hemorrhoids: they won't kill you—you just wish they would," and "The one sure cure of acne—old age."

They claim a fifteen hundred word article on a subject (like hospital-room etiquette) can contain up to eight humorous anecdotes or jokes and still be considered serious and informative. It isn't designed to keep the patient in stitches—he's probably already there.

The bible for selling magazine articles is the *Writer's Market*. Updated annually, it has a complete list of magazines, with names and addresses, that are looking for freelance material, including humor.

Anecdotes and Fillers

The *Courier-Journal* of Louisville, Kentucky, has been running "The Funny Bone," a joke column, in their Sunday magazine for more than thirty years. It uses subscriber joke contributions exclusively. Readers not only like the jokes, but take great pride in seeing their names, and those of their friends, published. Once when the column was possibly going to be dropped because it required too much staff time, readers protested so vigorously that "The Funny Bone" was kept, and continues to be one of the magazine's most popular features.

In articles, humor works best as a leadoff hitter. You can suck the reader into the story faster with a good anecdote. You'll find examples of that every day on the front page of the *Wall Street Journal*. A humor anecdote also works well as a sign off.

Anecdotes and fillers are used more often by magazines than newspapers. And of all the publications which solicit public contributions, the *Reader's Digest* is the Super Bowl of humor achievement. It is, by far, the most rewarding market for freelancers. With over fifty million readers, they pay the highest rates for anecdotes, jokes, and humorous quotes. To find the latest fees just turn to page four of the most recent *Digest* issue.

The term "filler" originated when type was set by hand or linotype. It refers to the one or two line tidbits printers used to quickly fill space at the end of a column or a page. Even though today's computerized typesetting has eliminated that need, fillers still appear in magazines—humorous ones, as leavening.

There is no precise formula for a filler. "A good filler," wrote Betty Johnston, a former *Digest* editor, "is one that the reader will want to quote or read aloud to a colleague." Because most magazines have four and five month editorial deadlines in advance of publication, fillers need a certain timeliness (or, better, timelessness) and relevance—a quote or anecdote from the past must have some special application for today.

Humor is integral. Regina Hersey of *Reader's Digest* told *The Comedy Roundtable* that in the magazine's monthly reader's poll, humor sections are consistently ranked first, and humor articles are a consistently favorite format. This really comes as no big surprise, because *Reader's Digest* has at least nine different areas for salable humor: "Toward More Picturesque Speech," "Points to Ponder," and "Quotable Quotes" specialize in zany or inventive play-on-words phrasing; "Life in These United States" tries for true, previously unpublished anecdotes; "Laughter, the Best Medicine" is a joke department that includes puns, topical humor, and celebrity quips. Humorous stories are reprinted in special sections: "Personal Glimpses," "All in a Day's Work," "Campus Comedy" and "Humor in Uniform." In addition, at the end of some articles, the magazine still uses miscellaneous anecdotes as old-fashioned fillers.

There are twelve staff editors who do nothing but prepare the humor anecdotes and fillers. Humor is read by two editors before being rejected so that the bad mood of one editor won't automatically eliminate a marginal possibility. Then the magazine submits all material seriously being considered for publication to an "index" department where it's checked for originality. (Beginning writers can ruin their reputations with a magazine by trying to pass off someone else's material as their own.) Finally, a research department checks original sources for verification.

Anecdotes about yourself are acceptable, but anecdotes about famous people are particularly desired because names make news (or the other way around).

Many general publications have taboos against bathroom humor, vulgarity, and stories that ridicule the handicapped. Put-down humor is acceptable when the joke is in the cleverness of the response. That's why, if the humor comes close to any of these areas, self-deprecating stories have a much greater chance of publication. Tell the story on yourself, don't make yourself the smart alec. The *Digest* is not above changing the point of view in these cases, but they'll always check with the writer.

A few magazines, like *Reader's Digest,* are also interested in reprinting good humor from other publications, and will pay readers handsomely for discovering it. *The New Yorker* delights in typos and short items with unintentionally weird or double entendre phrasing.

However, humor material in other major publications, like *Time, Newsweek,* and the *New York Times,* is so thoroughly covered by *Digest* staff personnel that it's rare freelancers can get credit. Over 800 newspaper columnists regularly send their columns to *Reader's Digest* in the hope of editorial selection. Therefore, the magazine is looking for reprint material from remote areas like small regional magazines, corporate newsletters, and local radio shows.

The winning combination for acceptability is a good sense of what's funny—and knowing how to present it. That gives the professional humor writer an advantage over the amateur contributor.

Stories must have a punch as well as a punch line. They should be written in less than 300 words, thus they can't require long introductions or lots of background information. The best material has a sense of truthfulness, rather than a contrived setup. People in incongruous situations make the funniest stories because the reader identifies with the "It could have happened" possibility.

A filler, unlike a regular article, is paid for only on publication. *Reader's Digest* gets thousands of submissions each month, so they won't return material even if you include a self-addressed, stamped envelope (SASE). If your piece was intended for publication but omitted because of space, no check! If they like it you'll generally hear within three months. But sometimes they may take up to a year, so everyone's unhappy if you've given up on them and submitted the humor elsewhere. If you *have* sold the item elsewhere and the magazine's research department calls to verify, never lie. You'll win that game only once, but will be blackballed forever.

Material should be neatly typed, double-spaced, each item on a separate sheet of paper, with your name, address, telephone number, and date of submission clearly identified.

Letters to the Editor

Even if you're just interested in writing a letter to the editor, you've got a better chance of being published if you use humor. The annual peeka-boo swimsuit issue of *Sports Illustrated* prompts more letters to "The 19th Hole" than many other issues combined. It gets a lot of subscriptions "re-nude." Here's an example of a letter that got published because of a basic reverse technique:

> I was shocked at the display of flesh [that issue] contained: what legs! what chests! Where did you find those Sumo wrestlers?

CHAPTER 18

The Scarce Comedy-ty: Writing for TV Sitcoms

AFTER TWENTY-FIVE CONSECUTIVE YEARS of being a majority of the top twenty TV programs, the sitcom format fell into disfavor in the early- to mid-eighties. The finger pointing was contagious: "Humor is not designed to command the depths of people's attention," claimed Sheldon Leonard. "The public's just sick of your product," wrote another critic. "Comedy has become too predictable. They want violence, mayhem, sex, and glamour."

Comedy writers who used to greet each other, "What a silly job being a sitcom writer—you're making *how much?*" were now asking, "I don't care if it is silly, where can I get a writing job?"

In 1985, without a six-gun or a screeching tire, the hero rode into town. His name, Bill Cosby. His family-oriented sitcom raised the consciousness of comedy and, in one year, the program broke total viewing and advertising records for a regular program.

Success bred change. The networks did another flip-flop (which might be better termed a successful flip) and twenty-nine sitcoms again dominated the next year's schedules. There were at least three every night of the week.

Cheaper by the Dozen
Once again it's a seller's market for those writers who can consistently produce acceptable material—and, once again, the key word is *consis-*

tently. Writers not only make good bread, they eat cake—with all the frosting. Not only are there as many sitcoms as before, but each show has realized the need for a squad of writers to maintain quality while maintaining night-crawling deadlines. A team of six writers is standard, but it's becoming increasingly more common to see as many as twelve writers on just one show. This is logical, because the story and the humor are the only variables, once the cast and program premise have been settled upon. And despite the buckets of money Guild writers are paid, they're the least expensive commodity on the show, when you compare actors' salaries, or production and distribution costs.

It isn't unusual for salaries to run as high as $10,000 per week for writers who have hyphenated titles like writer-director or writer-producer. And, of course, TV reruns generate residual payments. There is never a time when reruns of such legendary hits as *All in the Family, M*A*S*H, I Love Lucy,* and *The Jeffersons* aren't running somewhere around the globe. In their old age, some writers will have nurses endorsing residual checks.

THE LUCK OF THE DRAW

Until they learn the importance of being earners, however, comedy writers start out very lean and hungry.

To be a sitcom writer you must reflect your world, not through an ordinary mirror but through what Bert Andrews once called "a Coney Island mirror that distorts and makes amusing every little incident, foible, and idiosyncrasy." You must also be aware of the serious limitations to the creative process. A successful sitcom must satisfy the production company, the networks, the stars, the sponsors, the critics and, finally and the most important of all, a large enough segment of the viewing public to outdistance all competitive programming. That takes skill—and luck!

For example, since you must please the audience, the script must take advertising demographics into consideration. The major consumer market is women between the ages of eighteen and forty-nine, and since men of brawn (and some brains) are attractive to this audience, machos get as much exposure as well-endowed young ladies in tight jiggle outfits.

A Spec is a Little Piece of Dirt

One of the first and best ways to attain skill in sitcom writing is to write for an existing show. Not that you're going to sell the script, competing with a dozen pro writers who sweat the show weekly. It's just that these shows provide a benchmark for evaluating your scripts.

There are plenty of shows to choose from. *Daily Variety* and *The Hollywood Reporter* list shows in production and the names of producers to contact for script submission. Your public library will have addresses of these publications, and may have copies. Otherwise, you can watch a show's rolling credits for the name of the executive producer. *TV Market List* publishes the names of shows in development. Even submitting a sample script for an oldie in syndication permits agents to evaluate your ability and sales potential. Find a show that reflects the type of humor you feel comfortable with. Watch as many different episodes as you can, noting plot treatment, character development, set locations, timing, and running gags. If possible, record the program on video cassette for review, and audio cassette to remember where *you* laughed.

The names of agents, with notations on who will and who won't look at unsolicited manuscripts, are available through The Writer's Guild of America (West) in Los Angeles and the *Literary Market Place (LMP)*.

IT'S STILL THE SAME OLD STORY

One of the things you'll notice are recurring themes. Successful shows, like the *Bill Cosby Show*, spawn copies. *The Honeymooners* and *I Love Lucy* begat dozens of shows with bickering married couples, and don't forget that there was a radio show called *The Bickersons* in the '50s. When Phil Silvers starred as Sergeant Bilko, a dozen comedy service shows soon marched along in step. Hillbillies, cops, show biz, and talking apparitions each went in and out of favor. You can bet on one thing—they'll be back again some day to delight a new generation.

Another thing you'll notice is recurring story lines. Just review *TV Guide* to identify the crux of each story. By the way, unless you can summarize your plot in one simple sentence, it is probably too complex.

Humor is like magic. A magician still uses tried-and-tested tricks. The excitement comes from the new way he packages it. Well-tracked funny situations must be displayed in novel ways.

The heart of every sitcom is the "What if. . ." conflict. The plot fabrication is determined when the main character is placed in a unique, frequently uncomfortable situation. Not all sitcom dialogue is humorous. In fact, over 65 percent of a sitcom's time involves serious situations, which are highlighted by comic relief. Garry Marshall advised, "Trouble? Who doesn't have any? If the experience is painful to you, don't block it out. Save it. Maybe in three days it will be funny."

The following are ten of the most common recurring themes popular with audiences since the beginning of motion picture production—the grandfather of all contemporary sitcoms. Most of these themes are just exaggerations of ordinary situations. They frequently overlap, or two plots are running at the same time.

1. Family aggression
2. Workplace aggression
3. Mistaken assumptions
4. Intrusions
5. Heartbreak
6. Moral and ethical conflicts
7. Sympathy for the disadvantaged
8. Physical mishaps
9. Something of value
10. Failure to cope

Family Aggression

People in close contact develop basic competition. Husbands compete with wives, in-laws compete with married children, children compete with parents, and families, not just children, compete with relatives and neighbors. Laughter is created when characters interplay with love, illness, jealousy, prejudice, death, and cream pies.

The mother-in-law coming for a visit is still one of the hundred most common plots on TV. Someone in the family must always be the fall guy, because we'll watch the stupidity of others and feel superior. That's why stereotypes are still being used, but today the humor comes from our surprise at their normal behavior. This is one of the delights of the *Bill Cosby Show,* which has probably done more for race relations than all the other black family programs combined.

Workplace Aggression

Offices, factories, schools, even taxi dispatch stations provide the setting for thriving antagonisms. Workers resent bosses and each other. In every sitcom, close proximity produces enmity and your story must reveal the farce around the friction.

Some of the on-the-job plots used frequently today include a compliment goes to the boss's head, someone is expecting an important job promotion, and someone is accused of being a crook.

Names often express an important personality trait and keep the viewer focused on character expectations. "Hot Lips" was appropriate for her passion, Archie Bunker talked bunk, and Hawkeye Pierce sounded like a rascal, not a Park Avenue doctor.

Mistaken Assumptions

One essential ingredient in drama is that the audience be kept in the dark about something. In humor, it's just the reverse—the audience is clued in from the beginning, but one essential character is purposely not. In fact, if all the characters in a sitcom told the truth in the first three minutes, there would be no need for the other twenty. Examples are common: one character tries to hide his true ability, a body is hidden in a trunk, someone is hiding in the closet, a married couple pretend they're single, the boss is mistaken for a worker, a house painter is mistaken for a doctor, etc.

Intrusions

Anything that disturbs the status quo presents a conflict of emotions. Relatives, friends, objects and events cropping up at inconvenient times and places disturb the equilibrium, and the attempted cover-up provides the humor.

Examples of intrusions are workmen in the house, a pest of a kid comes for a visit, the surprise birthday party is held at the wrong time, or the house suddenly appears to be haunted.

Heartbreak

This is the oldest of all emotions next to love and frequently runs in tandem with it. In humor, it must focus on absurdities: an American GI falls for a Korean aristocrat, an old flame is discovered but is already married, a doctor must tell a patient the truth about her illness.

Then there's always the line, "I think I'm pregnant." Other typical plots in this category: a character finds a lot of money—but it's counterfeit, a role in a movie or play is on the line, there's a big bet on a sports event, or one character tries to save the life of another.

Moral and Ethical Conflicts

These scenarios—so obvious and predictable—are the kindergarten of original satirical humor. The protagonist is a lone dissenter, or wants to go to a class reunion without a date, or tries to crash a celebrity party. Deeper issues include fighting for women's rights, single parent families, and unique professional, business, or religious practices.

Typical plots include finding money, a lost lottery ticket, or jewelry, calling the police to report a crime committed by a well-known person, purposely ignoring new rules, and trying to hide a drunken friend from authority figures.

Sympathy for the Disadvantaged

Sitcom plots are getting into more and more delicate areas. Humor plots which deal with handicapped people, crime, sexual disabilities, and the elderly are fairly common. The audience instinctively feels for the underdog if there is some other fall guy on which to focus the humor.

Physical Mishaps
This is a variation on the previous theme category, but the plot conclusion generally indicates that an accident caused only a temporary disability: amnesia, broken bones, or impotency. These are the vaudeville shticks of slipping on a banana peel, falling down a manhole, and getting a pail of water flung in your face. No slapstick plot is more popular than two or more characters getting locked together in something and not being able to get out.

Something of Value
Everybody wants money, promotions, awards, or material goods, and many will create havoc to get it. The more oddball the need, the better. The audience even identifies with get-rich-quick schemes if the hero needs money, his own or someone else's.

Failure to Cope
These plots are based on the inability of the lead character to handle a new situation at home, on the job, in a social event, or at school. Becoming unemployed is one example; getting a divorce, or the Jeffersons living in an all-white apartment building, are others.

SCRIPT MECHANICS

The time element is important. Scripts are decided upon six months before air date and final taping takes place three to six weeks before airing. Therefore, writers must be thinking of what the world might be like a year in advance. That's normal. What happens if the show you're working on gets cancelled? That's normal, too!

Scripts must be timed precisely. In most cases, playing time is less than twenty-five minutes in every half hour. Commercials take three-and-a-half minutes, opening and closing titles may take more than a minute. Then, a varying amount of time is set aside for a promo of next week's show.

The first scripts are written with minimal stage directions. Only the final scripts are blocked separately for actors, cameramen, and sound effect specialists. Script format should follow the Writer's Guild guidelines. A copy of these guidelines (*Professional Writer's Teleplay/Screenplay*

Format) costs only $2.85 and can be ordered from Writer's Guild of America East, 555 W. 57th St., New York, NY 10019.

MAKE A SCENE

As you get used to timing, you'll develop a feel for the logical number of characters, sets, and possible scenes in any given show. You can't throw a lot of eggs up in the air to hatch a plot. Your story is really no more than a good excuse for your characters to interact in a humorous sketch.

Scenes usually start off sensibly, but then get silly and end abruptly with a cut to the next scene. *M*A*S*H* often opened with shots of serious operations; then the banter removed the seriousness.

When you've decided on one or more of your "What if . . ." ideas, expand them into a one-page outline. Then, by yourself or with a collaborator, brainstorm your ideas. How would the characters react? Who would take the lead in resolving them? Who would obstruct action? Why?

Break it down into the various acts and then into the necessary scenes. You only have three sets, so don't jump all over the globe. Your work will be filled with false starts, weak dialogue, and then—finally—sudden brilliance. Think of the rewriting process as a mandatory luxury, probably the only luxury in a writer's life that never seems to end.

It will help if you study as many successful sitcoms as possible. You can find collections of scripts in the libraries of many colleges and universities, particularly those with large drama departments. And if you have a video recorder, tape and analyze some of the many classic sitcoms now in syndication to develop a feel for pacing and a better understanding of how all the elements come together in performance.

Don't Fight City Hall

The biggest mistake beginning sitcom writers make is to write in new characters who share, let alone hog, the spotlight. For many good reasons the stars demand 80 percent of the dialogue. The audience, too, has been conditioned to see the whole show as a vehicle for the star they love. Don't fight it.

Whatever the problem, the lead characters always support moral goodness—a throwback to the American film code which insisted that crime does not pay. Characters continually fight for right against wrong, although their belief as to what's right and what's wrong may vary. Overprotective parents are all right, because they are really for their children's well-being. In sitcoms, characters may even be above the normal rules of morality because they are goofy and lovable, but never wicked.

No matter how tense your situations become within one episode, your story should end happily. This construction is reassuring for the audience, who looks forward to a familiar situation each week. But although your ending resolves the immediate problem, it never resolves the basic conflict of the series. That's the cliffhanger.

Seeing is Believing

TV is a visual medium, so what we see must be even more entertaining than what we hear. Otherwise, radio soap operas would still be popular. Characters must wear unusual clothing, flash signals with their face, hands, and body. Slapstick works only in visuals and there is nothing funnier than seeing the wall of a house fall on your victim, only to see him standing in a spot where a neatly cut-out window frame permits him to escape without a scratch.

It is not the mark of a poor writer to write in one particular style, but to be a good writer you must develop a unique style. You must learn from every comedian and every show. If you're writing for an existing show, that's the formula you must use. If you are conceiving your own show idea (about a ten thousand to one shot these days!) only then can you establish your own characters and style.

Said Selma Diamond, "You learn by doing it. I only learned by doing. I just kept writing and writing. I failed a lot. Then I found out, I was in great company."

"You're being fired, Wilson, because everytime I said, 'Stop me if you've heard this one,' you did!"

CHAPTER 19

This Is a Wrap:
The Most Commonly Asked
Questions About Humor
Construction

I think everybody is entitled
to my opinion!

—Victor Borge

What's a Topper?

Getting an audience laughing from a dead start is like pushing a truck stuck in the snow. It takes a great deal of effort and luck, and you can't start off by just gunning the motor—you'll end up spinning your wheels. First you've got to rock the truck (audience) back and forth carefully until the wheels catch. Then, when the weight is going forward, you've got to keep that momentum going with split-second timing. If it works, you're home free.

A topper is that second effort, and writing it is an art. It's a follow-up joke that builds on the first laugh and "keeps 'em rollin'." There are many variations of toppers. One of the variations is a humor challenge, where one comedian tries to top the partner:

First: I'm on a first name basis with the unknown soldier.
Second: Yeah, well I was a busboy at the Last Supper.
First: I remember you. How did you like my tip?

A topper can be a second line when the audience thinks the joke is already finished—the performer has paused. Then you surprise them again, they're delighted with the second effort.

Man rushes up to pedestrian:
"Have you seen a cop around here?"
"No."
"Good, then stick 'em up!"
(*Pause*)
"Stick what up?"
"Don't confuse me, this is my first job."

Jack Benny's writers used this device frequently because Benny's tightwad character was so strong, a laugh could come from every reference. For years, he had a running gag which resulted from a long pause after a robber asked him, "Your money or your life?" Finally, the robber asked, "Well?" And Benny would retort, "I'm thinking it over!"

In the following example, Benny uses a topper in a dialogue with a bum who begged for some money:

Benny: Here's a quarter. Buy yourself a pair of shoes.
Bum: With a quarter? (*small laugh*)
Benny: You'll need laces, won't you?

Here's another example of a topper. This time one story tops another. The second one is most funny when the first one has just been told.

Quasimodo, the hunchback of Notre Dame, wanted to take a vacation. He needed a replacement bell ringer, but the only one who showed up at the top of the bell tower was a man without any hands. "How can you expect to ring those heavy bells?" asked Quasimodo. "Easy," said the armless man, "Watch!" He ran full force at the bells, smashing into them with his head, and the bells swung back and forth. "I don't believe it," said Quasimodo. "How long can you keep that up?" "No problem," said the man, "I'll do it again. Watch!" And once more he ran full tilt into the bells, except that the bells were swinging out just as he got there. He missed the bells and fell twenty stories to his death. Quasimodo painfully rushed down the winding stairs. When he got to the street, a crowd had gathered around the smashed body. A policeman asked, "Does anybody know him?" "I don't know who he is," answered the hunchback, "but his face rings a bell."

The Topper

The next day another man showed up, also without hands. "That was my brother you saw yesterday," he said to Quasimodo. "I'm better than he was." Again he rang the bells with his face, but on the second attempt he also missed and fell to his death. "Who's this guy?" asked the policeman. "I don't know," said Quasimodo, "but he's a dead ringer for his brother."

The final example of a topper is a triple that builds, each line topping the other.

Do you know the definition of fame?
First man: Sure, fame is when I'm invited to the White House for a personal meeting with the President.
Second man: No, fame is when I'm invited to the White House, the phone rings and the President ignores it.
Third man: No, real fame is when the President answers the phone, listens for a moment and then says "It's for you."
—Robert Orben

Is a Topper the Same as a Running Gag?

No. A running gag (sometimes called a combo) is a line that comes early in a monologue and then is repeated as a payoff line for jokes scattered throughout the piece. The Russian-born comedian Yakov Smirnoff uses this technique in several of his stories.

Soon after I came to America, I went to Tennessee. They are always checking your hearing there. They keep saying, "Now, you come back. You hear?" I can hear. Then a farmer played a practical joke on me. He told me to milk his bull. Now when you milk a bull you've made a friend for life. The bull kept running down the field yelling, "Now you come back. You hear?"
—Yakov Smirnoff

The most famous running gags were Jack Benny's jokes about his parsimony and his age, Fibber McGee's closet, and Milton Berle's "make-up" line. Every time Berle used the word, a man would run on stage and hit him in the face with a giant powder puff.

What's a Saver?

It's a line used to save you from embarrassment when a joke bombs. Johnny Carson frequently uses, "I knew that joke wouldn't work." (If he knew, why did he use it?) Others are "That's the last time I buy a joke from (the president of the club)." Or, "When did you all become members of a jury?" Comedy writers have to prepare a fistful of savers for their clients. Your most dangerous time is when the fist is empty.

There are also savers when a performance is interrupted by an "unexpected" event—but no professional performer is ever unprepared.

A plane flies overhead: I hope it's one of ours.
Police siren: Here comes my ride home.
Electricity goes off: Call (Con Ed) and tell them the check is in the mail.
Pretty girl enters late: I thought I told you to stay in the tub.
Man enters late: Don't worry. I'll tell you what you missed.
A fire in the theater: Let's get the hell out of here.

The worst thing a performer can do about an onstage emergency is to publicly complain. A humorist should alleviate tension, not cause it.

How Do You Switch a Joke?

Woody Allen calls the old switcheroo "the big non sequitur." You take a familiar story and reverse or switch the ending.

He carried a bullet in his breast pocket. Someone threw a Bible at him and the bullet saved his life.   —Woody Allen

Said the Wolf to Red Ridinghood, "I'm going to eat you." So she shot him. "My god," she said, "doesn't anybody just screw anymore?"

What Do They Mean When They Say Humor is Written Backwards?

The last line—the joke—is created first. Then the anecdote or setup is written to prepare the audience. For instance, in a play on words (POW) you might accidentally discover a unique literal interpretation of a cliché or a reformed cliché (which can happen just as easily when you accidentally make a whittle typing error). But creating setups isn't easy; you might try half a dozen before the best one is apparent. Then you can spend hours changing words and whittling it down whittle by whittle.

Some say the reason there are so many Jewish comedians is because Hebrew lettering is read from right to left, i.e., backwards. But the one who's really a master of the art is Bill Cosby. His technique is to find the expression he wishes to use and then to start building his monologue. Here are four examples (italicized) in material which lasts only one minute, ten seconds. Note how Cosby uses introductory material to set up each punch line.

My mother could not stand my room. *My mother was an authority on pig sties.* "This is the worst looking pig sty I have ever seen in my life. And I want it cleaned up right now. How anyone can live in this filth is beyond me."

I love it when they give you "another think coming." "If you think that I was put on this earth to be your slave, you've got another think coming."

And mothers are always more interested in the condition of your underwear than in your body. "If you're ever in an accident. . . ." They tell you that, "I hope for my sake if you're ever in an accident you have on clean underwear." Well, I thought that was what an accident was. Look, you're driving a truck, here comes another truck who's going to hit you. Now whether you hit the truck or not you're going to have soiled underwear. Because first you say it, then you do it.

How Do You Localize Humor?

Localizing—tailoring material for specific audiences—is an important and common practice for professionals who play on the road or make frequent personal appearances at banquets. The audience wants to know that you care enough to use material personalized for them. Bob Hope is famous for inside material. He'll send a writer to a site a few days before his appearance to write dozens of opening lines about local people, places, and controversial activities.

If you need material for a hotel, do it this way:

A guest at (name of a posh local hotel) called room service. "I want three overdone fried eggs, hard as a rock, some burnt toast that crumbles at first touch, and a cup of black coffee that tastes like mud." "I'm sorry, sir, but we don't serve a breakfast like that." "No? Well, you did yesterday!"

If you need it for an airport, localize it this way:

> *Passenger to (name of airline) ticket agent:* "Ship this bag to New York. This second one to Kansas City, and this third one on your overseas flight to Calcutta." "We can't do that." "Well, you did when I was here last time!"

Another method is to have open-ended jokes in your files that can be completed by inserting local targets.

What About Recycled Humor?

Most writers write only on assignment, but material comes to mind frequently when there is no immediate need for it. Then ideas should be jotted down and warehoused for future delivery. More and more often, computers are being used for indexing. Recycling is taking previously used material and holding it for anticipated events: election jokes, holiday jokes, sick-in-bed material. Greeting card publishers aren't the only ones wise enough to plan seasonal humor material.

Every time there is news about the following events, out come the files and jokes are updated. If you haven't heard it before, it's new.

> *Airline problems:* They not only give you the arrival and departure quotes, they also give the odds.

> *Nuclear accident:* We've been getting glowing reports from (*accident site*). One man said to his wife, "Darling you look radiant today."

> *Elections:* I wouldn't say that (*name of candidate's wife*) is overconfident, but when it rained yesterday, she called the White House and told the First Lady to be sure to shut all the windows.

Retried jokes may be like refried beans. They're both better the second time around.

What is Telegraphing?

Generally, this is a sign of the beginner who gives too detailed an introduction, making the setup so obvious that the audience can anticipate the ending of the story.

Here's an example:

Jack Ellis, director of development (fund-raising) for Ohio University was being given a testimonial dinner. One speaker told the story of the carnival strong man who wet a towel and then squeezed every drop of water out of it. Then he offered to bet anyone in the audience fifty dollars that they couldn't squeeze out just one more drop. Up sprang our guest of honor, and sure enough, he squeezed out three drops. "Who in the devil are you?" asked the strong man. And the man said, "I'm a fund raiser for Ohio University."

Another fund-raising story, which doesn't telegraph the ending as much, would have been better:

You've probably all read about one of our most wealthy alums who has given many large gifts to our university. One day he was missing. His wife didn't know where he was. His business partners couldn't find him. Even the FBI couldn't locate him. The only one who knew where he was day after day was Jack Ellis.

What's the Secret of Timing?
In his book *Make 'em Laugh: Life Studies of Comedy Writers*, Dr. William Fry, Jr. quotes Herbie Baker on timing:

There are no rules. Timing comes from experience—waiting for the laugh, knowing when to come in. You get a feeling that the timing is right. When to start telling the next joke. When performers start out they step on their own laughs. They don't wait long enough, or worse, they wait for a laugh to die down completely, then have to start building all over again.

The trick is to create a laughing roll, waiting for the laughter to come down to about one-third its peak volume and then proceed immediately to your next line.

Comedy should be written so that each joke in the series is funnier than the previous one. Since the setup has already been established, the second, third, and fourth jokes are short, shorter, shortest. You can keep the roll building with physical action. When the audience laughs so hard that their sides ache, that's the equivalent of a home run with the bases loaded.

What is "Working the Audience" and How Do You Do It?

This is a performance technique which is a rare skill. It requires the performer to go into the audience and ask questions, then make brillant insult rejoinders regardless of the target's answer.

While difficult, it's no more mysterious than a magician's prepared hocus-pocus. The trick is that the performer be in control at all times, only asking questions or picking on people for whom his material has already been prepared. The questions are general—hometown, profession, clothing being worn, marital status, size of family, etc. Therefore, answers can be predictable. There are only so many states, professions, color of hair, etc. Even our ages can be categorized.

Because it runs counter to the warning of never threatening your audience, this ad-lib performance requires a great deal of practice and must be carefully plotted by the writers. Material is prepared, then tested over and over in similar situations.

Steve Allen, Johnny Carson, and Don Rickles have worked on their acts for years. Billy Crystal, Pudgy and Howie Mandell are still working on theirs.

> I love the complete fear when the curtain goes up. I never believe I am completely prepared.   —Howie Mandell

Audiences love it because the target of the humor is at the expense of someone else. Tension is high: "What if he comes over to me?" Others don't mind being insulted as long as they're the center of attention.

Beginners learn it by first using college audiences as a Greek chorus:

Performer: Hey, everytime I ask you a question, yell back "Shit, no!"
Crowd: Shit, no!
Performer: Having a good time tonight?
Crowd: Shit, no!
Performer: Am I your favorite entertainer?
Crowd (louder): Shit, no!
Performer: Are you going to get laid tonight?"
Crowd (very loud): Shit, no!
Performer: Hell, I could have told you that!

Why Is the Same Performance Great One Day and Terrible the Next?

Some psychologists believe outside factors account for the wide variety of humor appreciation from different audiences receiving identical humor material (as at a movie). The rule is that you can *not* hypnotize nor amuse an unwilling subject. External factors like bad weather, current news (the stock market went down sharply), or temporary physical irritations (the air conditioning broke down or the show started late) increase audience tension and take precedence over our initial desire to take a vacation from reality. No performer wants to face an audience daring him to abruptly change their mood.

> Audiences are really something else. When you're apprehensive and show a little fear and doubt because you're not getting any laughs, man, an audience will eat you alive. They sense fear, and it's like being in a confrontation with a wild animal that senses you're afraid. In both cases you're doomed.
>
> —Richard Pryor

What Does "Hiding the Joke" Mean?

This is the opposite of telegraphing a joke. Someone tells a story and the audience believes it to be a simple, true statement (followed by a short pause); they don't see the joke coming. That way, the surprise and the laughter are maximized.

> Ohio University was founded in 1804 and opened with a freshman class of twelve students. . . . And this year, eight of them graduated.

"Hide the joke" is Bob Hope's favorite admonition to his writers. He once told Gene Perret, "Don't write philosophy, write comedy."

What's a Premise?

A premise is an idea, a conflict—like deception—that may be raised by details of a plot. A common trap for humor writers is to believe that a single joke can be the basis of a premise. That rarely happens. In the end it's only one joke.

Woody Allen once wrote, "I try to develop a long story with as many laughs coming as close together as possible. After I'm finished, I have a lot of jokes and comments, but as I look at them I find 90 percent don't meet my standards."

What's a Pitch?

It's a query to an editor or a producer to suggest a story or script idea. In Los Angeles there are workshops that focus exclusively on "how to give a pitch." Written or verbal, a pitch should be very short. Ideas must be condensed into three or four sentences, like a program recap in *TV Guide*. Some ideas might be accepted on the basis of five words: "The President's mistress is pregnant."

Is There Such a Thing as a Natural Comedy Writer?

Yes! Like natural ability in athletics, singing, art, and dance, there are many who just seem to be fast learners and have an instinctive talent. As the saying goes, "We're all born equal. After that, we're on our own." Talent must be developed, or it won't go very far. Writing humor professionally is an all-consuming occupation. Your mind is your office and your office hours are every waking hour.

Can Anybody Make a Career at Comedy Writing?

No! Any intelligent person can learn humor, work at it and even produce it. The problem is that the commercial world won't pay enough for second best to let everyone make a living. In humor, good enough is no longer good enough. Only about 5 percent of those who study it go on to the professional world, but that's true of many professions. Since you're only as good as your last joke, there's a great deal of insecurity in comedy writing and a fast turnover of staff; for economic reasons many performers like to work with freelancers.

Should I Work Alone or with a Collaborator?

I recommend partners whenever possible. Despite the added difficulty of scheduling, teams of two or three writers spark each other, test and refine each other's ideas.

Finding someone in your own city is worth the effort. Together you should shut yourselves off from everything else during creative sessions—no telephone calls, no family chores, no long breaks, not even for lunch. Work for a solid morning, a solid afternoon, or a solid evening. Start with brainstorming. Write down as many ideas as the two of you can think of, then start to zero in on those you both agree have merit.

Eric Idle, of the Monty Python group, once wrote, "Getting six guys to agree on what's funny is easy. We read it aloud. If we laugh, it's in; if we don't, it's out. If four guys think something's funny and two guys think it's not, we solve that very simply: we take the two guys out and kill 'em."

"I love working with other writers," wrote Phil Lasker. "I have learned to appreciate surrounding myself with talent. Others may have better lines than you or better story points. You have to listen to those you respect, and it's also fun to notice that the great writers are listening to you."

Often a student will point out that the most famous comedies were written by one man—Charlie Chaplin or Neil Simon. The classic answer is "When you're Chaplin or Simon, we'll let you do it alone, too!"

Do I Need an Agent, and If So, How Do I Get One?

Agents are a great example of a Catch 22 situation. The big agents won't touch neophytes, but beginners can't get into any major undertaking without an agent. There are many exceptions, however, and your job is to find them. Abe Burrows said he thought of his agent, the William Morris agency, as family. When he paid them their 10 percent, he didn't think of it as a commission but as sending money home to mother.

There are directories at public libraries that provide names and addresses of agents. Just never give a new agent your wallet to hold when you go on stage.

Does Giving Author Credit to Someone Else Add or Diminish Audience Appreciation When You Retell a Joke?

Actually it may help beginners get bigger laughs, unless you do it every time. The audience respects famous comedians and is predisposed to laugh at something attributed to them. It's a fair deal. They get the credit and you get the laughs. When I encourage students in workshops to plunge immediately into active experiments, I use Woody Allen's story of how his father taught him to swim:

> My father took me out into the lake on a boat and then just threw me overboard. . . . It wasn't half bad once I got out of that sack.

If a Comic Says "Stop Me If You've Heard This One," Should I?

Absolutely not. A pro never stops another person from reciting. Here's why:

1. The other person has the spotlight, and you don't want to kill *his* laugh.
2. You might hear an even better way to tell the joke than the way you already know.
3. It may have a familiar opening, but it might have a new punch line.

Many jokes begin with a stereotyped setup. Here's a classic story about Hawaii:

A married couple, on their first vacation flight to Hawaii, argue about the island's pronunciation. As soon as they land, they walk into a delicatessen across the street from the airport and the man asks the waiter, "How do you pronounce this place? Ha-why-ee? Ha-vie-ee? Or Ha-vie-ee-ee?" The waiter answers, "Ha-vie-ee!" "Thank you," says the couple. And the waiter replied, "You're vel-come!"

If you had stopped in the middle of the first one, because you heard it before, you'd never learn that there's a second joke:

Same opening, they walk into delicatessen, but this time the man asks the waiter: "I want to know how you pronounce this place, so please say it very slowly." The waiter looks him in the eye and says, "Ir-ving and Mil-ton's Del-i-ca-tess-en."

A comedian rarely laughs out loud at a colleague's humor, but will compliment the friend, "That's a good bit, Joel." A pro watches the style of other pros. They listen to content, delivery, and timing. "I'm so busy thinking, who has time to laugh?" Stepping on an associate's lines is amateur night. It also may teach you how hard a punch you can take.

Do Humor Writers Have a Common Psychological Profile?

Yes. And this profile doesn't make a pretty picture. The average professional is serious, almost solemn. In a room, they sit in the back so they can see the world in front of them. They read voluminously, and are interested in a wide range of subjects. They're intelligent listeners, and have a good ear for incongruous language and actions. That's the good news.

The bad news is—male or female—comedians probably had an unhappy childhood, came from a large family, weren't the oldest, but more likely the youngest, child. The father was rarely involved in upbringing, and the mother's approval was most important. (One-upsmanship was when the child boasted to a friend, "My mother hits harder than your mother.") They probably weren't athletic, and acted as class clowns to cover their lack of interest in scholarship.

Many have some minor physical deficiency: being short, overweight or very skinny, bald, wearing glasses, big nose, and they may have a big mouth in more ways than one. Emotionally, they are insecure, always seeking approval, quick tempered, argumentative and, ironically, rarely use humor to defuse an actual conflict. They are frequently not dependable spouses and are often sexually frustrated. They are notoriously difficult husbands and fathers. Divorce is very common.

The nature of their working hours encourages heavy use of alcohol, tobacco, and drugs. Dr. Samuel S. Janus reports that approximately 40 percent of the humorists have had psychiatric therapy, and nearly 20 percent have been confined for a short time in mental institutions.

Why Are So Many Humor Writers and Performers from Minority Groups?

People whose backgrounds have included a good deal of fear, pain, and deprivation tend to be more creative because their minds have been constantly challenged on how to survive.

Jerry Lewis claims that not one great comedian ever came from a wealthy family and most come from a ghetto, street-smart background. At last count, 85 percent of the writers and performers were Jewish, but they are ambivalent about it. ("Are you Jewish?" one reporter asked Woody Allen. "Yes," he said, "but with an explanation.") It appears that a minority upbringing, filled with uncertainty, anxiety, warding off hostility, and catering to an in-group uniqueness, is fertile topsoil for humor. It is most likely the next major groups in humor will be blacks, Hispanics, and women.

How Do I Test My Humor?

Humor can't be tested in a vacuum. You need an audience, and it must be an audience receptive to humor. If you can't find a "comedy audience," try it on another humor professional—writer or performer. Don't walk up to a stranger and ask, "What d'ya think of this?" The only thing worse is to try it on your friends, your spouse, your parents, or your children. They are too subjective, too critical, and, instead of just relaxing and enjoying it, they turn into pseudo-analysts.

Only one out of every ten jokes will probably work the first time out. And no joke will ever please every person in the audience. It's impossible. Getting laughs from 50 percent is doing very well.

Speakers are urged to try new material—at most thirty seconds worth—at the very beginning of their talk. This is the toughest time because the audience is most skeptical, but if it goes over then, you know it has merit.

Jokes are like machine-gun bullets. They don't all hit the target, but if you shoot enough of them accurately at the audience, you'll kill 'em. Count one point for a twitter of laughter, two points for a solid laugh, and three points for applause. Throw out a joke that doesn't score any points after it's been tried at least three times. If it gets only one point, try rewriting it so your score is constantly going up. Don't fall in love with your own material, and don't blame it on the performer or the audience. Once you learn about flop sweat yourself, you'll never write bad material for a client.

My final advice is to test your humor material until you're sure it doesn't work. Then forget about writing and concentrate on teaching.

Why Aren't There More Comediennes?

In all of Shakespeare's comedies, women emerged as wittier and shrewder than the men, but the problem has been that since humor is brazen, audiences are uncomfortable seeing "ladies" being aggressive, sexually intimidating, and coarse. But, the more honest we become as a society, the more we appreciate the need for women to air their criticisms.

Numerically, women performers may soon come close to equaling the number of men. And in writing comedy, that equality is growing faster yet. Performers don't care who wrote the joke; they never give credit anyway.

What Kind of Sex Jokes Should Comediennes Use?

During the height of the feminist movement, female comedians (who even resent the word "comediennes") focused their sexual humor attacks against the virility of men, "our natural enemy." But the payoff in humor isn't advocacy, it's laughs. And the payoff was more silence than the feminists would have wished. According to Joanne Cantor, who researched the subject at the University of Wisconsin, the sad truth is that both women and men prefer sexual humor directed at women. The reason is, no matter how they try to cover it, that men are more sexually insecure and resent being ridiculed. In addition, men still make up the majority of comedy audiences and women usually don't laugh as loud. But despite the research and the statistics, comediennes are increasing the amount of anti-male sexual material. The best ones are getting away with it—and it's about time.

Does Sick Humor Make Us Feel Better?

Morbid humor appears after every tragic situation. Once upon a time, when the banker in the three-piece suit slipped on a banana peel it was funny only if he got up. Today, someone will make a joke out of it only if he breaks his neck.

Within hours after the Russian nuclear accident at Chernobyl the airwaves were filled with such humor as *"Question:* What has feathers and glows in the dark? *Answer:* Chicken Kiev."

Within the last few years, there have been sick jokes on: Senator Ted

Kennedy ("He's the star of two movies: *The Goodbye Girl* and *A Bridge Too Far*"); AIDS; the space shuttle; Tylenol, as well as Chernobyl. Perhaps it's the frenzied tempo of the world, but they seem to be getting more frequent and more vicious.

> *Question:* What's the fastest thing on two legs?
> *Answer:* A chicken in Ethiopia.

> Ferdinand Marcos, now known as the "Manila folder," doesn't get as much sympathy as his wife Imelda because a lot of American women would have liked to have been in her shoes.

> Jesus walked up to the registration desk of the Hilton hotel, threw three nails on the counter and asked, "Can you put me up for the night?"

Do sick jokes, frequently tasteless and insensitive, serve an important purpose? The consensus is that humor is one way of coping with tragedy. The more we're scared the more we create jokes to laugh away the fear.

> Black comedy is sick to those who don't get it and sickle cell anemia is not funny to blacks who do get it.   —Danny Abelson

Many of the most offensive jokes derived from current tragedies are *entre-nous* humor, told by one person to intimate friends but rarely performed in public.

> The other day Jim Brady, Reagan's original press secretary, who was badly wounded in Hinkley's assassination attempt, said he had half a mind to go back to work at the White House.

Psychologists have always been interested in explaining human behavior through humor. Humor is an important manifestation of what society really believes but dares not speak or teach. "We can't confront tragedy directly," suggests Professor Joseph Boskin of Boston University, "so we try to ease ourselves in a humorous way."

Laughing at negative facts frequently replaces them with positive feelings. Sigmund Freud, who studied humor, but not for the fun of it, theorized that jokes allow us to express unconscious aggressive and sexual impulses, a substitute in words for what we may not be able to accomplish in deeds.

But when it comes to sick humor, the real reason is much simpler—people tell such jokes to make themselves feel better by getting respect, because entertainment is a socially acceptable device to gain attention. Since we were young, we discovered that we could always get a laugh by dropping our pants or saying some taboo word. We may have grown older physically, but the desire to attract attention and gain approval through audacious humor remains.

The detonating cap that explodes humor is the element of surprise. Therefore, sick jokes on any specific subject are acceptable only as long as the public interest in that tragedy remains current.

Question: What's the only type of wood that doesn't float?
Answer: A Natalie Wood.

After that, the sick jokes are put back in the file, ready to be used when similar tragedy occurs. Dr. Jeffrey Goldstein recalls that thalidomide jokes in the sixties were similar to the AIDS jokes of today, such as: "AIDS—the only disease that turns a fruit into a vegetable."

And many of the Chernobyl jokes were only recycled gags heard years ago about Three Mile Island or, more recently, about the poison gas leak at Bhopal, India, known as Union Carbide's Asian production of *Gone With the Wind*.

Many comedians believe that they don't need sick humor once they're become established. Said Larry Wilde, "It's mainly done by the young comics anxious to be noticed. As you get older, you find that material on death and disease makes the audience feel uncomfortable."

In other words, a comic has to be brave enough to be clean. It may be only coincidental but a rather significant acronym results from the first letter of the three elements used by those who depend upon sick humor to attract attention: audaciousness, shock, and surprise. Put them all together, they spell ASS. Wonder what Freud would have had to say about that?

Are Computers Going to Have an Impact on Humor?

They already are. Obviously, they are a big help in indexing and word processing. But above that, computer technology can now record on audio tape and evaluate the intensity of laughter, give each joke a numerical rating and indicate which jokes in the files work best by demographic profile of audience.

Are There Organizations I Can Join to Help Me with My Speechmaking Ability?

Yes, Toastmasters International and the National Speakers Association offer a wide range of seminars, workshops, and performance opportunities at every meeting. An updated list of these and other organizations can be secured from *The Executive Speaker* (a newsletter), Box 292437, Dayton, OH 45429.

What Advice Do You Have for a Beginning Humor Writer?

Writing humor is an eighteen hour-a-day assignment, which means new ideas pop into your head anytime, anyplace. Some claim humor can be conceived even when you dream, so keep a notebook by your bedside.

Once you've learned the basic techniques, don't let anybody talk you out of writing your own way. Humor styles change with each generation and, while formulas rarely vary, standard subject matter, formats, fads, and characterizations are constantly being challenged. New ideas are the lifeblood of comedy, as they are of most businesses. And most new ideas take at least three years to germinate.

There are two other essential elements—luck and perseverance. Some claim they go together—that the luckiest people are those who worked the hardest. In any case, you must be your own publicist. That generally means having confidence in your own material and ability. The business is so competitive that self-effacing writers rarely make it. If you can't sell yourself, how are you going to have the ability to sell a few sheets of paper with gag lines on them? You'll more likely gag first.

How Do You Start "Thinking Funny"?

Watch. Look for the absurdities of life. Notice the physical actions which bring a smile to people's lips.

Read. If you read something funny, make a note of it. Notice the construction. Start a joke file.

Listen. Try to remember how people phrase things, what Mel Brooks calls "the rhythm of human speech." Things that look good on paper don't always perform well. We don't speak in full sentences, and sometimes skip words. We almost always use contractions. We don't give full background details.

Speak. Do your own stand-up. Don't hesitate to deliver your own material in a meeting, at private parties, to dinner guests. You'll notice how audiences differ, how your performance differs, and how important it is to have the right material for the right audience.

Write. Now that you've finished this book on *how* to write, get started doing it. I'm betting my reputation that now you really can write funny and make money.

APPENDIX A

Books for a Humor Writer's Library

REFERENCE

Bartlett's Familiar Quotations, Little Brown and Company, Boston, MA (revised every seven years)

A Browser's Dictionary, by John Ciardi, Harper & Row, New York (1980)

The Columbia Viking Desk Encyclopedia, The Viking Press, New York

Comedians: Annual Directory of Comedians and Comedy Clubs, Creative Concepts, Great Neck, NY (annual)

Dictionary of American Slang edited by Harold Wentworth and Stuart Berg Flexner, Thomas Y. Crowell Company, New York (1975)

A Dictionary of Catch Phrases by Eric Partridge, Stein and Day, New York (1977)

Dictionary of Quotations edited by Bergen Evans, Avenel Books, New York (1978)

A Pronunciation Dictionary of American English, G & C Merriam Company, Springfield, MA

Roget's International Thesaurus, Thomas Y. Crowell Company, New York

Webster's Dictionary of the English Language, G & C Merriam Company, Springfield, MA

Webster's Biographical Dictionary, G & C Merriam Company, Springfield, MA

Webster's Treasury of Synonyms, Antonyms and Homonyms, Avenel Books, New York

Writer's Market, Writer's Digest Books, Cincinnati, Ohio (annual)

HUMOR WRITING TECHNIQUES

Comedy Techniques for Writers and Performers by Melvin Helitzer, Lawhead Press, Athens, OH (1984)

The Craft of Comedy Writing by Sol Saks, Writer's Digest Books, Cincinnati, OH (1985)

The Great Comedians Talk About Comedy by Larry Wilde, Citadel Press, Secaucus, NJ (1968)

How the Great Comedy Writers Create Laughter by Larry Wilde, Nelson-Hall, Chicago, IL (1976)

How to Write Columns by Olin Hinkle and John Henry, Iowa State College Press, Ames, IA (1952)

How to Write and Sell Your Sense of Humor by Gene Perret, Writer's Digest Books, Cincinnati, OH (1983)

Jokes, Form, Content, Use and Function by Christopher Wilson, Academic Press, London (1979)

Make 'em Laugh by William I. Fry, Jr. and Melanie Allen, Science and Behavior Books, Palo Alto, CA (1975)

BIOGRAPHY

The Autobiography of Will Rogers by Donald Day, AMS Press, New York (1949)

Bob Hope, a Life in Comedy by William Robert Faith, Putnam, New York (1982)

Comedy: a Critical Anthology (plays) edited by Robert W. Corrigan, Houghton, Mifflin, New York (1971)

The Comic Mind: Comedy and the Movies by Gerald Mast, Bobbs-Merrill, New York (1973)

Encyclopedia of Comedians by Joe Franklin, Citadel Press (1979)

Funny Men by Steve Allen, Simon & Schuster, New York (1956)

Funny People by Steve Allen, Stein and Day, Briarcliff Manor, NY (1981)

The Great Columnists edited by Jerry D. Lewis, Collier Books, New York (1965)

The Great Movie Comedians by Leonard Maltin, Crown Publishing, New York (1978)

Groucho and Me by Groucho Marx, AMS Press, New York (1959)

Growing Up With Chico by Maxine Marx, Prentice-Hall, Englewood Cliffs, NJ (1980)

Heartland by Mort Sahl, Harcourt, Brace, New York (1976)

How to Talk Dirty and Influence People by Lenny Bruce, Playboy Press, Chicago, IL (1966)

I Remember Jimmy, the Life and Times of Jimmy Durante by Irene Adler, Arlington House, Westport, CT (1980)

Ladies and Gentlemen—Lenny Bruce by Albert Goldman, Random House, New York, (1974)

The Laugh Makers: A Pictorial History of American Comedians by William Cahn, G. P. Putnam, New York (1957)

In Method of Madness: The Comic Art of Mel Brooks by Maurice Yacowar, St. Martin's Press, New York (1981)

No Laughing Matter by Joseph Heller and Speed Vogel, Putnam, New York (1986)

Loser Take All: The Comic Art of Woody Allen by Maurice Yacowar, Fredrick Ungar, New York (1979)

Off Camera by Leonard Probst, Stein and Day, New York (1975)

On Being Funny: Woody Allen and Company by Eric Lax, Charterhouse, New York (1975)

The Redd Foxx Encyclopedia of Black Humor by Redd Foxx and Norma Miller, Ward Ritchie Publishing, Pasadena, CA (1977)

Selected Works of Artemus Ward edited by Albert Jay Nock, AMS Press, New York

Show·People: Profiles in Entertainment by Kenneth Tynan, Simon and Schuster, New York (1979)

Stan: The Life of Stan Laurel by Fred Lawrence Guiles, Stein and Day, New York (1980)

Teamwork—The Cinema's Greatest Comedy Teams by Jeffrey Robinson, Proteus, New York (1982)

The Tonight Show by Robert Metz, Playboy Press, Chicago, IL (1980)

HUMOR MEDIA

Cartoons

Cartoonists and Gag Writer's Handbook by Jack Markow, Writer's Digest Books, Cincinnati, OH (1967)

The Funny Pages: A Serious Guide to Comedy Artists, 12050 Hartsook Street, North Hollywood, CA 91607

Films

The Comic Mind: Comedy and the Movies by Gerald Mast, University of Chicago Press, Chicago, IL (1979)

Movie Comedy by Stuart Byron and Elizabeth Weis, Grossman Publishing, New York (1977)

On Movies by Dwight McDonald, Prentice-Hall, Englewood Cliffs, NJ (1969)

Professional Writer's Teleplay/Screenplay Format, Writer's Guild of America East, 555 W. 57th St., New York, NY 10019

Literature

The Best of Modern Humor edited by Mordecai Richler, Alfred A. Knopf, Inc., New York (1983)

Comic Relief: Humor in Contemporary American Literature edited by Sarah Blacher Cohen, University of Illinois Press, Urbana, IL (1978)

The Last Laugh: Humor in Contemporary American Novel by Ronald Wallace, University of Missouri Press, Columbia, MO (1979)

The World of Victorian Humor by Harold Orel, Appleton-Century-Crofts, New York (1961)

Stage

American Vaudeville edited by Charles W. Stein, Alfred A. Knopf, Inc., New York (1985)

Male-Female Comedy Teams in American Vaudeville (1865-1932) by Shirley Staples, University of Michigan Research Press, Ann Arbor, MI (1984)

Vaudeville, U.S.A. by John E. Dineglio, Bowling Green University Press, Bowling Green, OH (1973)

Stand-Up Comedy

Breaking It Up! The Best Routines of Stand-Up Comics edited by Ross Firestone, Bantam Books, New York (1975)

If You Have to be a Comic by Robert Orben, The Comedy Center, Wilmington, DE (1963)

Speechmaking and Selling

How to Handle Speechwriting Assignments by Douglas P. Starr, Pilot Books, New York (1978)

How to Hold Your Audience with Humor by Gene Perret, Writer's Digest Books, Cincinnati, OH (1984)

How to Make a Speech by Steve Allen, Waldenbooks, New York (1983)

How Speakers Make People Laugh by Bob Bassindale, Parker Publishing, West Nyack, NY (1976)

How to Speak Like a Pro by Leon Fletcher, Ballantine Books, New York (1983)

The Speech Writing Guide by James J. Walsh, John Wiley & Sons, New York (1968)

How to Tell a Story and How to Have One for Any Occasion by Harry Hornblower, self-published (1984)

How to Write and Deliver a Speech by John Ott, Trident Press, New York (1970)

How to Write and Give a Speech by Joan Detz, St. Martin's Press, New York (1984)

Humor Power by Herb True, Doubleday, Garden City, NY (1980)

Podium Humor by James C. Humes, Harper & Row, New York (1980)

Talk Your Way to the Top by James C. Humes, Stein and Day, New York (1980)

We're Roasting Harry Tuesday Night: How to Plan, Write and Conduct the Business/Social Roast by Ed McManus and Bill Nicholas, Prentice-Hall, Englewood Cliffs, NJ (1984)

The World's Greatest Speeches edited by Lewis Copeland and Lawrence W. Lamm, Dover Publications, New York (1973)

Therapy

Anatomy of an Illness by Norman Cousins, Norton, New York (1979)

The Comic Vision and the Christian Faith by Conrad Hyers, The Pilgrim Press, New York (1985)

In the Presence of Humor: A Guide to the Humorous Life by E. T. Eberhart, Pilgrim House, Salem, OR (1983)

Zen and the Comic Spirit by Conrad Hyers, Westminster Press, Philadelphia, PA (1973)

Television and Radio

American History of American Television by John E. O'Connor, Frederick Ungar Publishing, New York (1983)

The End of Comedy: The Sitcom and the Comedic Tradition by David Grote, Anchon Books, Hamden, CT (1983)

Radio Comedy by Arthur Frank Wertheim, Oxford University Press, New York (1979)

HUMOR THEORY

The Act of Creation by Arthur Koestler, MacMillan, New York (1964)

An Anatomy of Laughter by Richard Boston, London (1974)

The Anatomy of Satire by Gilbert Highet, Princeton University Press, Princeton, NJ (1972)

The Argument of Laughter by D. H. Munro, Notre Dame Press, South Bend, IN (1963)

Comedy by Henri Bergson, Doubleday, Garden City, NY (1956)

Comedy High and Low by Maurice Charney, Oxford University Press, London (1978)

Comedy is a Serious Business by Harry Ruskin, Dramatic Publishing, Chicago, IL (1974)

Comedy in Space, Time and Imagination by Paul H. Grawe, Nelson-Hall, Chicago, IL (1983)

Enjoyment of Laughter by Max Eastman, Simon & Schuster, New York (1936)

The Handbook of Humor Research (two volumes) by Paul E. McGhee and Jeffrey H. Goldstein, Springer-Verlag Publishers, New York (1983)

Humor: Classification and Analysis by Warren Shibles, The Language Press, Whitewater, WI (1978)

The Humor of Humor by Esar Evans, Bramhall House, New York (1952)

Humor and Laughter: Theory, Research and Applications by Anthony Chapman and Hugh Foot, John Wiley and Sons, New York (1975)

Humor and Laughter: An Anthropological Approach by Mahadev L. Apte, Cornell University Press, Ithaca, NY (1985)

Humor and Humanity by Steven Leacock, Henry Holt Publishing, Los Angeles, CA (1938)

Humor: Its Origin and Development by Paul E. McGhee, Freeman and Company, San Francisco, CA (1979)

Humor and Social Change in Twentieth Century America by Joseph Boskin, the Boston Public Library, Boston, MA (1979)

Humor: Theory and Technique by Stephen Leacock, Dodd, Mead, New York (1935)

In Praise of Comedy by James K. Feibleman, Russell and Russell, New York (1939)

It's a Funny Thing, Humor edited by Anthony J. Chapman and Hugh C. Foot, Pergamon Press, New York (1977)

Jokes and Their Relation to the Unconscious by Sigmund Freud (1905), translated by James Strachey, W. W. Norton, New York (1960)

Laughing and Crying by Helmuth Plessner, Northwestern University Press, Evanston, IL (1970)

Laughing and Liberation by Harvey Mindess, Nash Publishing, Los Angeles, CA (1971)

Motivation in Humor by J. Levine, Atherton (1969)

No Laughing Matter: Analysis of Sexual Humor (formerly *Rationale of the Dirty Joke*, 1968) by Gershon Legman, Indiana University Press, Bloomington, IN (1975)

The Origins of Wit and Humor by Albert Rapp, E. P. Dutton, New York (1951)

Personality and Sense of Humor by Avner Ziv, Springer, New York (1984)

The Psychology of Humor by Jeffrey H. Goldstein and Paul E. McGhee, Academic Press, New York (1972)

The Psychology of Laughter by Ralph Piddington, Gamut Press, New York (1963)

The Rise and Fall of American Humor by Jesse Bier, Holt, Rinehart and Winston, New York (1968)

Satire's Persuasive Voice by Edward and Lillian Bloom, Cornell University Press, Ithaca, NY (1979)

The Secret of Laughter by A. M. Ludovici, Constable Books, London (1932)

Semantic Mechanisms of Humor by Victor Raskin, D. Reidel Publishing, Boston, MA (1984)

The Study of Humor edited by Harvey Mindess and Joy Turek, Antioch University Press, Venice, CA (1982)

Sweet Madness: a Study of Humor by William F. Fry, Jr., Pacific Books, Palo Alto, CA (1963)

Taking Laughter Seriously by John Morreall, SUNY Press, Albany, NY (1983)

The Theory of Comedy by Elder Olson, Indiana University Press, Bloomington, IN (1968)

Theories of Comedy edited by Paul Lauter, Doubleday, Garden City, NY (1964)

Understanding Laughter by Charles D. Gruner, Nelson-Hall, Chicago, IL (1978)

The World of Laughter by Kalton C. Lahue, University of Oklahoma Press, Norman, OK (1966)

HUMOR COLLECTIONS AND ANTHOLOGIES

The most prolific authors of joke collections and humor anthologies are listed below. Each has written (or edited) more than ten books; Larry Wilde has over thirty titles of category jokes to his name.

Mark Harris, McGraw Hill, New York

Robert Orben, Doubleday & Company, New York
  2,100 Laughs for All Occasions
  2,000 Sure-Fire Jokes for Speakers and Writers
  2,000 New Laughs for Speakers
  The Encyclopedia of One-Liner Comedy

Laurence J. Peters, William Morrow, New York
  The Laughter Prescription, with Bill Dana (1982)

Jack Prelutsky, William Morrow, New York

Alvin Schwartz, Harper & Row, New York
  Tomfoolery, Trickery and Foolery with Words (1973)
  A Twister of Twists, A Tangler of Tongues (1972)
  Wit, Cracks, Jokes and Jests From American Folklore (1973)
  Whoppers: Tall Tales And Other Lies (1973)

Larry Wilde, Pinnacle Books, New York

In addition, a recommended library of jokes and anthologies would include all of the following titles:

The Big Book of Jewish Humor by William Novak & Moshe Waldoks, Harper & Row, New York (1981)

The Comic Encyclopedia by Evan Esar, Doubleday, Garden City, NY (1978)

An Encyclopedia of Modern American Humor edited by Bennett Cerf, Doubleday, Garden City, NY (1954)

A History of Negro Humor in America by William Schechter, Fleet Press, New York (1970)

Humor in America edited by Enid Veron, Harcourt, Brace, New York (1976)

Laughter, the Best Medicine (annual), The Reader's Digest, Pleasantville, NY

Puns by Walter Redferm, Basil Blackwell, New York, (1983)

A Subtreasury of American Humor edited by E. B. White, AMS Press, New York (1941)

The Toastmaster's Treasure Chest by Herbert Prochnow, Harper & Row, New York (1942)

Treasury of Humor by Isaac Asimov, Houghton, Mifflin, New York, (1971)

A Treasury of Laughter by Louis Untermeyer, Simon & Schuster (1946)

With Malice Toward All by Dorothy Hermann, Putnam, New York, (1984)

APPENDIX B

Humor Journal Addresses

(Reprinted with permission from *World Humor and Irony Membership Serial Yearbook* (WHIMSY), edited by Don L. F. Nilsen and Alleen Pace Nilsen. Updated lists are available from WHIM, English Department, Arizona State University, Tempe, AZ 85287.)

A Propos, Stephan Furtounov, Editor, House of Humour and Satire, 5300 Gabrovo, P.O. Box 104, Bulgaria

American Humor, An Interdisciplinary Newsletter, Larry Mintz, Editor, American Studies Program, University of Maryland, College Park, MD 20742

Ballast Quarterly Review, Roy R. Behrens, Editor, 2968 North Prospect Avenue, Milwaukee, WI 53211

Belch and Fart, Marcia Blackam, Editor, Box 6342, Terra Linda, CA 94903

Benedicta Newsletter, Reinhold A. Aman, Editor, 331 S. Greenfield Avenue, Waukesha, WI 53186-6492 (414) 542-5853

Bingo Humor, Fred Shaw, Editor, Empire Press, 4711 W. Armitage Avenue, Chicago, IL 60645

Bits and Pieces, Arthur F. Lenehan, Editor, The Economics Press, 12 Daniel Road, Fairfield, NJ 07006 (201) 227-1224

Canard Enchaine, A. Ribaud, Editor, 2 Rue des Petits-Peres, Paris (2e), France

Cartoon World, George Hartman, Editor, P.O. Box 30367, Lincoln, NE 68503 (402) 435-3191

Cheesecake Newsletter, Louisa Otis, Editor, 3636 NE 117th Street, Seattle, WA 98125

Comedy and Comment, Mack McGinnis, Editor, 448 North Mitchner Avenue, Indianapolis, IN 46210

The Comedy Round Table, Ed Hercer, Editor, P.O. Box 13, King of Prussia, PA 19406 (215) 354-2574

Cracked, Paul Lamont, Editor, Larken Communications, 535 Fifth Avenue, New York, NY 10017

Cracked, Robert C. Sproul, Editor, Major Magazines, Inc., 235 Park Ave. South, New York, NY 10003

Creativity, Arnold Green Short, Editor, Instituto de Idiomas, Yazigi SC, Av 9 de Julho 3, 166-CEP 01406, Sao Paulo-SP, Brasil

Deadfromtheneckup, Inc, Chuck Shepherd, President, P.O. Box 57141, Washington, DC 20037

The Dull Men's Quarterly, Joseph L. Troise, Editor, The Rather Dull Press, Waldo Point Harbor, #E-25, Sausalito, CA 94965 (415) 331-3050

The Freedonia Gazette, Paul G. Wesolowski, Editor, Darien 28, New Hope, PA 18938 (215) 862-9734

The Freedonia Gazette, Raymond D. White, Editor, 137 Easterly Road, Leeds LS8 2RY, England

Funny Bone Bulletin, Tom Royer, Editor, P.O. Box 30134, Indianapolis, IN 46230

Funny Funny World, Martin Ragaway, Editor, 1172 Casa Verde Way, Palm Springs, CA

The Funny Pages, Susan Sweetzer, Publisher, 12050 Hartsook Street, Suite 3, North Hollywood, CA 91607

The Gag Recap, Al and Jo Gottlieb, Editors, P.O. Box 86, East Meadow, New York, NY 11554

Games. Ronnie Shushan, Editor, (also Curtis Slepian and Suzanne Gardiner), 515 Madison Avenue, New York, NY 10022

The Gelosophist, Lauren I. Barnett Scharf, Editor, Lone Star Publications, P.O. Box 29000, Suite 103, San Antonio, TX 78229 (512) 433-6076

Glimpse, Russel Joyner, Editor, International Society for General Semantics, P.O. Box 2469, San Francisco, CA 94126 (415) 543-1747

The Goofus Office Gazette, S. T. Godfrey, T. J. Finegan, C. Morris, and L. Stanley, Editors, 4 Rockland Avenue, Nanuet, NY 10954 (914) 623-6154

Humor Events, Barbara Cummings, Editor, P.O. Box 23334, Workshop Library on World Humour, Washington, DC 20026 (202) 484-4949

Humor Magazine, Edward Savaria, Jr. and Suzanne Tschantz, Editors, 144 Gay Street, Philadelphia, PA 19127 (215) 482-7673

Humor News, James W. Roland, Managing Editor, 1010 Vermont Ave., NW, Suite 910, Washington, DC 20005

Humor Newsletter, Douglas Shaw, Editor, 2210 Arbor Blvd, Dayton, OH 45439

Humormarket, 1239 W. Nopal Place, Chandler, AZ 85224

Inside Joke, Elayne Wechsler, Editor, P.O. Box 1609, Madison Square Station, New York, NY 10159 (718) 435-7284

International Journal of Creature Communication, Charles Larson, Editor, Communication Studies, Northern Illinois University, Watson Hall 205, DeKalb, IL 60115; 212 South Main, Sycamore, IL 60178 (815) 895-9490

The Intra-Tent Journal, Rick Greene, Editor, Sons of the Desert, 9215 Sepulveda Boulevard, #23, Sepulveda, CA 91343 (818) 894-7718

Jewish Language Review, David L. Gold, Editor, 67-07 215 Street, Oakland Gardens, NY 11364

Journal of Irreproducible Results, Alexander Kohn, Editor, Department of Virology, Israel Institute for Biological Research, Ness Ziona, Israel, 70450; George H. Scherr, Associate Editor, Chem-Orbital, Box 234, Chicago Heights, IL 60411 (312) 755-2080

Journal of Polymorphous Perversity, Glenn C. Ellenbogen, Editor, Wry-Bred Press, Inc., P.O. Box 1454 Madison Square Station, New York, NY 10159 (212) 689-5473

Just for Laughs, Hut Landon, Anne Fox, and Jon Fox, Coeditors, 22 Miller Avenue, Suite G, Mill Valley, CA 94941 (415) 383-4746 or (415) 775-7795.

Krokodil, A. S. Pianov, Editor, 101455, G.S.P., A-137 Bumazhnyi Proezd, Dom 14, Moscow, U.S.S.R.; 250-10-86 or 212-21-73.

The Laff-Letter, L. Katherine Ferrari, Editor, International Laughter Society, 16000 Glen Una Drive, Los Gatos, CA 95030, (408) 354-3456 or (408) 354-LAFF

Last Laugh: A Serious Humor Magazine, Michael W. Carden, Editor, P.O. Box 2704, Santa Rosa, CA 95404

Last Month's Newsletter, Monroe Harnish, Editor, Procrastinator's Club of America, 1111 Broad-Locust Building, Philadelphia, PA 19102 (215) 546-3861

Latest Jokes Newsletter, Robert Makinson, Editor, GPO Box 3341-J, Brooklyn, NY 11202 (718) 855-5057

Laugh Factory, Jamie Masada, Bill Taub, and Mindy Shultheis, Editors, 400 S. Beverly Drive, #214, Beverly Hills, CA 90212 (213) 656-1336

Laugh Lovers' News, Virginia Tooper, Editor, P.O. Box 1495, Pleasanton, CA 94566 (415) 462-3470

The Laugh Makers, Cathy Gibbons, Editor, Fun Technicians, P.O. Box 160, Syracuse, NY 13215 (315) 492-4523

Laugh Time U.S.A., Maxwell Miller, Editor, Maxwell Miller Publications Co., P.O. Box 42303, Philadelphia, PA 19101

Laughing Matters, Joel Goodman, Editor, The Humor Project, 179 Spring Street, Saratoga Springs, NY 12866 (518) 587-8770

Laughter in God, History and Theology (LIGHT), *Salvation and Laughter Together* (SALT), Robert J. Larremore, Editor, 4421 McCart, Box 6928, Fort Worth, TX 76115 (817) 923-1921, ext. 275

Libsat Newsletter, John Love, Editor, Gananoque Public Library, 100 Park Street, Gananoque, Ontario K7G 2Y5, Canada (613) 382-2436

Limerick Sig Newsletter, Arthur Deex, Editor, P.O. Box 365, Moffet, CA 94035

Lingua Pranca, Tom Ernst and Evan Smith, Coeditors, Indiana University Linguistics Club, 310 Lindley Hall, Bloomington, IN 47405

Lone Star Humor Digest, Lauren I. Barnett Scharf, and Ashleigh N. M. Lynby, Editors, P.O. Box 29000, Suite 103, San Antonio, TX 78229 (512) 433-6076

Lone Star: A Comedy Monthly, Lauren I. Barnett Scharf, P.O. Box 29000, Suite #103, San Antonio, TX 78229 (512) 433-6076 (Lauren Scharf also edits a journal entitled *Lone Star*)

Lucy Newsletter, Thomas J. Watson, Editor, P.O. Box 480216, Los Angeles, CA 90048

Mad Magazine, Nick Meglin and John Ficarra, Editors, E. C. Publications, Inc., 485 Madison Avenue, New York, NY 10022 (212) 752-7685

Maledicta, Reinhold Aman, Editor, 331 South Greenfield Avenue, Waukesha, WI 53186-6492 (414) 542-5853

Mark Twain Journal, Thomas A. Tenney, Editor, Cyrel Clemens, Emeritus Editor, English Department, The College of Charleston, Charleston, SC 29424 (803) 723-0487

Minne Ha! Ha!, Lance Anger, Editor, P.O. Box 14009, Dinkeytown Station, MN 55414

National Lampoon, Larry Sloman, Editor, 635 Madison Aven, New York, NY 10022 (212) 688-4070

Newsletter of the Church of the Subgenius, The Subgenius Foundation, Ivan Stang, Editor, P.O. Box 140306, Dallas, TX 75214

Orben's Current Comedy, The Comedy Center, Robert Orben, Editor, 700 Orange Street, Wilmington, DE 19801 (302) 656-2209; or 1200 North Nash Street, Arlington, VA 22209

Pangloss Papers, Bard Dahl, Editor, Box 18917, Los Angeles, CA 90018 (213) 663-1950

The Peter Schickele Rag, Peter Schickele and William Crawford, Editors, Box 325, Woodstock, NY 12498 (212) 535-8157

Phantastic Phunnies, John Fultz, Editor, 1343 Stratford Drive, Kent, OH 44240 (216) 673-5095

Phoebe: The Newsletter of Humor, James MacDougall, Editor, 511 5 & 20, Waterloo, NY 13165 (315) 539-8051

Playfulness, Revelry, Nonsense (PRN), Elaine Teutsch and Pat Rushford, Editors, 3401 S.W. Illinois, Portland, OR 97201 (503) 225-7709

Porlock Society Journal, Russ Meyer, Editor, English Department, University of Missouri, Columbia, MO 65201

Punch, Alan Coren, Editor, 23-27 Tudor Street, London, England EC4Y OHR, telephone: 01-583-9199

Punchline: The National Humor Newsletter, William W. Travis, Editor, National Museum of Humor, Shades Mountain Plaza, P.O. Box 26026, Birmingham, AL 35226-0026

The Pundit, John S. Crosbie, Editor, P.O. Box 5040, Station A, Toronto, Ontario, Canada M5W 1N4; or 107 Ridge Drive, Toronto, Canada M4T 1B6 (416) 486-1282

The Puns Corps Press, Robert L. Birch, Editor, P.O. Box 2364, Falls Church, VA 22042-2364

Quagmire, Dale Lowdermilk, Editor, *Not-Safe*, P.O. Box 5743, Montecito, CA 93108 (805) 969-1185

The Ralph Newsletter, Peter Crescenti and Bob Columbe, Editors, C. W. Post College, Greenvale, NY 11548 (516) 229-2622

The Realist, Paul Krassner, Editor, Box 1230, Venice, CA 90294 (213) 392-5848

Red Rubber Noses, Barbara Allen Smith, Editor, Institute for Sharing Amusing Anecdotes in Church/Synagogue (ISAAC), an Affiliate of the Workshop Library on World Humour (WLWH), P.O. Box 10, Nashville, TN 36221

Rip Off, Gilbert Shelton, Editor, P.O. Box 14158, San Francisco, CA 94114

SALT Newsletter, Robert J. Larremore, Editor, Box 6928, Fort Worth, TX 76115 (817) 923-1921, ext. 275

Scrooge Newsletter, Charles G. Langham, Editor, 1447 Westwood Road, Charlottesville, VA 22901 (804) 977-4748

Sharing Ideas, Dottie Walters, Editor, 600 W. Foothill Blvd., Glendora, CA 91740

The Snooze News, J. D. Stewart and C. L. "Prosy" Anderson, Editors, International Dull Folks, Unlimited, P.O. Box 23584, Rochester, NY 14692 (716) 334-3398

The Stark Fist of Removal, Ivan Stang, Editor, P.O. Box 140306, Dallas, TX 75214 (214) 823-8534

Sting, Lois Fad, Editor, Alpha Publications, 1079 De Kalb Pike, Center Square, PA 19422 (215) 277-6342

Studies in American Humor, John O. Rosenbalm, Editor, English Department, Southwest Texas State University, San Marcos, TX 78666

Studies in Contemporary Satire, C. Darrel Sheraw and D. R. Wilmes, Editors, English Department, Clarion State College, Clarion, PA 16214

The Subterranean Sociology Newsletter, Marcello Truzzi, Editor, Sociology Department, Eastern Michigan University, Ypsilanti, MI 48197

T.A.A.S.P. Newsletter, Ann Marie Guilmette, The Association for the Anthropological Study of Play, P.O. Box 40, Clark Hall, Faculty of Education, Brandon University, Brandon, Manitoba, Canada R6A 6A9

Thalia: Studies in Literary Humor, Jacqueline Tavernier-Courbin, Editor, Department D'Anglais, University of Ottawa, Ottawa, Ontario, Canada K1N 6N5 (613) 231-2311 or (613) 744-1993

Thoughts for All Seasons, Michel P. Richard and P. Kellogg, Editors, Department of Sociology, State University of New York, Geneseo, NY 14454 (716) 245-5336

The Twainian, Chester L. Davis, Editor, Mark Twain Research Foundation, Perry, MO 63462

Uneeda Review, J. Parkhurst Schimmelpfennig, Editor, Nick Lyons Books, 31 West 21st Street, New York, NY 10010

The Upstart Crow, William E. Bennett, Editor, English Dept., University of Tennessee, Martin, TN 38238

Variety (weekly entertainment industry newspaper) 154 West 46th Street, New York, NY 10036

View From the Ledge, Chuck Shepherd, Editor, *Deadfromtheneckup,* P.O. Box 57141, Washington, DC 20037

Weirdo, Peter Bagge, Editor, Last Gasp of San Francisco, Box 34, Kirkland, WA 98033 (206) 885-4201

The Whole Mirth Catalog, Allen Klein, Editor, 1034 Page Street, San Francisco, CA 94117

Word Ways: The Journal of Recreational Linguistics, A. Ross Eckler, Editor, Spring Valley Road, Morristown, NJ 07960 (201) 538-4584

World Humor and Irony Membership Serial Yearbook (WHIMSY), Don and Alleen Nilsen, Coeditors, English Dept, Arizona State University, Tempe, AZ 85287

APPENDIX C

Humor Organizations

(Reprinted with permission from *World Humor and Irony Membership Serial Yearbook* (WHIMSY), edited by Don L. F. Nilsen and Alleen Pace Nilsen. Updated lists are available from WHIM, English Department, Arizona State University, Tempe, AZ 85287.)

America's Favorite Jokes, 119 S. Osborn, Youngstown, OH 44509

American Comedy Conferences, John Bryant and Augustus Kolich, Directors, Committee on American Studies, 1011 Liberal Arts Tower, The Pennsylvania State University, University Park, PA 16802

American Federation of Comedians, Richard Knight, Director, P.O. Box 1589, Beverly Hills, CA 91213

American Humor Guild, Herb True, President, 1717 East Colfax, South Bend, IN 46617

American Humor Studies Association, an affiliate of the Modern Language Association, 10 Astor Place, New York, NY 10003 (212) 475-9500

Animal Town Game Co., Ken and Jann Kolsbun, P.O. Box 2002, Santa Barbara, CA 93120

Antioch Humor Project, Harvey Mindess, Psychology Department, Antioch University, 300 Rose Avenue, Venice, CA 90291

The Association for the Anthropological Study of Play, Frank E. Manning, President, Department of Anthropology, The University of Western Ontario, London, Ontario, Canada N6A 5C2

The Association of Comedy Artists, Barbara Contardi, President, 2 Bond Street, New York, NY 10012 (212) 677-1409

Association for the Promotion of Humour in International Affairs (APHIA), Alfred E. Davidson, John E. Fobes, and Richard H. Moore, P.O. Box 357, Webster, NC 28788 (704) 586-9705

Association Pour la Promotion de l'Humour dans les Affaires Internationales, Alfred E. Davidson, 5 Rue de la Manutention, F-75116 Paris, France

Association for the Study of Jewish Languages, 1610 Eshkol Tower, University of Haifa, Haifa 31 999, Israel

Balloon-a-grams and Clowns, Ellen Maggs (Kookoo the Clown), 2157 West Mulberry Drive, Phoenix, AZ 85015

Bulwer-Lytton Fiction Contest, Scott Rice, English Dept., San Jose State University, San Jose, CA 95192-0090

Burlington Liars Club, John Soeth and Donald Reed, Presidents, 149 Oakland Avenue, Burlington, WI 53105

California Lovers of Wit and Nonsense (CLOWN), Arthur Asa Berger, Director, Broadcast Communication Arts, San Francisco State University, 1600 Holloway, San Francisco, CA 94132

Cartoon Art Museum of California, Malcolm Whyte, 333 Richardson Drive, Mill Valley, CA 94941

Cartoon World, c/o George Hartman, P.O. Box 30367, Lincoln, NE 68503

Cartoonists Across America, Debra Leighton, 1641 W. Beaver Lake Drive S.E., Issaquah, WA 98027 (206) 391-1115

The Cat Club, 76 East 13th Street, New York, NY 10012. Features the annual "Charlie" Comedy Awards.

The Cat's Pajamas, P.O. Box 1517, North Myrtle Beach, SC 29598

Centre for the Study of Creature Communication, Charles U. Larson, Director, Communication Studies Department, Northern Illinois University, DeKalb, IL 60115 or 612 South Main, Sycamore, IL 60178 (815) 895-9490

The Church of the Subgenius, Ivan Stang, P.O. Box 140306, Dallas, TX 75214 (214) 823-8534

Clearinghouse for Speech and Humor (Eastern Office) Suite 1809, 1270 Avenue of the Americas, New York, NY 10020

Clearinghouse for Speech and Humor (Western Office), Mick Delaney, President, P.O. Box 15259, Wedgewood Station, Seattle, WA 98115

Clown, Mime, Puppet and Dance, Box 24023, Nashville, TN 37202

The Comedy Center, Robert Orben, 700 Orange Street, Wilmington, DE 19801 (302) 656-2209

The Comedy Center, James W. Roland, Director, P.O. Box 9582 Friendship Station, Washington, DC 20016

The Comedy Workshop, Paul Menzel, Director, 2105 San Felipe (at Sheperd), Houston, TX 77019

The Comedy Writer, Roger (Wilko) Wilkerson, 1747 Lincoln Blvd, Suite 314, Santa Monica, CA 90404 (213) 335-7216

Comedy Writers' Association, Robert Makinson, President, G.P.O. 3341, Brooklyn, NY 11202 (718) 855-5057

Crack Me Up, Arnold Hiura, Director, American Studies, University of Hawaii, Honululu, Hawaii 96822

Creative Cartoon Service, Peter Vaszilson, Director, 3109 West Schubert Avenue, Chicago, IL 60647

Creative Media Group, Inc., Chic Thompson, Manager, 123 4th Street NW, Charlottesville, VA 22901

Creative with Words Publications, Brigitta Geltrich-Ludgate, Director, P.O. Box 223226, Carmel, CA 93922

Creative Lunatics, Red Bilodeau, President, 10000 Imperial Highway, Downey, CA 90242 or 1251 West Sepulveda #169, Torrance, CA 90501

Daypunch, P.O. Box 4984, Kansas City, MO 64120

Deadfromtheneckup, Chuck Shepherd, Director, P.O. Box 57141, Washington, DC 20037

Densa, Steve Price, President, P.O. Box 214338, Dallas, TX 75221

Dial-a-Joke, J. Edward Thornberg, Department Ho-Ho, The National Humor Hall of Fame, P.O. Box 242, Clear Lake, IA 50428 (515) 357-HOHO

Dull Men's Club, 3364 22nd Street, #7, San Francisco, CA 94110

Flat Earth Society, Charles Johnson, Director, P.O. Box 2533, Lancaster, CA 93539-2533

Franklin J. Meine Library of American Humor, University of Illinois, Urbana, IL 61801

Fun-Dynamics!, Mary Lou Galacian, Director, 917 East Laguna Drive, Tempe, AZ 85282

Fun-Technicians, Inc., Cathy Gibbons, P.O. Box 160, Syracuse, NY 13215 (315) 492-4523

Fun Technicians, 108 Berwyn Avenue; Syracuse, NY 13210

Funny Bone Productions, Tony DePaul, 1745 Beloit Avenue, #218, Los Angeles, CA 90025

Funny Farm, Bob Taylor, 31130, Apt. 20, South General Kearny Road, Temecula, CA 92390 (714) 676-4614

Those Generics, Michael Gonzalez, 3122 Bretton #B, North Canton, OH 44720

Half-S Enterprises, Wally and Douglas Lindsey, Director, Box 531, Cortaro, AZ 85652

The Happy Press, Dave Morice, Director, Box 585, Iowa City, IA 52244

Heartland Humor Company, Bob Rubright, Director, 340 East Jefferson, Kirkwood, MO 63122 or 214 South Bemiston Avenue, St. Louis, MO 63105

Holy Fools, William J. Peckham, P.O. Box 1828, Springfield, IL 62705 (217) 753-3939

The House of Humor and Satire, Stephen Furtounouv, Director, P.O. Box 104, Gabrovo 5300, Bulgaria

The Humor Bank, Elvin T. (Cy) Eberhart, 1637 Westhaven Avenue, NW, Salem, OR 97304 (503) 362-4030

The Humor Communication Company, Art Gliner, Director, 8521 Grubb Road, Silver Spring, MD 20910

The Humor Project, Joel Goodman, President, Sagamore Institute, 110 Spring Street, Saratoga Springs, NY 12866 (518) 587-8770

Humor Program, Kidd's Corner, South Fulton Hospital, 1170 Cleveland Avenue, East Point, GA 30344

Humor Program, Connie LaFont, Lincoln General Hospital, 2827 Ponca NE, Lincoln, NE 68506

Humor Program, Marvin C. Mengel, The Living Room, Humana Hospital, Diabetes Unit, 1200 E. Hillcrest Street, Orlando, FL 32803

Humor Program, The Living Room, William Stehlin Foundation for Cancer Research, St. Joseph's Hospital, Houston, TX 77002

Humor Program, David J. Steel, Presbyterian Medical Center, Box 77, Conju, Korea-52

Humor Program, Ethel Percy Andrus Gerontology Center, University of Southern California, University Park/MC-0191, Los Angeles, CA 90089-0191

Humor Club International, C. Govindarajulu, Chair, 46 Venkatachala Mudali Street, Madras-600004, India

Humor, Comedy and Laughter League (HCLL), An Affiliate of the Workshop Library on World Humor (WLWH), Peter Crofts, President, 24 Station Street, Sandringham, Melbourne, Victoria, Australia 3191, 613-598-3671

Independent Publications, 7001 N. Clark, Room 323, Chicago, IL 60626

Institute for the Advancement of Human Behavior, Gerald Piaget, Director, P.O. Box 7226, Stanford, CA 94305; or P.O. Box 94305, 4370 Alpine Road, Portola Valley, CA 94025; or P.O. Box 7226, Stanford, CA 94305

Institute for Sharing Amusing Anecdotes in Church/Synagogue (ISAAC), P.O. Box 10, Nashville, TN 37221

International Association for the Child's Right to Play (IPA), Secretariat, 61000 Ljubljana, Jugoslavija

International Association of Professional Bureaucrats (INATAPROBU), James H. Boren, President, 1032 National Press Building, Washington, DC 20045 (202) 347-2490

International Dull Folks Unlimited, an affiliate of DENSA, J. D. "Dull" Stewart, Chairman of the Bored, P.O. Box 23584, Rochester, NY 14692 (716) 334-3398

International Dull Man's Club, Joseph L. Troise, President, Walso Point Harbor, E E-25, Sausalito, CA 94965 (415) 331-3050

International Geletology Institute, William F. Fry, Jr., M.D., 888 Oak Grove, Menlo Park, CA 94025 (415) 324-4965

International Humor Advisory Council, 3908 East Fourth Street, Long Beach, CA 90814 (213) 438-3424

International Laughter Society, L. Katherine Ferrari, President, 16000 Glen Una Drive, Los Gatos, CA 95030 (408) 354-3456

International Maledicta Society, Reinhold A. Aman, President, 331 S. Greenfield Ave., Waukesha, WI 53186-6492 (414) 542-5853

The International Save the Pun Foundation, John S. Crosbie, Chairman, Box 5040, Station A, Toronto, Canada M5W 1N4 (416) 486-1282

Irish Bull Society, Desmond McHale, Director, An Affiliate of the Workshop Library on World Humour (WLWH), Math Dept., University College, Cork, Ireland

Jenkins and Associates Humor Workshop, Joe Jenkins, Director, 200 West Mercer St., Suite 201, Seattle, WA 98119

Jest for the Health of It, Patty Wooten, 1762 Hamilton Avenue, San Jose, CA 95125 (408) 265-7507

Joke of the Month Club, 1106 Glenwood Avenue, Nashville, TN 37204

The Joke Tracking Center, Dave Barry, Director, P.O. Box 011509, Miami, FL 33101

The Jokesmith, Edward C. McManus and Bill Nicholas, 44 Queen's View Road, Marlborough, MA 01752

Laboratory of Applied Humor Research, Martha R. Ortiz, Director, 3811 Chanel Road, Annandale, VA 22003

Laugh Factory Magazine, Jamie Masada, Editor, 400 S. Beverly Drive #214, Beverly Hills, CA 90212 (213)656-1336

Laugh-In Club, Eddie Rose, President, 12807 Jade Stone Drive, Sun City West, AZ 85375 (602) 584-5769

Laugh Therapy, Annette Goodheart, Director, P.O. Box 40297, Santa Barbara, CA 93103

Laugh-Makers Camp, Richard Snowberg, University of Wisconsin, 1725 State Street, La Crosse, WI 54601 (608) 785-8058

Laughter Therapy, Bob Basso, 10700 Bluffside Drive, Suite 6, Studio City, CA 91604

Laughter Unlimited, Pinkie Barclay, 951 W. Orange Grove, #03204, Tucson, AZ 85704

The Laughter Project, Phame Camerena, Director, Sabina White, Co-Principal Investigator and Nancy Nuzum, Project Coordinator, Student Health Service, Dept. of Sociology and Health Education, University of California, Santa Barbara, CA 93106

The Levity Company, Joe Bly, President, P.O. Box 1961, Asheville, NC 28802, (704) 298-3629

The Lighter Side, 35075 Automation Drive, Mt. Clemens, MI 48043

The Limerick Special Interest Group, Arthur Deex, Box 365, Moffett, CA 94036

Little Apple and Assorted Fruits (LAAF), Clyde Colwell, Director, College of Education, Kansas State University, Manhattan, KS 66506

The Loonies, Barry Gantt, President, P.O. Box 20443, Oakland, CA 94620 (415) 451-6248

The Marx Brothers Study Unit, Paul O. Wesolowski, President, c/o the Freedonia Gazette, Darien 28, New Hope, PA 18938 (215) 862-9734

Messies Anonymous, Sandra Felton, President, 5025 B SW, 114th Avenue, Miami, FL 33165

The Murphy Center, Paul Dickson, Director, Box 80, Garrett Park, MD 20896.

Museum of American Humor, Leopold Fechtner, 84-51 Beverly Road, Kew Gardens, NY 11415 (212) 846-2002

Museum of Cartoon Art, Ashley Hunt, Manager, Comly Avenue, Port Chester, NY 10573

Nanny Goat Productions, Joyce Farmer, Director, P.O. Box 845, Laguna Beach, CA 92652

National Coalition to Legalize Freedom, P.O. Box 4394, Santa Barbara, CA 93103

National Ding-a-Ling Club, Box 2188, Glen Ellyn, IL 60137

The National Humor Hall of Fame, J. Edward Thornberg, Director, Department Ho-Ho, P.O. Box 105, Clear Lake, IA 50428; or Pat Welch, Communications Director, Box HO HO, LeClaire, Iowa 52753

National Laugh Report, Maxwell Miller Publications Co., Box 42303-C, Philadelphia, PA 19101

National Museum of Humor, William W. Travis, Curator, Shades Mountain Plaza, P.O. Box 26026, Birmingham, AL 35226-0026

National Organization Taunting Safety and Fairness Everywhere (NOT-SAFE), Dale Lowdermilk, Director, Box 5743; Montecito, CA 93108 (805) 969-1185

National Speakers Association, Robert H. Henry, President, 4323 North 12th Street, Suite 103, Phoenix, AZ 85014-4506

The New York Comedy School, Robert Vare, Director, New School for Social Research, 66 West 12th Street, New York, NY 10011 (212) 741-5690

Nobody Press, Derek Evans and Dave Fulwiler, 10746 Esmeraldas Drive, San Diego, CA 92124

Northern California Cartoonist and Humor Association, Ken Kirste, Director, 294 Waverley Street #6, Menlo Park, CA 94025

Nulle and Voyd Enterprises, Max M. Feibelman, 5064 Campo Road, Woodland Hills, CA 91364 (213) 870-6576 or (213) 391-8276

Nurses for Laughter, Deborah Leiber, Director, Department of Community Health Care Systems, Oregon Health Sciences University, 3401 SW Illinois, Portland, OR 97201 (503) 225-7709

Order of the Almond Tree, Niyi Oladeji, Vice President, Dept. of English Language, University of Ife, Il-Ife (Oyo State), Nigeria

Other Covers, Fanta Graphics Books, 196 West Haviland Lane, Stamford, CT 06903

Phantastic Phunnies Comedy Service, 1343 Stratford Drive, Kent, OH 44240

Play World, Leo Rutherford, 58 Westbere Road, London, England NW2 3RU, telephone: 01-435-8174

Popular Culture Associations, J. Fred MacDonald, President, Bowling Green State University, Bowling Green, OH 43403

Procrastinators' Club of America, Les Waas, President, 1111 Broad-Locust Building, Philadelphia, PA 19102 (215) 546-3861

Productivity Games, Inc., Bob Basso, Director, 10700 Bluffside Drive, No. 6, Studio City, CA 91604

Professional Comedians Association, Abby Stein, President, P.O. Box 222, New York, NY 10185 (212) 614-1123

The Puns Corps, Robert L. Birch, Coordinator, Box 2364, Falls Church, VA 22042

The Punster's Press, P.O. Box 405, Glenview, IL 60025

Republic of Twerpwyck, Al Schatz, Governor, A Division of Educators' Press, 6907 Sherman Street, Philadelphia, PA 19119

Ripley's Believe it or Not, Barbara Gregson, 8489 West Third Street, Los Angeles, CA 90048 (213) 655-6040

Royal Association for the Longevity & Preservation of the Honeymooners (RALPH), Peter Crescenti and Bob Columbe, C. W. Post College, Greenvale, NY 11548 (516) 299-2622

Salvation And Laughter Together (SALT), Robert J. Larremore, President, 4421 McCart, Fort Worth, TX 76115

Samuel LaRue Finley Humorous Writing Competition, John Sisco, Director, School of Communication, Northern Arizona University, Flagstaff, AZ 86011

San Francisco Academy of Comic Art, Bill Blackbeard, Director, 2850 Ulloa Street, San Francisco, CA 94116 (415) 681-1737

Sarcastics Anonymous, P.O. Box 1495, Pleasanton, CA 94566

Schmulowita Collection of Wit and Humor, Johanna Goldschmid, Special Collections Librarian, San Francisco Public Library, Civic Center, San Francisco, CA 94102

Sidetracked Home Executives, P.O. Box 5364, Vancouver, WA 98663

Sniglets, Rich Hall, P.O. Box 2350, Hollywood, CA 90078

Society to Curtail Ridiculous, Outrageous, and Ostentatious Gift Exchanges (SCROOGE), 1447 Westwood, Charlottesville, VA 22901 (804) 977-4648

Society of Dirty Old Men (SODOM), L. Robert Quarles, II, Vice President, Box 18202, Indianapolis, IN 46218

Sons of the Desert, John McCabe, Orson Bean, Al Kilgore, Chuck McCann, and John Minicino, 9215 Sepulveda Boulevard, #23, Sepulveda, CA 91343 (818) 894-7718

Subgenius Foundation, Ivan Stang, President, P.O. Box 140306, Dallas, TX 75214

Thaler's Riddle and Joke Club, Mike Thaler, President, Box 223 R.D. 1, Stone Ridge, NY 12484

Toastmasters International, P.O. Box 10400, Santa Ana, CA 92711

The Very Bad Poets Club, Patty P. "Swell" Bell, President, 1325 W. Guadalupe Road, #318-C, Mesa, AZ 85202

WJOK Radio, Robert Cobbins, President, 2201 Watkins Mill Road, Gaithersburg, MD 20879 (301) 428-3555

We Love Lucy, Thomas J. Watson, President, P.O. Box 480216, Los Angeles, CA 90048

Will Rogers Memorial, P.O. Box 157, Claremore, OK 74017

Wittenburg Door, Youth Specialties, 1224 Greenfield Drive, El Cajon, CA 92021

Workshop Library on World Humour, Herb J. Cummings, President, P.O. Box 23334, Washington, DC 20026 (202) 484-4949

The World Game, University City Science Center, 3508 Market Street, Philadelphia, PA 19104 (215) 387-0220

World Humor and Irony Membership (WHIM), Don and Alleen Nilsen, Co-Chairs, English Department, Arizona State University, Tempe, AZ 85287

Writer's Guild of America, East, Inc., 22 West 48th Street, New York, NY 10036

Wry-Bred Press, P.O. Box 1454 Madison Square Station, New York, NY 10159 (212) 689-5473

INDEX

Other Books of Interest

General Writing Books

Getting the Words Right: How to Revise, Edit and Rewrite, by Theodore A. Rees Cheney $13.95

How to Get Started in Writing, by Peggy Teeters (paper) $8.95

How to Write a Book Proposal, by Michael Larsen $9.95

How to Write & Sell Your Personal Experiences, by Lois Duncan (paper) $9.95

How to Write & Sell (Your Sense of) Humor, by Gene Perret (paper) $9.95

Knowing Where to Look: The Ultimate Guide to Research, by Lois Horowitz $18.95

Pinckert's Practical Grammar, by Robert C. Pinckert $12.95

The 29 Most Common Writing Mistakes & How to Avoid Them, by Judy Delton $9.95

Writer's Block & How to Use It, by Victoria Nelson $14.95

Writer's Market, edited by Becky Williams $21.95

Nonfiction Writing

Basic Magazine Writing, by Barbara Kevles $16.95

How to Sell Every Magazine Article You Write, by Lisa Collier Cool $14.95

Writing Creative Nonfiction, by Theodore A. Rees Cheney $15.95

Writing Nonfiction that Sells, by Samm Sinclair Baker $14.95

Fiction Writing

Creating Short Fiction, by Damon Knight (paper) $8.95

Fiction is Folks: How to Create Unforgettable Characters, by Robert Newton Peck (paper) $8.95

Fiction Writer's Market, edited by Laurie Henry $18.95

Handbook of Short Story Writing, by Dickson and Smythe (paper) $8.95

How to Write & Sell Your First Novel, by Oscar Collier with Frances Spatz Leighton $14.95

Writing the Modern Mystery, by Barbara Norville $15.95

Writing the Novel: From Plot to Print, by Lawrence Block (paper) $8.95

Special Interest Writing Books

The Children's Picture Book: How to Write It, How to Sell It, by Ellen E.M. Roberts (paper) $14.95

The Craft of Comedy Writing, by Sol Saks $14.95

How to Write Tales of Horror, Fantasy & Science Fiction, edited by J.N. Williamson $15.95

How to Write the Story of Your Life, by Frank P. Thomas $14.95

Mystery Writer's Handbook, by The Mystery Writers of America (paper) $9.95

Nonfiction for Children: How to Write It, How to Sell It, by Ellen E.M. Roberts $16.95

The Poet's Handbook, by Judson Jerome (paper) $8.95

Poet's Market, by Judson Jerome $16.95

Travel Writer's Handbook, by Louise Zobel (paper) $10.95

TV Scriptwriter's Handbook, by Alfred Brenner (paper) $9.95

Writing Short Stories for Young People, by George Edward Stanley $15.95

The Writing Business

A Beginner's Guide to Getting Published, edited by Kirk Polking $10.95

How to Bulletproof Your Manuscript, by Bruce Henderson $9.95

How to Understand and Negotiate a Book Contract or Magazine Agreement, by Richard Balkin $11.95

How to Write Irresistible Query Letters, by Lisa Collier Cool $10.95

Literary Agents: How to Get & Work with the Right One for You, by Michael Larsen $9.95

Professional Etiquette for Writers, by William Brohaugh $9.95

To order directly from the publisher, include $2.00 postage and handling for 1 book and 50¢ for each additional book. Allow 30 days for delivery.

Writer's Digest Books, Dept. B, 1507 Dana Avenue, Cincinnati OH 45207
Prices subject to change without notice.

For information on how to receive Writer's Digest Books at special Book Club member prices, please write to:

Promotion Manager, Writer's Digest Book Club, 1507 Dana Avenue, Cincinnati, Ohio 45207